The Deadliest Men

To Emily, a good writer.

The Deadliest Men

The World's Deadliest Combatants throughout the Ages

Paul Kirchner

Paladin Press · Boulder, Colorado

The Deadliest Men:
The World's Deadliest Combatants throughout the Ages
by Paul Kirchner

ISBN 1-58160-271-5
Printed in the United States of America

Published by Paladin Press, a division of
Paladin Enterprises, Inc.
Gunbarrel Tech Center
7077 Winchester Circle
Boulder, Colorado 80301 USA
+1.303.443.7250

Direct inquiries and/or orders to the above address.

PALADIN, PALADIN PRESS, and the "horse head" design
are trademarks belonging to Paladin Enterprises and
registered in the United States Patent and Trademark Office.

Visit our Web site at www.paladin-press.com

Contents

Preface

He hefts his battleax.
She stands en garde,
rapier poised.
He thumbs down the safety on
his .45 automatic.
Each faces a superior
number of armed and deter-
mined enemies, but no matter.
Within moments, those ene-
mies will either have fled or
lie dead.

Invincible heroes have fascinated us from the epics of Homer to the action films of Hollywood. They routinely fight for their lives, survive terrible wounds, pull off hairbreadth escapes, triumph against overwhelming odds, and leave their enemies in heaps. But how many such people have there really been? This book profiles nearly 50, ranging from a Viking to a samurai, a Texas Ranger to a Detroit Tiger, a contemporary Los Angeles shopkeeper to a Colonial-era housewife.

Each fought as an individual. I chose not necessarily those who racked up the highest body counts, but those who consistently prevailed in a violent environment, whether or not they had to kill. While there are fencing masters and combat pistol shooters who may have demonstrated greater skill than my subjects, they are not covered here unless they fought for blood, not sport.

Obviously, no collection such as this can aim to be comprehensive, and I limited it by certain parameters. Falling under my definition of "masters of personal combat" are fighter pilots, but not those who led armies or captained ships. I wanted only those who faced their foes on an even footing or at a disadvantage, so I haven't covered snipers. I sought the widest variety of subjects, balancing the well known with the obscure, the contemporary with the ancient, the civilian with the soldier, men with women, and Americans with heroes of other nations, while leaving out stories that were too similar. There are simply too many great fighter pilots, Western gunfighters, and combat infantrymen to give each his due, and a succession of such stories can get repetitive.

Why did they fight? All had legitimate causes—war, law enforcement, affairs of honor, or self-defense—but I think that two reasons underlie them.

First, for the most part, they *liked* to. They found the clash of blades and the whiz of bullets stirring; in the words of a Viking poem, they were "battle-glad" and "strife-eager." Describing this quest for danger, Andrew Steinmetz, a 19th-century chronicler of dueling, wrote: "Few sensations are more delightful than those we enjoy upon finding ourselves secure after our lives have been placed in imminent peril, and men who have once known the pleasure of escaping danger often seek it, or are, at least, careless about exposing their persons, hoping again to experience similar gratification." Russian general Mikhail Skobelev put it more vividly when he said, "The risk of life fills me with an exaggerated rapture. The fewer there are to share it, the more I like it. . . . Everything intellectual appears to me to be reflex, but a meeting of man to man, a danger into which I can throw myself headfirst, attracts me, moves me, intoxicates me. I am crazy for it, I love it, I adore it. I run after danger as one runs after women; I wish it never to stop."

Secondly, they were motivated by honor, a concept that's easier to understand than it is to define. In its crudest form, it is little more than a truculent demand for respect, as expressed by John Wayne in *The Shootist*: "I won't be wronged, I won't be insulted, and I won't be laid a hand on. I don't do these things to other people and I require the same from them." At its more refined, it involves an absolute commitment to one's word, reputation, and comrades. It holds that there are things more important than life, and that they are worth fighting—and dying—for. Honor is inextricably bound up with courage, for it takes courage to sustain honor and, after anger's hot blood has cooled, honor to sustain courage. Like courage, it is not an inherently moral quality, but we admire it even in our enemies because it represents a triumph over the fear of death.

It's a paradox, but life achieves its highest value only when it is held less precious than other things. Those who value nothing above their own safety lead diminished lives, but the hero, by valuing honor more than his life, transcends his own mortality. This is often literally true. The cliché holds that it is better to be a live coward than a dead hero, but the coward, hampered by what Patton called "the weakening instinct of self-preservation," may lose his life while the hero, focused solely on victory, survives.

Along with the ever-present possibility of violent death, what makes these stories compelling is the variety of characters involved. Some, like Jean-Louis and Bryce, were masters of their fighting arts, while others, such as Duston or Thomas, won their battles on sheer never-say-die mind-set. Francisco and Hamer were powerful men who towered over their opponents, while Allen and Murphy were no less formidable despite their small stature. Some, like Pizarro and Shaka, suffered harsh poverty in their youth and seemed driven by a lifelong need to command respect, while others, like Alexander and Churchill, were born to wealth and privilege yet displayed the same craving for glory. Some, like Jackson, created successful peacetime careers with the determination that had carried them through combat; others, like Boyington, seemed to lose their bearings without a tangible enemy to fight. Cobb, who exemplified the crudest sort of honor—mere aggressive self-assertion—fought in a berserker rage; York, who exemplified honor's highest ideals, fought in a state of sanctifying grace.

When reading these stories, the reader may wonder to what extent they are true. As someone who's not sure how much to believe of what I read in the daily paper, I can't provide a satisfactory answer. Combat is by nature chaotic, and accounts of an event often conflict, even when provided by the same person. Furthermore, a hero may be tempted to put the best possible spin on his adventures, and if he doesn't, others will. Before the 20th century, historians generally didn't consider it their duty to let facts get in the way of a good story. As for national heroes, glittering deeds accrue to them long after their deaths. I consider the more recent stories the most reliable: I wouldn't put much stock in a Viking saga, but no one receives the Medal of Honor unless his heroic act has been verified by at least two witnesses, and figures such as Bryce and Thomas were subject to press scrutiny and police investigation. At any rate, these are the generally accepted versions of events. I've done my best to cross-check and verify them, but I didn't set out to debunk. I have included stories I suspect have been embellished, but rejected those in which the embellishment has clearly overtaken the facts. (Sir Bevis of Hampton was under consideration, but I lost faith in the accounts after he slew his third dragon.) I think that Alexander's biographer Arrian had a valid perspective. After describing one of his subject's remarkable deeds, he wrote, "If it so happened, I have nothing but praise for Alexander. If the historians told it because they thought it the sort of thing Alexander would do, I still have only praise for Alexander."

Acknowledgments

This book could not have been written without the generous advice and assistance of Rosco Benson, Dr. Thomas Berger, Tom Conroy, Jeff Cooper, Lance Edwards, Thomas Kirchner, Dave Lawrence, Sandy Rabinowitz, Martial Ricart, Kenneth Robinson, Ian Tetrault, Lance Thomas, Barrett Tillman, Kurt Wahlner, and Joe and Lindy Wisdom.

I'd also like to thank the staff of the Miller Memorial Library, Hamden, Connecticut; the New Haven Public Library; the New York Public Library; the National Archives and Records Administration; Gaylynn Childs of the Geary County Historical Society, Junction City, Kansas; Laura Carter of the Western History Collections, the University of Oklahoma; the Mountain

View, Oklahoma, public library; the Metropolitan Library, Oklahoma City; the Oklahoma State Historical Society; the Federal Bureau of Investigation, Office of Public and Congressional Affairs, Research and Communications Unit; and Paul MacDonald of MacDonald Arms, Edinburgh, Scotland.

NOTE: Illustrations were done from photographs or portraits, with the exceptions of Egil Skallagrimsson, Jean-Louis, La Maupin, and Lewis Wetzel, whose likenesses were based on physical descriptions.

The author welcomes reader comments, either through the publisher or directly at deadliestmen@yahoo.com.

1 Alexander the Great

When I chose to organize this collection alphabetically, Alexander turned out to be the opening entry. Though the grandeur of his career makes my focus on him as an individual warrior seem myopic, he remains the most fitting first entry. He was the personification of the classic heroic ideal—suffused with the conquering spirit and larger than life, even in his faults.

From childhood Alexander craved glory. His father, Philip II, was the greatest king Macedonia had ever had, but when Alexander was told of his father's latest victories he would sigh and pout that soon nothing would be left for *him* to conquer. Conflict appealed to him because it offered an opportunity for demonstrations of courage and the attainment of honor; a settled kingdom and a life of wealth and luxury did not.

1

At 16, Alexander served as regent while Philip led his army to Byzantium. Alexander's court was visited by Persian diplomats, who brought him gifts they thought appropriate to an athletic young man: a polo mallet and ball. Holding up the ball, Alexander portentously told his visitors, "This ball is the world, and I am the stick that will move it as it wishes."

During his regency rebellion broke out among the Thracians, a northern border tribe, and Alexander led a flying column to the area and crushed it.

When Alexander was 18, Philip gave him command of the left wing of the cavalry at the Battle of Chæronea while he led the right. Alexander played a pivotal role in the battle, in which Macedonia conquered Greece.

Two years later Philip was assassinated. Alexander seized the kingdom's reins, even as many of its provinces erupted in rebellion. Some among his counselors advised negotiation, but Alexander preferred to act with brutal resolve, so that others would not be tempted to challenge him. A great believer in signs and omens, he visited the oracle at Delphi in search of a divine mandate. He arrived unannounced and dragged the seer forcibly into the temple. The priestess was known for her ambiguous pronouncements, but Alexander got a straight answer: "As if conquered by his violence, she said, 'My son, thou art invincible,'" Plutarch wrote.

In 334 B.C., with his kingdom secured, Alexander set out to conquer the Persian Empire.

He first fought the army of King Darius on the banks of the Granicus River, only two marches from the Hellespont. The Persian nobles planned to kill the Macedonian king at the outset of the battle, knowing that if he were eliminated the invasion would collapse. As he led the charge he could not have been difficult to identify in his glistening armor and a helmet that had a plume of white feathers on each side. Mithridates, Darius' son-in-law, flung a javelin at Alexander that pierced his shield and penetrated his cuirass. Alexander pulled Mithridates' spear

ALESANDRO MAGNO.

free and, spurring his famed steed, Bucephalus, forward, drove his own spear into Mithridates' breastplate. At this display of prowess, nearby ranks in both armies roared their approval. Alexander's spear snapped off against Mithridates' armor.

Mithridates drew his sword, but Alexander thrust his splintered spear handle into his face, knocking him to the ground. While Alexander was focused on one foe, two brothers, Rhosaces and Spithridates, attacked him. As Alexander exchanged sword blows with Rhosaces, Spithridates swung his battle-ax down on Alexander's helmet, shearing through the metal and opening his scalp to the bone. Reeling under the impact, Alexander nonetheless managed to kill Rhosaces. Spithridates raised his ax again, but before he could deliver a coup de grâce, Cleitus, the brother of Alexander's nurse and leader of the royal guard, lopped off his arm at the shoulder. Alexander collapsed and battle raged over his unconscious body until he recovered sufficiently to mount Bucephalus and again led his troops.

The Persian force finally asked for quarter, which Alexander refused to grant. Some 2,500 Persians were killed and wounded, and 2,000 prisoners were sent back to Macedonia as slaves.

During the roughly five years of the Persian campaign, Alexander grew concerned that his men would grow soft as they accumulated slaves and loot, warning them that "the end and perfection of our victories is to avoid the vices that have made our enemies so easy to subdue." To keep his edge he hunted lions and led raids, practiced his archery daily, and would often jump from his moving chariot, run alongside, and then remount it.

At one point during the campaign, while his army was laying siege to Tyre, Alexander took part in a raid behind enemy lines on Mount Antilibanus. As night fell, he saw at some distance a great many scattered fires of the enemy. He ran straight to the nearest, killed two of the enemy that sat by it, snatched up a lighted brand, and returned with it to his own men. They immediately made a great fire, which so alarmed the Tyrians that most of them fled and the rest were routed, according to Chares' account.

Alexander enjoyed comparing battle scars with his men.

Among his wounds were a sword thrust in the thigh; a catapult-fired bolt in the shoulder; an arrow in the leg, which so shattered his shin that bone splinters had to be taken out; and a violent blow from a stone upon the nape of his neck, which dimmed his sight for a period.

By 330 B.C. Alexander had conquered Persia and moved his army against India. When he besieged a city set on a supposedly inaccessible rock, he asked one of his men whether its ruler, Sisimithres, was a brave man. When he was told that on the contrary, Sisimithres was the greatest coward alive, Alexander responded, "Then you tell me that the place may easily be taken, since what is in command of it is weak." And in little time he had done so. It was Alexander's view that nothing was impossible for the man of courage, and nothing secure for the coward.

At Aornus, a fortified plateau at Pir-Sar, which Heracles himself was said to have tried and failed to capture, Alexander led a force of 700 in scaling the sheer cliffs and was the first to reach the summit. He and his men fell upon their terrified foes, killing them and driving them off the precipice. He could now boast that he had taken the fortress that had defied Heracles.

As his conquests continued, Alexander began to insist that he be acknowledged as a god. No one was permitted to question his judgment. When Cleitus, the faithful servant who had saved his life at Granicus, dared to criticize him, he stabbed him to death. Though we might consider Alexander a megalomaniac, his was not an unreasonable claim in the cosmology of the Greeks. Psammon, an Egyptian philosopher, told him that "that which is chief and commands is divine," and an Indian, in response to his query as to how a man might become a god, responded, "By doing that which was impossible for men to do." As an individual warrior, Alexander also had a seemingly godlike dominion over death, meting it out while remaining beyond its grasp.

In eight years Alexander's troops never lost a battle. They conquered an area of over a million-and-a-half square miles, fighting in mountains and deserts, crossing rivers, taking many great cities by siege, and establishing over 70 new ones. But in 326 B.C. they stopped at the river Beas in India and refused to continue. Alexander sulked in his tent, Achilles-like, hoping they would agree to go on. When he relented after three days, his men rejoiced, saying, "Alexander has allowed us, but no other, to defeat him."

As Alexander made his way home, he continued to make his weary troops fight at every opportunity. While attacking a walled city of the Mallians, he felt his men were too slow in climbing the ladders and went up one himself, crouching beneath his shield. At the top, he slew the enemies on the battlement and for a moment stood alone on top of the wall, exhorting his men. Moments later he was joined by three of his closest aides: General Leonnatus; General Peucestas, his shield-bearer; and Abreas, a highly decorated officer in the Guards. Alexander's bold stroke had its desired effect of shaming his troops, but as they rushed forward to join him their weight broke the ladders, leaving him without immediate hope of assistance.

Coming under a shower of arrows as he stood on the battlement, Alexander decided that if he were to be killed it would be while fighting. He leapt down inside the fortress. With his back to the wall, one side protected by a tree and his friends on the other, he took on all comers. Perhaps, like Hector in *The Iliad*, he thought, "Let me at least sell my life dearly and have a not inglorious end, after some feat of arms that shall come to the ears of generations still unborn."

As the Macedonians frantically battered at a nearby gate, Alexander and his band held off a crush of attackers, killing a number of the Mallians who closed in on them, including their commander. Abreas was the first to die, shot in the face by an archer. Then an arrow pierced Alexander's cuirass and entered his chest just above the lung. He managed to dispatch another attacker before a blow from a club dropped him. Peucestas covered Alexander with the sacred shield from the temple at Troy and continued to fight off the horde. Finally a group of Macedonians broke through the gate, another scaled the wall, and Alexander's army took the fortress.

The arrow was removed from Alexander's chest, and for a week he hovered near death. As the morale of his troops dwindled, Alexander knew he must resume command. Drawing on his seemingly limitless reserves of willpower and strength, he mounted his horse and rode slowly through the camp. As his men saw him they burst into cheers, and his officers touched him to assure themselves that he was indeed alive.

In Babylon, in 323 B.C., the 33-year-old Alexander became seriously ill. As he lay on his deathbed his men were permitted to file past him; he acknowledged each with a look or a slight nod. Asked to whom he bequeathed his kingdom, he gasped out, "To the strongest." But no one else had the strength to hold Alexander's empire together, and within a few years it had broken apart.

2 Tom Allen

He succeeded in doing lots of good where men without his roughness would have failed.
—George W. Martin, Junction City mayor

G lory is by no means fairly parceled out. It goes to some based on dubious or exaggerated exploits, while others remain obscure though their deeds are far more remarkable. One of the latter is Tom Allen. He was the city marshal of Junction City, Kansas, from 1871 to 1904. During those years, encompassing the roughest period of the Wild West, he never backed away from a fight—and never lost one either. He rarely used his gun, preferring to enforce the law with his "fistic ability." He could split an inch-thick hardwood board with one punch and had a left hook that never failed him.

Tom Allen was born Thomas Allen Cullinan in Kilrush, Ireland, in 1838, to well-to-do parents. A life of ease lay before him, but his adventurous nature demanded more. At age 11 he went to sea and spent six years traveling the world until he decided to make his home in the United States. He worked a year as a seaman on the Great Lakes, survived a shipwreck on Lake Erie, and became a qualified Mississippi River pilot. In 1857 he went to the Rocky Mountains as an employee of the American Fur Company, hunting and trapping from Yellowstone to the Taos valley. He spent the summer of 1858 at the New Mexico ranch of Lucien Maxwell and Kit Carson, who offered him a partnership. His wanderlust not yet satisfied, he turned them down. He relocated to the Denver area to do some mining and staked a 90-acre claim with three other men. Their right to the land was in dispute, so they strengthened their bargaining position by building themselves a substantial log blockhouse with a firing port in each wall. When a company of 80 armed men rode up to dislodge them, Allen permitted one to come forward, showed him their defenses, and made it clear that ousting them would require a fight to the death. The delegate reported back to the group, which, after due consideration, elected to ride off. (Ironically, the claim didn't pan out and the property was sold for a pittance.)

While in Denver, Allen had his first noteworthy fistfight. After he saw a man strike a woman in public, he challenged him to a no-holds-barred engagement and spent nearly an hour and a half delivering a lesson on the evils of domestic violence. He also had a run-in with a bully known as the Terror of the Gulch, whom he had caught stealing his sluice water. Allen first tried to reason with him and when that failed offered to settle the matter either "according to the rules of the ring" or "rough-and-tumble." The Terror chose the latter form, which allowed for head butting, stomping, biting, and eye gouging. A crowd watched as Allen demonstrated the nuances. The Terror subsequently left the area, perhaps in hopes of terrorizing some more manageable gulch elsewhere.

Denver merchants hired Allen and two of his associates from the land claim to explore the Colorado River eight years before Maj. John Wesley Powell's expedition. They might have succeeded had Utes not stopped them after some 250 miles. The Utes held them captive, but when one of the braves took the liberty of pulling Allen's ear, Allen knocked him flat. He then told the chief that he thought the Utes were cowards and that he could whip the best man in his tribe. The account does not make it clear whether he proceeded to do so or whether the chief was simply tickled by his doughtiness, but in any case Allen and his friends were released.

Allen enlisted in the Union army during the Civil War and served as a scout in the eastern states. He was in Leavenworth, Kansas, in 1863, when the town was taken over by a band of Jayhawkers, or paramilitary ruffians. The marshal was run out of town, and two policemen were shot. At the urging of the authorities, Allen took over as chief of police. With a judicious application of rough-and-tumble, he restored order in 30 days, then turned in his badge.

Allen married in 1865 and in 1871 accepted the job as marshal of Junction City, Kansas. "The post was not a sinecure," as Mayor George Martin dryly observed. Saloons and brothels attracted roughneck troops from nearby Fort Riley, as well as transients passing through on one of the intersecting railway lines, but Allen was not fazed. As the *Junction City Union* put it on April 25, 1885,

> We never heard of another single officer who could corral or lock up a gang of six or seven men at once. Tom Allen has done it frequently. One evening a couple of years ago six men came from a hay camp at Riley with the purpose of having a time. The marshal warned them not to attempt it. They started along the street overturning boxes and disturbing everybody. He overtook them and in less time than we can tell it four of them lay on the ground.

Another time he took without assistance six soldiers out of a gang of eight, shooting two of them slightly. In all his service he has never killed a man, although suffering at times great aggravation and taking desperate chances.

One recruit from Fort Riley, a self-styled tough guy accompanied by a dozen friends to cheer him on, came into town with the intention of pinning the marshal's ears back. Allen sent him back to the fort in an ambulance. On another occasion, eight soldiers were tearing apart a saloon when Allen entered. One at a time he knocked them out and hauled them to the hoosegow. By the time he had impounded seven, the eighth fled. The next morning Allen went over to Fort Riley to arrest the eighth one, and when the captain heard Allen was there he said, "Great Scott, that's the man who licked my sergeant! He can have him."

There was occasional talk of replacing Allen with an officer who would work for less money, but such talk was quashed by those who felt he was well worth his pay. They regarded his integrity and judgment as beyond reproach and allowed him considerable latitude in interpreting the law. If Allen thought a man should be arrested and brought before a judge, he did so; if he thought a man just needed a little aversion therapy, he could deliver that as well.

Allen was once called to deal with a drifter who, as newspaper accounts put it, had offered "a beastly offense to a little girl." He confronted the man, who was over 6 feet tall, and laid out the situation: on the one hand, the man could go to court, people would have to testify, he would be fined $10 that he didn't have, and the city would have to lock him up and feed him; on the other, Allen could give him a beating. To the drifter, who towered above the 5-foot 9-inch marshal, the latter sounded like a good bet, but Allen delivered the beating as promised.

Allen's fists not only packed punishment, but evidently rehabilitation as well. A drunk he had locked up numerous

Kansas State Historical Society

times precipitated a donnybrook in a local drinking establishment and afterward, according to the *Union*'s account, "stood out in the street with a rock in each hand when Tom arrived. 'Looking for a fight, are you?' remarked the peace officer as he gave him a wipe on the jaw, knocking him down and punishing him severely. This individual has never drank a drop since, and has thanked Tom repeatedly for that thrashing."

In 1884, trouble drifted into town in the person of a tall, redheaded stranger. He was raising a ruckus in a general store, brandishing a Colt and frightening people, when Allen showed up. Allen let him know that the next train was leaving in a half-hour and he expected him to be on it. The man ignored the advice and staged another scene that evening at his hotel. Allen again told him to get out of town. The following day, Allen had to intervene once more as the troublemaker disturbed the decorum of a local dive. "Now," said the marshal, "I will take you in."

On the way to the jail the man stopped and said, "You're not man enough to take me in" and slapped Allen across the mouth. The gauntlet having been thrown, Allen lit into him, beat him bloody, disarmed him, and threw him in the clink. When the next train stopped in town, Allen tossed him on it, still covered in dried blood encrusted with bits of crumbled masonry from the cell floor. According to George Martin, Junction City mayor at the time, "I think this was his last experience with amateur prize-fighters who came to test his mettle."

Tom Allen served 33 years as marshal. He was not responsible for a single death, was never injured, and died in bed on June 18, 1904.

3 James Bowie

> *By Hercules! The man was greater than Caesar or Cromwell—nay, nearly equal to Odin or Thor. The Texans ought to build him an altar!*
>
> —Thomas Carlyle

I f even half of the stories told about him are true—and perhaps half of them are—James Bowie must have gotten the glad hand from Odin himself when he sauntered into Valhalla.

It is said that, growing up in the bayou country of Louisiana at the turn of the 19th century, his favorite recreation was fighting alligators. With a knife clamped between his teeth, he would jump on the back of one as it lazed in the shallows, wrapping his arms and legs around it and hanging on tight while the animal plunged into deep water, rolling and twisting to dislodge him, or at least to loosen the grip of an arm or a leg long enough to bite down on it and tear it off. Timing his move just right, Bowie would suddenly grab his knife and plunge it into the alligator's vitals.

To provide meat for the family table, Bowie and his brother Rezin hunted the region's wild longhorn cattle. Sometimes they would shoot one, but other times they would lasso it, bring it to the ground, and then run in, dodging its horns, and cut its throat with a knife.

After leaving home, Bowie supported himself by sawing lumber and operating a plantation. He grew into a muscular 6-foot 1-inch, 180-pound man, noted for his powerful grip and penetrating gray-blue eyes. Intelligent and ambitious, he aspired to advance himself socially and developed the style and manners of a gentleman. As his renown as a fighting man spread, his pleasant and soft-spoken demeanor made him seem all the more lethal.

As of 1808 it was illegal to import slaves into the United States, and the only slaves who could be traded were those already here. Bowie formed a partnership with the pirate Jean Lafitte, who smuggled slaves in from the Caribbean, and for two years Bowie sold them throughout the South, earning some $65,000, which he invested in land.

Bowie made Alexandria, Louisiana, the headquarters of his business enterprises. There he quickly became an enemy of Maj. Norris Wright, for reasons ranging from financial to political. Wright was a notorious duelist who'd had at least five encounters, killing two men. One day, as he saw Bowie on the street, Wright pulled a gun and fired on him without warning. The bullet reportedly was deflected by a silver dollar in Bowie's pocket. Bowie drew his own gun, only to have it misfire. He then launched himself at the major and would have killed him with his bare hands had friends not pulled them apart. After this incident, Bowie vowed that he would never again be without a reliable weapon and had a leather rig made so that he could carry a large knife between his shoulder blades.

The hostility between Bowie and Wright grew and ended violently on September 19, 1827, a year after the original incident, at the Vidalia sandbar, a popular dueling spot on the

Mississippi some 70 miles north of Alexandria. Bowie had gone there as part of a group backing one of the parties, Samuel Levi Wells III, in an affair of honor. Among Wells' other supporters were Maj. George McWhorter and Gen. Samuel Cuny. Wright supported Wells' opponent, Dr. Thomas Hardy Maddox, as did Col. Robert Crain, the brothers Carey and Alfred Blanchard, and several others. All in all, some 16 men were present, all armed to the teeth. Major Wright had not yet arrived as the duel commenced.

When the signal was given, Wells and Maddox fired at each other and missed. After another bloodless exchange, they agreed that honor had been satisfied, shook hands, and suggested their parties share a drink of wine. However, as the opposing factions approached, the rancor between them boiled to the surface. Samuel Cuny, who had been feuding with Crain for some time, reached for his pistol and called out to him, "This is a good time to settle our difficulty, here and now." Crain, who carried a brace of dueling pistols, fired first, missing Cuny but hitting Bowie in the hip and knocking him off his feet. Cuny and Crain then exchanged shots. Cuny's shot grazed Crain's arm, but Crain's ball struck Cuny in the chest and killed him. Bowie, who had managed to get back on his feet, pulled his knife and charged Crain. Crain struck him so hard on the head with his empty pistol that its stock broke. Bowie dropped to his knees, and Maddox jumped on him and wrestled him to the ground. Bowie recovered his strength and had thrown him off when Major Wright arrived and shot at him. Bowie shot back and hit Wright, who exclaimed, somewhat prematurely, "The damned rascal has killed me!"

Wright drew his sword cane and plunged it into Bowie's chest, but its point turned against the breastbone. While Wright stood over him, trying to free his blade, Bowie reached up, grabbed him by his shirtfront, and yanked him down onto his knife. As the blade plunged into Wright's viscera, Bowie pulled it upwards and disemboweled him. As Bowie later said, "I twisted the knife until I heard his heart-strings sing." Wright died on the spot.

As Bowie stood up and pulled the sword from his chest, Alfred and Carey Blanchard fired at him, and he was hit once in the arm. Though wounded four times now, he turned savagely on Alfred and sliced a good-sized slab from his forearm. Carey fired again at Bowie but missed. As the brothers turned to flee, Carey was shot and wounded by McWhorter.

The Battle of the Sandbar was over, having lasted only about 10 minutes. Two men had died and four—Bowie, Crain, and the Blanchard brothers—were injured. In the days when the expression "he killed his man" bespoke respect, it had firmly established James Bowie as someone to be reckoned with. It took him months to heal, but the strength and will to live that carried him through the battle facilitated his recovery.

In 1829, a wealthy cotton planter and friend of Bowie's, Dr. William Lattimore, sent his son to Natchez, Mississippi, to sell the year's cotton crop and deposit the proceeds in a bank. Young William Lattimore was enticed into a gambling den run by "Bloody John" Sturdivant, a gangster known to have killed at least three of his enemies and to have burned down the homes of four others. Lattimore was plied with drinks and quickly fleeced of thousands of dollars. Despondent, he wandered the streets until he bumped into Bowie.

Bowie, an experienced gambler, assured Lattimore that he would recover his bankroll. Seating himself at a faro game in Sturdivant's saloon, Bowie slammed his knife into the table and told the dealer that if he caught him cheating, its point would rearrange his innards. Perhaps the poor man's concentration was unfairly disturbed, but Bowie soon won back Lattimore's money.

Sturdivant fancied himself the equal of any man in a scrap and had previously claimed that had he been a participant in the Battle of the Sandbar the renowned Jim Bowie would not have survived. Now that his dealer had been caught cheating and he had had to relinquish a few thousand dollars, Sturdivant felt sufficiently wronged to issue Bowie a challenge. Bowie cheer-

The UT Institute of Texan Cultures at San Antonio

fully accepted. They agreed to fight with knives, their left wrists bound together with a scarf. Bowie gave his pistol to Lattimore, with instructions to use it on any of Sturdivant's cronies who might be tempted to intervene.

As the contest began, Sturdivant stabbed at Bowie. Bowie parried the move, and with a quick thrust slashed Sturdivant's right arm to the bone, severing the tendons and causing his blade to drop from his limp fingers. In the time-honored tradition of chivalrous heroes, Bowie announced he could not kill a helpless man and let Sturdivant's friends attend to him. Sturdivant, in the time-honored tradition of villains, seethed and plotted revenge.

It was at about this time that the knife that bears Bowie's name was designed. There are different accounts of its genesis, but one has it that Bowie hired James Black, an Arkansas blacksmith renowned for the superior steel he used, to make up a knife with a foot-long blade and a guard separating the blade from the hilt. The guard was to be made out of relatively soft brass so that it would be more likely to catch and hold an attacker's stroke than to let it glance off. The blade of this knife was heavy enough to be capable of chopping through bone, yet, with its clip point positioned along its centerline, it was as effective in the thrust as in the cut. It was destined to become the classic American fighting knife, the weapon of choice among men who put their faith in cold steel.

Meanwhile, Sturdivant hired three assassins to ambush Bowie. Knowing that Bowie and a servant were traveling from Arkansas to Texas, the ambushers waited in a patch of canebrake and fired on the two men as they rode through at night. Having killed the servant and wounded Bowie, the assassins moved in to finish the job. Presumably, they were unaware of two salient facts: Bowie had just taken delivery of his new knife, and being shot made him testy. When the first desperado seized the bridle of Bowie's horse, Bowie leaned forward and stabbed him in the neck, killing him. A second man, armed with a knife, slashed at Bowie's calf, and Bowie jumped from the saddle and disemboweled him with an upward swing. The third hireling, reconsidering the odds, turned and ran. Bowie caught up with him and split his skull.

The gunfire had attracted men with lanterns, who shouted, "Who's there?"

Bowie replied, "Five of us. One alive."

In 1830, Bowie settled in Texas, then still part of Mexico. He became a Mexican citizen and was elected a colonel in the militia that later became the Texas Rangers. In 1831, he married Ursula Veramendi, daughter of a wealthy and well-connected family, and is believed to have fathered two daughters.[1] Family life didn't change his restless nature, though, and he continued to pursue far-flung business opportunities and chase Indians with the Rangers. In December 1832, while searching for the fabled San Saba silver mine, he and eight other men were attacked by 150 Comanches. Throwing together a rough circular fortification of stone, they crouched behind it and held off the attack for a full day. Their ammunition almost gone, they had resolved to fight to the end with their knives when the Indians pulled back. His group had one man killed and three wounded, whereas Bowie claimed to have seen 21 Comanches fall.

During this period Bowie is said to have participated in several exotic set-tos. In one, he and a Spaniard faced each other straddling a bench, their legs tied beneath it to hold them in place. While the Spaniard drew back his long blade for a thrust, Bowie, with his shorter knife, struck first and killed him. In another, he is supposed to have accepted a challenge from a Creole in New Orleans. Bowie's terms: knives, bare feet, a pitch-black locked room. When the door was unlocked, only Bowie walked out.

A journalist, William McGinley, witnessed Bowie in action in 1832 while he was traveling the Cumberland Road by stagecoach. Besides Bowie, the other passengers included the statesman Henry Clay, a young woman, and an unidentified pipe smoker. The young woman politely asked the smoker to extinguish his pipe, because it was making her ill. The man replied that "he had paid his fare and would do as he pleased." Bowie

---

1.   Bowie's family died two years later in a cholera epidemic.

may have been ignorant of the perils of secondhand smoke, but he recognized an insult to a lady. According to McGinley, he "drew from the back of his neck a wicked looking knife, the worst I had ever seen," sprang forward and pressed it to the smoker's throat, giving him one minute to throw his pipe out of the window. The pipe was tossed and tranquility restored.

Another time, Bowie witnessed a man whipping a slave tied to a tree and demanded he stop. When the man refused, Bowie cut the slave's bonds. This infuriated the slave's owner. He tried to shoot Bowie, but his pistol misfired. Bowie leaped on the man and nearly severed his gun hand, but he then wrapped a kerchief around the man's wrist and took him to a doctor.

In 1833, Bowie once again came to the rescue of a hapless gambler swindled by cardsharps. The venue this time was the *Orleans*, a riverboat, and the victim a young bridegroom traveling back to Natchez from a trip north. After his bride told Bowie of their woes, he joined in the crooked game. When the pot reached $100,000, he spotted the dealer's accomplice slipping him an extra card. Drawing his knife, Bowie told the dealer to lay down his cards, threatening to kill him if there were six. The dealer angrily demanded his name. At the response "James Bowie," the other card players fell back, but the dealer, not knowing whom he was dealing with, challenged him. They went to the hurricane deck, where each climbed on top of one of the wheelhouses, which were 12 yards apart. There was a count of *one . . . two . . . three . . . fire . . . stop*. The cardsharp fired before the signal, on the count of three, but missed. A second later, at the command to fire, Bowie shot and killed him, and the body rolled off the deck into the river. Bowie gave the bridegroom back what he had lost and kept the rest. This is the only duel Bowie is known to have fought with pistols.

After Texas came under the dominion of General Antonio López de Santa Anna, the American settlers rebelled. Three hundred Texas irregulars drove 1,400 Mexican troops from San Antonio and the fortified mission known as the Alamo. A counterattack was expected, so the rebellion's leader, Sam Houston, ordered Bowie to go and supervise an evacuation. Upon arriving, Bowie decided against carrying out his orders. Santa Anna would be forced to retake San Antonio before moving north, and Bowie reasoned that a spirited resistance at the Alamo would buy the rebellion time.

While helping to raise a cannon to the top of a wall, Bowie fell and fractured his hip. He became ill, possibly with pneumonia, and was confined to bed. William Barret Travis took command. Despite Bowie's illness, when Travis drew a line in the sand and asked every man to cross it who wished to fight with him to the end, Bowie asked that his cot be carried across, according to one witness who left the fortress.

Bowie is said to have been bayoneted to death when the Alamo was overrun on March 6, 1836. No one survived to provide an account, but it is assumed he went out fighting. When she heard he had died, his mother is supposed to have reflected a moment and said, "I'll wager no wounds were found in his back."

4 Gregory "Pappy" Boyington

> *Just name a hero and I'll prove he's a bum.*
>
> —Gregory Boyington

Gregory Boyington earned his Marine Corps wings in 1935. As a fighter pilot he was top notch—it was with life's other challenges that he had difficulty. He was a heavy drinker who got into numerous car accidents and fist-fights and was in almost constant trouble with his superiors. His marriage was in trouble as well, and his wife divorced him in 1941. Heavily in debt, Boyington resigned from the marines and went to China as a mercenary in Claire Chennault's American Volunteer Group (AVG), the renowned Flying Tigers, who helped to fight the Japanese invaders.

Life in the AVG was not conducive to long-range plans. Boyington slept in a barracks whose metal roof was ventilated by bullet holes and one rather large opening through which a dud bomb had fallen. Between missions he spent his time drinking in the officer's club. Once, when the airfield was strafed, he ran out the door, hurdled a railing, and landed in a slit trench, only then realizing that he had instinctively maintained his priorities: in each hand he held an unbroken bottle of Scotch. He fought as hard as he drank and claimed six kills,[2] even though he was flying the Curtiss P-40, which was no match for the Mitsubishi AGM Zero.

In July 1942, Boyington left the AVG for the United States rather than be drafted into the U.S. Army Air Corps. As far as he was concerned, he was strictly a marine. To his chagrin, his loyalty was not reciprocated—the marines did not seem to want him back. He spent months in Seattle, parking cars for a living, all the while firing off letters to Washington demanding reinstatement. He finally got back in as a marine pilot, but even after his being returned to the Pacific, more than a year went by before he saw any action. At 31, he was considered old for combat, and a broken leg suffered in a drunken brawl left him temporarily unfit for duty. He whiled away his time performing rear-echelon duties, going mad with frustration.

In August 1943, Boyington proposed to his old friend Colonel Sanderson that he be allowed to scrape together a temporary fighter squadron under the number of an inactive unit, to be filled with unattached veterans and replacement pilots from the pilots' pool and equipped with training Corsairs. Permission was granted, and VMF 214, the "Black Sheep Squadron" was born.[3] The pilots chose that name out of deference to public sensibilities—their first choice was "Boyington's Bastards," but they were told it would have had a chilling effect on press coverage.

The F4U Corsair had twice the horsepower of the Zero and a devastating array of six .50-caliber machine guns, but most of the men in the Black Sheep Squadron had little or no combat

2.   The U.S. Marine Corps accepted the figure, although the AVG credited Boyington with only three and a half.
3.   Boyington's version of the unit's genesis is contradicted by other accounts.

· KIRCHNER ·

experience. Boyington, dubbed "Pappy" because he was 10 years older than most of his men, created an esprit de corps with nightly parties and sing-alongs, where he imparted his own hard-earned knowledge of aerial combat. He asked his men to consider every possible combat problem and figure out a solution in advance, because there would be no time to think when a problem actually arose. In the split-second world of aerial combat, actions had to be preprogrammed, reflexive. He told them to get above the enemy, come in on a high stern pass, hold their fire until they were within good, close range, then let him have it. Afterward, they should dive out, climb away, and come back to the battle with altitude and speed. The Corsair could outclimb and outdive the Zero, but Boyington warned his men not to try to loop or turn with one or the Japanese plane would end up on their tail. Above all else, he told them, get in the fight. Boyington knew that aggressive spirit mattered more than skill or tactics—no man ever shot down an enemy plane unless he wanted the kill more than anything else in the world.

On September 16, on their third flight providing cover for bombers flying from Guam to Bougainville, the Black Sheep ran into a flock of about 40 Zeros. Boyington was caught by surprise, having not even turned on his electric gun sight or charged his machine guns. A Japanese pilot, as confused as he was, pulled up alongside him and waggled his wings in the standard "join up" gesture, then pulled ahead. Boyington fired a burst into him at 50 yards that sent him plunging straight into the sea. Boyington dived down to where the Japanese were attacking the bombers and exploded a Zero at a range of 50 feet, protectively throwing his arm over his face as he flew through its debris, which left dents on his cowling and wings.

Boyington knew how rarely a pilot gets a chance to score against the enemy and was determined to make the most of it. So, as a Zero looped out of an attack on a pair of U.S. Navy FGF Hellcats, Boyington caught it at the top of its arc and put a burst into its belly, sending it spiraling down in flames. He spotted another Zero flying just above the water and bore down on it. As he was getting into firing position, his instincts told him the situation was too easy, a setup. Cutting a tight turn, he sent a burst into the Zero that was closing in on his tail. Streaming heavy smoke, the Zero glided at a shallow angle for about 10 miles until it splashed in. While searching for his original prey, Boyington spotted another at 600 yards and opened up on it. He saw it pouring out smoke but got no confirmation of it as a kill or even as a probable. With fuel running low, he turned back toward base. He saw a Corsair that was being used for target practice by two Zeros and made a run on them when suddenly four of his guns went out of action. The closer Zero pulled almost straight up, and Boyington followed and hit it with a burst of his two functioning .50s for his fifth kill of the day. His speed too low, he stalled and pitched into an inverted spin before regaining control. He returned to the base with his fuel gauge bouncing on empty and learned that four of his guns had expended their 400-round belts and the other two had only 15 rounds left each.

When Boyington wasn't fighting the Japanese, he fought the brass, some of whom took exception to his casual approach to regulations and discipline. Between battles in this two-front war, he indulged his appetite for women, gambling, and whiskey-and-sodas. "He was an alcoholic in the days when we didn't know what an alcoholic was," said one of his men, who added, "but I've always maintained that he could fly better drunk than most people could sober." Awakened for predawn missions, Boyington often crawled out of his tent and looked toward the mess hall light, seeing it multiplied anywhere from two to six times. He dunked his head into a tub of water as many times as it took for the number to dwindle to one, then figured he was good to go.[4]

Once, in a bar, Boyington overheard a drunken fellow pilot bemoaning "Pappy's luck." As that pilot saw it, every time

---

4.   Boyington's debauchery was actually outdone by a pilot in the Japanese navy, Temei Akamatsu, who refused to attend pilot briefings or wait on the flight line, and at mission time had to be summoned from a nearby brothel. He would then tear onto the airfield in a jalopy, waving a half-empty whiskey bottle as he staggered drunkenly to his plane. He had frequent fistfights with superiors as well as subordinates. Though repeatedly disciplined and broken in rank, Akamatsu was a genius in the air whom the Imperial Navy could not do without. In the powerful but clumsy Mitsubishi J2M *Raiden*, he shot down more than 10 of the superior Mustangs and Hellcats, as well as at least one B-29. He survived six full years of aerial combat and is credited with about 50 kills. He claimed 350.

Boyington happened to sober up long enough to fly a mission, he got lucky: "He is surrounded by Japs and has to shoot his way out to get back to the free brandy to cure his hangover." Boyington allowed as how he normally would have decked a guy for a comment like that, but the bar had short hours and he couldn't spare the time.

Boyington, a varsity wrestler in college, was always game for a tussle. He once got into an argument over who had the advantage in a fight, a wrestler or a boxer, with a pilot trained in the latter art. The two men decided to settle it. Boyington's face was punched to a bloody pulp, but once he got his arms around his opponent he wrestled him to the ground and repeatedly bashed his head against the floor. Afterward, as the two men swigged beers, the other pilot said, "That was a lucky hold you got."

They went at it again. Pummeled a second time, Boyington's opponent conceded the point.

Within a month of the birth of the Black Sheep, the lightly armored Zeros had become wary of engaging Pappy's Corsairs, preferring to concentrate their efforts on the lumbering U.S. bombers. It was getting harder and harder for pilots to raise their tallies, a malady Boyington termed "lackajaps." On the night of October 16, as the Black Sheep caroused at the Hotel de Gink on Guadalcanal, Boyington's men gave him a beer shampoo and chanted, "Get us a Jappy, Pappy!"

The following day was overcast as the Black Sheep flew cover for a bombing mission on Kahili, the Japanese base on Bougainville. As usual, they searched unsuccessfully for enemy fighters as the bombers dumped their loads. Once the bombers headed home, the squadron turned with them, every man frustrated with the lack of action. Boyington was desperate. At his age, he figured he was unlikely to get another tour.

Halfway back to Guadalcanal, Boyington had an inspiration. He turned his boys back toward Kahili and began acting the part of a leader of a bomber group radioing for a fighter escort. He gave his location and an altitude reading of 20,000 feet. Moments later, he received a promise of prompt assistance from one of the English-speaking Japanese radio operators who monitored all American radio traffic.

A few minutes later, a formation of 30 Zeros roared in at 25,000 feet, searching the air below for the unprotected American bombers. There were none to be seen; the 20 Corsairs of the Black Sheep squadron were 5,000 feet above them. As Pappy opened his canopy and tossed out his cigarette, the squad dived.

The lead Zero disintegrated under the hammering of Boyington's six .50s. Boyington flew straight across the top of the Japanese formation, downing another, and still another just over the ocean surface. Tracers were weaving a wild pattern all around him, but he was too busy to worry about them. He clawed his way back up for more altitude, searching for prey, but the game was already over. The Zeros that were still in the air were fleeing back to Kahili. The Black Sheep had shot down 20 planes and had not lost one of their own.

As Boyington's score reached 19, pressure on him grew to surpass the American record of 26 kills set by World War I ace Eddie Rickenbacker. The press began interviewing him every time he returned from a sortie, asking him when he thought he would break it. But aerial combat was getting harder to arrange. Trying to stir some up, Boyington flew once more over Kahili, taunting the Japanese over his radio and challenging them to come up and fight. "If you're so brave, Major Boyington, why don't you come down here?" was the usual response. Boyington once accepted the invitation and strafed Kahili's landing field, flying off after one pass, chased by antiaircraft fire.

On Christmas Eve, 1943, the Black Sheep sat around Boyington's tent in the wilting tropical heat, batting at mosquitoes and shooing away oversized centipedes. They sang bawdy songs and drank an improvised eggnog fortified with medicinal whisky. Talk got around to Pappy and his 26th kill. As much as they wanted to see him break the record, his men told him they didn't want him to get killed doing it.

"Don't worry about me," responded Boyington. "They can't kill me. If you guys ever see me going down with 30 Zeros on my tail, don't give me up. Hell, I'll met you in a San Diego bar six months after the war, and we'll all have a drink for old times' sake."

They raised a toast to that San Diego bar.

On Christmas[5] of 1943, Boyington was flying his daily patrol when he spotted a dozen or so Zeros heading for the Japanese stronghold of Rabaul on New Britain. He closed in until he was a mere 50 feet behind one. The Japanese pilot was completely unaware of his presence, so Boyington took his time checking his gun chargers and trimming his rudder and stabilizer tabs. He placed the Zero precisely in the center of his sights before squeezing off an economical burst. The pilot bailed out as the plane burst into flame. Boyington then moved in on a two-Zero formation, settling in 100 feet behind one and shooting it down. As the other pilot circled his parachuting companion, giving him cover, Boyington came out of the sun and delivered a burst. The Zero rolled onto its back and hit the ocean upside down. He decided to swing by Rabaul, and there spotted a nine-plane patrol. Gliding down, again from out of the sun, he opened up on the last plane in the formation from 300 yards, feeling his Corsair buck against the heavy recoil of the six .50s as the Zero burst into flame. The other Zeros regrouped and chased Boyington, but he eluded them. While heading home, he spotted a surfaced Japanese submarine and put a long burst into its conning tower. A hell of thing for one guy to do to another on Christmas, he mused, but then, Christmas was never his favorite holiday.

By December 27, Boyington was just one short of matching Rickenbacker's record. It wasn't getting any easier, though. On December 28, the Black Sheep lost three men during a fighter sweep, and when Boyington returned to the base he lost his

---

5. Black Sheep records indicate that it was actually December 23 on which Boyington flew this mission. He may have identified it as Christmas by mistake—or purposely, in order to make a better story.

patience with reporters who continued to badger him. "You don't give a damn whether I beat that record or not!" he exploded. "It will make just as good a story if I get killed in the attempt to beat it or if I tie it."

On January 3, 1944, Boyington and his wingman, George Ashmun, spotted 10 Zeros off Rabaul. Ashmun took a covering position while Boyington lit into them. Ashmun called out, "Gramps, you got a flamer!" It was Boyington's twenty-sixth. According to Boyington, he and Ashmun each downed another but found themselves under attack from 20 Zeros that had been waiting in the clouds above. Ashmun's plane took some hits and began throwing smoke. Boyington claimed that he had shot down another Zero while trying to clear the Japanese off Ashmun's tail but realized he had troubles of his own as bullets began to stitch his wings and slam the armor plate at his back. Flames engulfed Ashmun's plane, and it hit the ocean. Boyington went into a dive to outrun his pursuers. As he pulled out, just over the water, his main gas tank exploded, turning the cockpit into a blast furnace. With one hand, Boyington grabbed the rip cord of his parachute and with the other unfastened his safety harness. He didn't have time to open his canopy, so he kicked the stick forward and was thrown through it by the negative g force. His chute blew open and he splashed into the water.

When Boyington did not return, every available plane went out on a desperate search but found no trace of him. With just a few days left in their combat tour, the Black Sheep wreaked vengeance on the Japanese, shooting up boats, barges, gun positions, buildings, encampments, and supply dumps and strafing troops. They also shot down four more Zeros. The press had a great story: Boyington declared missing in action on the very mission in which he had surpassed Rickenbacker.

On January 8, 1944, the original Black Sheep squadron was broken up, its members scattered as replacements, its designation assigned to a new group of pilots. In 12 weeks, its 51 pilots had shot down 97 planes; Boyington alone accounting for 22.

The Marine Corps, which had never even awarded him a Purple Heart, put him in for the Medal of Honor.

Boyington wasn't out of surprises, though. When the war ended, he was released from a POW camp.

Boyington got a chuckle when he learned that he had been awarded the Medal of Honor "posthumously." He figured the brass would never have allowed him to receive it if they suspected he would turn up alive to embarrass them. Imprisonment had enforced a cold-turkey treatment for his alcoholism, but after returning home he kept his pledge to meet his men for a drink, and soon he was making up for lost time. His drunk-driving arrests, marital problems, and run-ins with the law became the main focus of press coverage about him. He seemed determined to validate his dictum, "Just name a hero and I'll prove he's a bum."

It didn't have to be that way. Had the Marine Corps not accepted Boyington's claim of six kills with the AVG, and his last two, for which there was no independent confirmation, its highest ranked ace would have been Joe Foss, a far more respectable hero, with 26 kills. Too much of a gentleman to press the point, Foss went on to become a brigadier general in the Air National Guard, governor of South Dakota, and president of the National Rifle Association (NRA). Boyington did little with the rest of his life but burnish his image as the hard-drinking, two-fisted rebel who, for a few months in the cockpit of a fighter plane, found glory.

5 Delf A. "Jelly" Bryce

He never missed. Never. He was a perfect shot.

—Leah Rhymer,
childhood friend of Bryce

There were gunmen who were introduced to firearms at an early age, but few as early as "Jelly" Bryce. According to his sister, "When he was a baby they let him teethe on Daddy's unloaded pistol. They propped him up with pillows there in the crib and let him go after it."

Of Cherokee descent, Bryce was born on December 6, 1906, on a Kiowa reservation near the small town of Mountain View, Oklahoma, where, as he said, you could look farther and see less than any other place on earth.

Before he entered school he had his own .22 rifle and practiced with it constantly, soon proving himself a shooting prodigy. He shined shoes to earn money for ammunition, and his doting grandfather began subsidizing his shooting expenses. Every summer from 1922 to 1926 Bryce attended a 30-day civilian military camp at Ft. Sill, Oklahoma, where he trained on the pistol, submachine gun, rifle, and machine gun. Competing against hundreds of other trainees, he took first place with both rifle and pistol.

Bryce's great passions were hunting and fishing, and he went to work as a Oklahoma State Game Ranger in August 1927. For some reason he resigned after a year and set out for the University of Oklahoma. En route, he learned of a pistol match in Shawnee, sponsored by the Oklahoma Sheriffs and Peace Officers Convention, and decided to enter it.

Climbing out of his car at the event, Bryce met Clarence O. Hurt, Oklahoma City's assistant chief of police and head of its shooting team, and asked if he could enter. Hurt was dubious of "Joe College" in his natty white slacks and sweater, but decided to see whether he had any talent. He stuck an envelope against a tree, paced off the regulation distance, and told him to shoot at it.

Bryce drew and fired fast, putting six shots from his well-worn .38 Special into a 2-inch circle. Flabbergasted, Hurt declared, "You are now a member of the Oklahoma City Police Department."

Hurt had an ulterior motive for hiring Bryce on the spot. He badly wanted his team to win that day's pistol match, and with Bryce's participation it did. Bryce took home the first prize, $100 in gold.

After he had been on the job a few months, on November 6, 1928, his skill with the pistol proved of far greater value. Working plainclothes in the Auto Theft Bureau, Bryce and his partner, B.D. "Chick" Faris, had been tailing two known car thieves, John Robinson and Johnny Walker, when they observed the former getting into a parked car. Bryce walked up and opened the driver's-side door. Robinson, who was trying to hot-wire the vehicle, looked up at the dapper 21-year-old and snarled, "Who are you?"

"A police officer," answered Bryce.

At that, Robinson pulled a pistol and swung it on Bryce, but before he could shoot, Bryce drew his own revolver from under his jacket and shot him in the arm. Robinson and Walker surrendered. (Even though news accounts described Robinson's wound as slight, Bryce's police file reports it as fatal.)

During his police career Bryce carried either a .38 Special or a .44 Special he called his "lucky gun," its ivory grips decorated with a black cat and the number 13 on one side, a steer head on the other. Bryce practiced his draw for hours a day in front of a three-way mirror in the police station locker room and honed his marksmanship on the department's indoor range.

On March 10, 1929, Bryce and Faris arrested car thieves Kilroy Gage, George Vaughn, and Earl Johnston. A pistol was taken from Gage. Faris got into the stolen vehicle to accompany the three suspects to the police station while Bryce followed in the patrol car. Gage drove, Vaughn sat in the passenger seat, and in the backseat, Johnston sat on the left and Faris on the right. As they drove, Gage suddenly told Vaughn to take the wheel, whirled round, and threw himself at Faris. As the two fought for the policeman's gun, Bryce jumped out of his car and climbed onto the stolen car's right-hand running board. Faris was slightly wounded in the arm before he was able to wrest his gun from Gage. Bryce shot Gage in the small of the back and then shot Vaughn twice under his arm, killing him, while Faris shot Gage in the shoulder and abdomen. Johnston stayed out of the fight, a decision that undoubtedly saved his life. The running gun battle ended in front of the Orpheum Theater, where a show was just letting out.

There are several explanations of how Bryce got the nickname "Jelly," but according to one, as Gage crawled from the car and collapsed on the Orpheum Theater's steps, he looked up at Bryce in his white Palm Beach suit, Panama hat, and two-toned brown shoes and groaned, "I can't believe I got it from a jelly bean like you." Jelly bean was a slang term for a fancy dresser, particularly a sissyish one. Bryce liked the nickname so much that in 1958 he had it legally made part of his name.

The newspapers treated Faris as the hero in this incident; he had killed a man in a gun battle just a week before, but he admitted he was not sure his shots were effective this time. Bryce's police dossier credits him with both kills.

An unfortunate incident occurred in late 1930, when Bryce and an unnamed partner responded to a radio call regarding a burglary in progress at a grocery store on the outskirts of the city. As they arrived, a man later identified as W.L. Johnson was coming out the door with a sack of money in one hand and a revolver in the other. Bryce and his partner identified themselves as police officers and called on Johnson to drop the gun, but he began shooting at them. They returned fire and killed him. Afterward it was learned that Johnson, who had been drinking heavily, was the store's owner. Bryce and his partner were exonerated after an investigation.

Bryce and H.V. Wilder made the front pages after a January 18, 1933, gun battle when they pursued a robbery suspect on city streets. The suspect was shooting from his getaway car, but the officers held their fire until they were out of the populated area. Then they opened up and hit the car 37 times and, by shooting out a rear tire, caused it to crash into a ditch. Bryce's police dossier lists the unidentified suspect as having died of his wounds. He was on the lam from a robbery-homicide in Tulsa, his getaway car equipped with a supercharged engine and a police-band radio.

On December 29, 1933, authorities got a tip that escaped convict Wilbur Underhill was holed up in Shawnee, 40 miles east of Oklahoma City. Underhill, known as the Tri-State Terror, had been on a seven-month bank-robbing and murder spree and was a suspect in the Kansas City massacre in which four lawmen were killed. That night Bryce, carrying a Thompson submachine gun, was one of seven policemen and FBI agents who approached the back of Underhill's hideout.

Hurt and a federal agent saw Underhill through a rear window and called on him to surrender, but Underhill grabbed a pair of Lügers and began firing. Bryce and the others fired back. Underhill went down but somehow got back on his feet, grabbed a shotgun, and ran out the front door spraying buckshot. After losing his pursuers in a ground fog, he broke into a downtown furniture store where he was later found lying in a bed, bleeding from 11 bullet wounds. He died a week later in a prison hospital.

A character as colorful as Bryce tends to inspire tall tales. One has it that he accompanied the FBI agents sent to arrest Vern Miller, then public enemy number one. Miller made a dash for his car and drove away as the agents closed in, and Bryce emptied the 50-round drum of his Thompson after him. Miller was so unnerved that he stopped at the next town and surrendered, insisting he needed protection "from that wild Indian." An agent examining Miller's car counted forty-nine .45-caliber holes in it, and couldn't resist needling Bryce about the missing bullet. "I think I was shorted," responded Bryce.

On July 18, 1934, Oklahoma City police got a tip that three gangsters, one of whom was wanted for the murder of a policeman in McPherson, Kansas, were holed up at the seedy Wren Hotel on West Main Street. Today a SWAT team would be sent in, but then the equation was simpler: three gangsters, three detectives.

The hotel was owned by 28-year-old Merle Bolen, but it was her mother that Bryce and his two associates found running the desk. They asked to see Bolen, whose room the mother led them to. She knocked perfunctorily and opened the door, then recoiled in surprise and began closing it. Jamming his foot in the crack, Bryce said, "I told you, we're police officers." He shoved the door open and entered the room, his revolver still holstered under his jacket. On the bed, along with Bolen, lounged J. Ray O'Donnell, one of the gangsters the detectives had come for. As Bryce later described it, "When I looked into the room there he was, up on his elbows with a gun in both hands, aimed right at me. He was lying on the near side, and the woman was on the other side of him. I jumped to one side, out of the line of fire, grabbed my gun and tore him up."

To reiterate: O'Donnell held a semiautomatic pistol on Bryce, steadying it with both hands. In the instant before the gangster could squeeze the pistol's trigger, Bryce reached under his jacket, drew his .44, and started shooting. His first five bullets went into O'Donnell and the last into the mattress. It may be the most impressive practical demonstration of the fast draw on record.

In its November 12, 1945, issue, *Life* magazine featured Bryce in a three-page photo spread, drawing and firing in a stroboscopic multiple exposure. Bryce started with his right hand outstretched, shoulder high, a silver dollar on the back of his fingers. He yanked his hand back, drew his revolver, and was ready to shoot before the coin had fallen past his waist. Elapsed time: two-fifths of a second. The spread also shows a silhouette target that Bryce fired upon at 21 feet, the average range of a gunfight, with six shots grouped tightly in its center.

As he reached for his gun he would step quickly to the left to create a space between his body and his jacket into which his hand could slip unimpeded. He fired one-handed, feet spread, knees bent, and crouched, under the theory that if he were hit he would fall forward and could keep shooting. Asked to compare his swooping, circular draw to the style of the Old West, Bryce described the latter as "a four-count draw: one, reach for gun; two, pull gun from holster; three, aim gun. The fourth move was to fire, but the man wasn't alive anymore by that time." Bryce didn't use his sights except for slow, precise shots. Though his technique was called "instinct" or "reflex" shooting, it relied on neither instinct nor reflex, but rather on precise, painstakingly honed eye-hand coordination. Few had the natural talent and determination that enabled Bryce to master this technique, which remained the law enforcement

KIRCHNER

standard for a generation. It has since been replaced by the two-handed Weaver or isosceles stances (in which the shooter stands erect and uses his sights), techniques in which it is far easier to attain proficiency.

Most FBI agents were lawyers or accountants, but in 1934, after a number of them were killed in shootouts, the bureau began recruiting law enforcement officers with proven gun-fighting abilities.[6] Bryce submitted an application on May 8 of that year. From it we learn that he was 5 feet 8 inches and weighed about 150 pounds, had a horsefly tattooed on one shoulder and "Mom" on the other, had a bullet wound through the left side of his chest from when he was 16, and was divorced and had a son. His police file included the notation, "This officer has worked in Auto Theft Department, Raiding and Vice Department, Detective Bureau, on general and special cases. Always selected when rounding up badly wanted men. Is a crack pistol shot." Hoover seems to have been especially impressed by Bryce's performance in the O'Donnell shooting, and in November Bryce was sworn in. He is rumored to have been involved in the four-hour gun battle that brought an end to the Barker gang in January 1935, but the extent of his involvement in this and other high-profile cases remains unknown. As Bob McMillin, an Oklahoma newsman who followed his career, put it, "He very seldom talked about himself or anything he did. He was credited with being one of those people who got Pretty Boy Floyd [in October 1935]. He never admitted it, but he never denied it either."

In 1935 Smith & Wesson (S&W) brought out the .357 magnum, presenting the first production model to J. Edgar Hoover in April. Bryce won one for himself in September in a competition at the Camp Perry Police Pistol Matches against S&W vice president of sales Doug Wesson. Wesson, holding a cocked

---

6.   In May 1934 Bryce's friend Assistant Chief Hurt joined the FBI. He was one of the men who shot John Dillinger outside Chicago's Biograph Theatre two months later.

revolver, was unable to pull its trigger before Bryce drew his revolver from its holster and fired twice. Bryce carried his prized .357 from then on. The medal he won at the matches was forwarded to him by Hoover himself, along with a letter congratulating him on his performance.

Bryce was a great admirer of Hoover and is said to have emulated his conservative style of dress, retiring his more flamboyant outfits for snap-brim hats and gray double-breasted suits. In June 1941, he had the opportunity to defend his director's honor when a man walked into the El Paso office and told him, "I just want you to know what I think about your boss, J. Edgar Hoover. Personally, I think he is a half-nigger son of a bitch." Bryce wrote Hoover that the period at the end of that sentence was formed by the hole in the plaster wall where he pushed the man's head through it. Hoover wrote back to express his "sincere appreciation" at Bryce's handling of the situation.

During the war years Bryce investigated German-American Bund members operating in the border region. When he cornered the notorious Nazi sympathizer Dale Maple, who habitually dressed in a German uniform, he jammed his .357 under his chin and snarled, "You son of a bitch, I'm fighting a war." The Harvard-educated Maple broke down, ultimately helping Bryce expose one of the largest World War II sabotage conspiracies ever uncovered. When the case was taken over by U.S. Army Intelligence, Bryce angrily expressed his frustration to a friend in the press, Martin O'Neill: "I told them if they'd give me 50 men who piss hard against the ground, I'd . . ." He trailed off, clenching and unclenching his fist. When O'Neill said that he might have to report the story, Bryce responded, "If you do, I'll kill you." O'Neill detected no hyperbole.

While on business in Roswell, New Mexico, Bryce spotted the most beautiful girl he had ever seen, walked up to her, introduced himself, then said, "I just thought you'd want to know— I'm going to marry you." Bryce and Shirley Bloodworth married in 1944 and had a son.

In the mid-1940s, when the *Life* spread appeared, Bryce was considered the best shot among the FBI's 4,000 agents. He trained other agents at Quantico, Virginia, and gave public demonstrations of his skill all over the United States as well as in Mexico and Canada. With a .22 rifle he could hit a Mexican peso tossed into the air, even specifying that he would hit it close to the edge to make a watch fob out of it. With a pump shotgun he could break five clay pigeons tossed up at once, the last usually just a foot above the ground. He could even bust clays in the air with his .357 magnum. He often demonstrated his ability to draw and fire his revolver before a volunteer from the audience could drop the hammer on one that was cocked. He also indulged his wicked sense of humor: borrowing an expensive watch from someone in the audience, he claimed he would put a bullet right next to it without hitting it—instead, his shot would smash the watch to pieces. Bryce would let the shock register for a few moments before revealing that he had palmed the borrowed watch and destroyed a dime-store replacement. As a grand finale, he would turn his back on a clay pigeon 20 feet away and shoot at it over his shoulder, holding his left hand close to his eye and aiming in a reflective facet of his large diamond ring. If his shot left a large fragment of the four-inch target intact, he would fire again and obliterate it. (At one of these performances, someone asked Bryce if there was a story behind the big diamond ring. "Yes, there is," replied Bryce. "I saw it, I wanted it, had the money to pay for it and bought it.")

In the course of his 23-year career, Bryce served as special agent in charge in El Paso, Albuquerque, San Antonio, and Oklahoma City. Whenever there was a standoff with an armed and dangerous criminal, Bryce was summoned to negotiate his surrender. If the criminal refused, Bryce did his negotiating in about two-fifths of a second. His peers used to say of any perp who went up against Bryce, "If he blinks, he'll die in the dark." His FBI file contains few details, but there are numerous letters from J. Edgar Hoover commending Bryce on his "resourcefulness and aggressiveness" or "caution and good judgment" in making high-profile arrests.

Whenever he was asked how many men he had killed, Bryce would reply with a terse "no comment." According to Oklahoma City Police Chief Bob Wilder (son of Bryce's onetime partner), Bryce had been in 19 shootings, most of which were fatal for the other party. Bryce was once asked if he wasn't interested in "bringing 'em back alive." He answered, "I'm more interested in bringing *me* back alive." Bryce's advice to a young officer was, "Approach every man with a smile on your face and homicide in your heart."

Bryce retired from the FBI in 1958 to run as an independent candidate for governor of Oklahoma on a reform platform, promising, among other things, that he could name every Communist in the state and that none would hold a position of trust under him. After his defeat, he settled in Mountain View and worked as a private investigator. He continued to pursue his interest in hunting and fishing. He killed every type of big game on the North American continent except moose but claimed that his ability as a fisherman far outshone his ability as a gunman.

Bryce's beloved wife Shirley died of injuries suffered in a car accident in 1973, and he died of a heart attack at a convention of retired agents a year later, at 67.

6 Lloyd L. Burke

I couldn't see leaving my guys up there without trying to do something.
—Lloyd L. Burke

In 1943, when Lloyd L. Burke was 18, he dropped out of college, joined the army, and served two years with the combat engineers in Italy as an enlisted man. He wasn't greatly impressed by most of the officers he met and vowed that if he ever achieved rank he would do better. After he was discharged, he returned to Henderson State College in Arkansas and joined the ROTC. In 1950 the owlish, 120-pound, 5-foot 8-inch Burke, who looked more like a clerk than a soldier, graduated as the Distinguished Military Graduate. He accepted his commission and five months later was in Korea, leading Company G, 2d Battalion, 5th Cavalry Regiment.

After the Chinese poured across the Yalu River, enveloping the UN forces there, he guided his platoon to safety, for which he received a Silver Star and Distinguished Service Cross. He also was awarded two Purple Hearts.

In October 1951, his tour being up, Burke was at the regimental rear, his plane ticket in his pocket, eager to get home to see his wife and infant son. Meanwhile, 2 miles away, his company was trying to cross the Yokkok-chon River, its efforts blocked by a large Chinese force well entrenched on Hill 200. The battle went on for days, with the 2d Battalion's assault repeatedly thrown back. Lieutenant Burke anxiously kept up with the reports until he could stand it no longer and headed back to the front. "I couldn't see leaving my guys up there without trying to do something," he said.

When Burke arrived at the base of Hill 200, he was stunned to find his company reduced to 35 shell-shocked survivors. "These men were completely beat," he said. "They lay huddled in foxholes, unable to move. They all had the thousand-yard stare of men who'd seen too much fighting, too much death."

Burke hauled up a 57mm recoilless rifle and fired three rounds at the nearest enemy bunker, a wooden-fronted structure covering a cave dug into the hillside. A hail of grenades continued to pelt the Americans from out of the Chinese trenches, so Burke aimed an M1 rifle at the trench line. Each time a Chinese soldier popped his head up to toss a grenade, Burke swung his rifle on him and fired. He kept shooting, but the grenades kept coming. After firing off an eight-round clip, he began to wonder if he could be missing. "I considered myself a pretty fair shot, but this was getting ridiculous. I had to do something," he recalled.

He lay down his rifle, grabbed a grenade, and ran about 30 yards to the Chinese trench line. He threw himself at the base of the 2-foot-high dirt berm that fronted it and also protected him from enemy fire. When the firing died down momentarily, Burke vaulted into the trench, a grenade in one hand and his pistol in the other. Five or six dead Chinese lay sprawled at his feet, each with a hole in his forehead. His bullets had found their mark.

Two Chinese soldiers rushed him from farther down the trench, and he took two quick shots at them. Then he tossed a grenade in their direction, leaped out, and lay against the outside of the berm. The Chinese knew where he was and began lobbing grenades at him. Most rolled down the hill and exploded harmlessly, but some went off nearby. Burke caught three and tossed them back. Meanwhile, his own men were throwing grenades, some of which fell short of their Chinese targets and exploded dangerously close to Burke. "You'd better get out of here," he told himself.

Burke couldn't head straight back to his lines in the middle of a grenade-tossing match, so he crawled off to the side, where he found a gully to take cover in. The gully ended farther up the hill at a high-topped Korean burial mound. Burke edged his way up the hill and sneaked a look over the top of the mound. He couldn't believe what he saw: Not more than 100 yards away, exposed in enfilade, was the main Chinese trench, curving around the hill, filled with troops. They seemed surprisingly at ease—some sat, chatted, and laughed as others fired mortars and hurled grenades at his 2d Battalion. There were enough to overwhelm the Americans easily.

Burke made his way down the gully to Company G's position and told the senior NCO, Sgt. Arthur Foster, "Get 'em ready to attack when I give you a signal!" and then loaded himself up with the company's last working Browning model 1919 machine gun and three cans of ammunition. The combined load weighed almost as much as the skinny lieutenant himself, but he dragged it back up the hill, hoping that he hadn't been spotted. Once more on top of the burial mound, he mounted the machine gun on its tripod, set the screw to free traverse, fed in one of the 250-round belts, and aimed at the nearest part of the trench, where the mortars were set up. For a long moment he took in the view over his sights, then pressed the trigger. He hosed the Chinese mortar squads until he was certain that everyone who had caused his company so many casualties was

National Archives

dead. He then moved his fire to a machine gun emplacement and quickly wiped that out as well.

The Chinese troops were too stunned by Burke's attack to react. He fired up and down the trench, mowing them down like "ducks sitting on a pond." After several minutes they fled down the trench, clambering over each other in a panic.

Burke kept firing until his Browning jammed. While he worked to clear it, an enemy sneaked toward him and began throwing grenades. Burke ignored him and attended to the malfunction, even when fragments from one blast tore open the back of his hand. As soon as his machine gun was working again, he finished the nettlesome grenadier with a quick burst.

Burke called out to Sergeant Foster, who led a small group to Burke's position, where it added its firepower to his own. Convinced that they were under attack from a full-sized force rather than a few determined skirmishers, the Chinese retreated, but Burke did not intend to let them get away. Having attacked every target visible from atop the grave mound, he removed his field jacket and wrapped it around the Browning's hot barrel sleeve, jerked the 31-pound gun off its tripod and, with its ammo belt draped over his shoulders, walked toward the trench, firing at stragglers. Sergeant Foster and his men went with him. When Burke ran out of ammunition, he used grenades and his .45 automatic to clear out bunkers.

Hill 200 had blocked the 2d Battalion for days. Lt. Lloyd Burke cleared it in minutes, killing over 100 men and destroying three machine-gun nests and two mortar emplacements.

Burke received the Medal of Honor at a White House ceremony on April 11, 1952.

He served in Vietnam until a helicopter in which he was flying was shot down, forcing him to return to the United States for lengthy hospitalization. In all, he spent 35 years in the military, served as the army's liaison officer to Congress, and retired with the rank of full colonel.

7 Ned Christie

He was at one time a member of the Executive Council of the [Cherokee Nation]. He was a blacksmith by trade and was a brave man.

—Inscription on Ned Christie's tombstone

That a man's home is his castle is a cliché of English common law, but no Englishman ever took the principle as seriously as did a full-blooded Cherokee, Ned Christie.

In the 1830s, the U.S. government forcibly drove the Cherokee from their lands in the Carolinas and Georgia to the northeastern part of what is now Oklahoma. Thousands died as they traveled what they called the Trail of Tears. The 74,000-square-mile area in which they were settled came to be the Cherokee Nation, or Indian Territory, with its capital, Tahlequah.

Christie, called Ne-de Wa-de in Cherokee, was born near Tahlequah on December 14, 1852. He learned to handle guns early and by age 10 had earned a reputation as an excellent marksman. His father, Watt, was a top-notch blacksmith and gunsmith, and Ned too mastered those trades. He grew tall—6 feet, 4 inches—and cut a striking figure, wearing his hair long in the traditional style. He served as a member of his tribe's executive council and a bodyguard to its principal chief, Dennis Bushyhead, and was a respected leader in the Keetowa Society, a religious order that opposed white encroachment on Cherokee sovereignty.

As settlement in the West increased, the federal government grew more concerned with the situation in the Indian Territory, which had become an outlaw haven. In 1875, Judge Isaac C. Parker was sent to the federal court in Fort Smith, capital of the Western District of Arkansas, with authority to bring law and order to the region. On the evening of May 4, 1887, one of the marshals working for him, Dan Maples, was in Tahlequah searching for a fugitive when, acting on a tip, he went to see Jennie Schell, a suspected whiskey dealer. As he approached her cabin, he was shot from ambush and died the following day.

Pressure mounted to find Maples' killer. His hometown of Bentonville, Arkansas, offered a $500 reward, to which the governor added $1,500. Chief Bushyhead pledged $300. Schell was questioned and said that John Parris and Ned Christie, both very drunk, had left her home shortly before Maples was shot. Parris was soon picked up and, under interrogation, said that Christie had shot the marshal. The following day, as Christie left his hotel to attend a session of the Cherokee Executive Council, a friend approached him and told him of the accusation. Christie swore he knew nothing about the crime, claiming that shortly after leaving Schell's place he had passed out, waking up the next morning in the grass. He considered turning himself in and pleading innocent, but his friend argued that that would be suicide. A murder warrant signed by Parker, the "hanging judge," was tantamount to a death sentence, especially for a Cherokee.

Christie returned to his home, some 10 miles southwest of

KIRCHNER

Tahlequah, determined to resist arrest. For armament, he had a muzzle-loading .58-caliber Springfield rifle as well as two 1860 army .44 pistols his father had carried during the Civil War. As ample proof of his gunsmithing expertise, Christie had converted the cap-and-ball revolvers to fire .44–40 cartridges after studying the method developed by Colt. He needed a repeating rifle and persuaded his neighbor Eli Wilson to sell him a lever-action Winchester '73, which took the same kind of ammunition as the revolvers. Christie stocked up on cartridges and made four leather ammunition-carrying aprons that he could sling around his neck.

The first of many deputies who would attempt to deliver Judge Parker's warrant was Joe Bowers. As Bowers rode through the forested, rolling hills of the Going Snake district toward Christie's cabin, Christie surprised him from ambush and shot him in the leg, then allowed him to ride away. A charge of assaulting a federal officer was filed against Christie.

The next lawman to try to make the arrest, Deputy John Fields, approached Christie's cabin early in the morning and called on him to surrender. Christie burst out of the cabin door, Winchester in hand. Fields wheeled his horse around and gave it the spurs, but Christie fired and hit him in the neck. He was not seriously wounded, and Christie let him ride off. Christie put out the word that he didn't want to kill a marshal, but he would not tolerate one on his property.

A third charge was added to the others, and the deputies riding out of Fort Smith were told to "quit trying to take him alive." But every time a posse headed into the Going Snake district, Christie seemed to be waiting for it. He had a network of watchful neighbors, but many believed he also had a sixth sense that warned him of danger.

One posse fled after Ned wounded three of its members. After the shootout, Eli Wilson came to Christie's cabin to see that he was all right. Wilson's children picked up spent shell cases for Ned to reload, and afterward Ned played marbles with the children while his cousin, 16-year-old Arch Wolfe, stood guard in case the posse returned.

In September 1889, Heck Thomas took up the challenge. Thomas, who had captured the train robber Sam Bass and was later to kill the notorious Bill Doolin, was one of the West's most famous lawmen. He enlisted the aid of Deputy L.P. "Bones" Isbel, who knew the area. Together with a posse of three, they rode south from Vinita, traveling slowly and cautiously to escape the vigilance of Christie's neighbors. On the night of September 26, they tied their horses a long way from Christie's cabin and made their way on foot under cover of darkness, closing in from different directions. Christie's watchdogs caught their scent, though, and began barking. Christie ran to his loft, kicked a board loose, and opened fire.

Thomas positioned himself behind a small outbuilding used as a blacksmith shop and ordered Christie to surrender. Receiving no answer, Thomas then set the shop on fire, hoping to draw him out.

Meanwhile, Isbel, who was firing at the cabin from behind a tree, leaned out to get a better look. That brief exposure was long enough for Christie to draw a bead on him and shoot him in the right shoulder, sending him staggering back, badly wounded. As Thomas came to Isbel's assistance, Christie's wife, Nancy, sprinted out of the cabin and into the safety of the woods.

A shifting wind blew the flames from the smithy against the cabin, setting it on fire. Christie's only son, Jim, 13, leaped from the burning structure and ran for the treeline. Mistaking Jim for his father, the deputies shot him.

As Thomas tried to stop Isbel's bleeding, Christie jumped from his cabin and ran. Thomas snapped off a shot from his rifle. Christie reeled and grabbed at his forehead, but made it into the forest.

Thomas and the posse searched the woods for Christie but were unable to find him in the predawn gloom and had to leave

to get Isbel to medical attention. Christie and his son were rescued by friends and taken to a tribal doctor. Jim was wounded
in the lung and hips but recovered. Christie had been hit in the
bridge of his nose, the bullet tearing through his right eye and
lodging above his temple. His once handsome features were
grotesquely marred, and he would never see out of his right eye
again. At the same time, Isbel's career as a lawman was over
because he permanently lost the use of his right arm.

The tribe hid Christie on top of a hill about a mile north of
his burned-out house, and for shelter built him a rough fort nes-
tled among boulders and foliage. (The hill is still known as Ned
Fort Mountain, and the foundation of the fort remains.) When
he recovered, he visited the ruins of his home along the Bidding
Creek. Embittered against the government, Christie vowed that
U.S. marshals would never take him alive. He knew that the
effort to capture him would intensify and decided to rebuild in
a more defensible location, on the high ground across the creek
from his former home, near a spring.

He bought himself a steam-driven saw and milled the lumber with which he built a fort two stories tall, its walls constructed from two layers of logs with sand between them, pan-
eled on the inside with oak 2 x 4s. There were no windows on
the ground floor, only a stout door, and the second floor was
pierced with narrow firing slits. Christie cleared all the brush
and stones from the surrounding area, so that an attacker would
have no cover close to the house.

Deputy Marshal Dave Rusk was the next to try to bring
Christie in. Though standing only 5 feet, 4 inches, Rusk was a
formidable lawman who had been a captain in the Missouri
Cavalry of the Confederate States Army (CSA) in the Civil War
and had worked several seasons as an exhibition pistol shooter
in a traveling circus. He gathered a posse of Cherokees loyal to
the federal government and closed in on Christie's stronghold.
As they took positions at the edge of the forest, they came under
a fusillade. It was apparent that Christie had gotten advance

warning. Between shots, a strange cry emanated from the fort, sounding like a cross between a wolf howl and a turkey gobble. Posse members identified it as the Cherokee death call. Rusk had to call off the attack after four of his men fell wounded.

Later, on two occasions, Rusk tried to approach the fort alone, hoping to catch the elusive desperado unaware. In both instances, Christie saw him first and sent a bullet through the crown of his black Stetson. Through an intermediary, Christie placed a taunting message in the *Cherokee Advocate*: "I thought I saw a big, black potato bug in my garden, but it turned out to be the hat of that 'little marshal'—Dave Rusk!"

Rusk decided to give up his solo forays, knowing full well that Christie could easily have put a bullet through his head.

Two other deputies, Heck Bruner and Barney Connelley, also crept up to Christie's place. Hidden by brush, they fired warning shots and demanded that Christie surrender. They weren't prepared for the furious response. Showered with clipped-off bits of foliage as bullets whizzed through their position, they beat a hasty retreat, declaring Christie's fort "well-nigh impregnable."

Rusk made his home in Oaks, a small town north of Tahlequah, where he ran a general store to supplement his deputy marshal's income. Worried for his family's safety, he moved them to Joplin, Missouri, to stay with relatives. His precaution was well timed: while he was away, Christie, his son, and Arch Wolfe staged a raid. Christie entered the store on horseback and held the clerk, William Israel, at gunpoint while the others dismounted and ransacked the place. They were especially angered that Israel, a Cherokee, would work for the marshal. They tarred and feathered him, poured a bottle of whiskey down his throat, and sent him fleeing into the woods a few steps ahead of a hail of bullets. Then putting Rusk's store to the torch, Christie must have taken grim satisfaction from seeing it burn.

The raid made Christie one of the Old West's most wanted

outlaws, and he was blamed for every crime within a 100-mile radius. While it is true that Christie fought more battles and wounded more deputies than any other outlaw in his time, he did his best not to kill, counting on near misses, grazing shots, or minor wounds to get his message across.

On October 11, 1892, deputy marshals Dave Rusk, Charley Copeland, Milo Creekmore, and D.C. Dye gathered near Christie's stronghold for another assault, assisted by Joe Bowers and John Fields. Backing up Christie were Jim, Arch Wolfe, and a boy named Charles Hare. In the initial exchange of gunfire, Bowers was wounded in the ankle and Fields was hit in the neck. (Fields died from the wound about a week later.) It was clear that the lawmen's only hope was to burn Christie out. The deputies found his old lumber wagon, filled it with brush and scraps of timber, set it on fire, and gave it a tremendous push toward the fortress. It crashed into Ned's outhouse and ground to a halt. The outhouse burned, but it was too far from Ned's fort to pose any danger.

Copeland had come equipped with a bundle of dynamite. He lit the fuse and tossed it at the fort, but it bounced off and the fuse was knocked loose, sizzling brightly on the ground until it sputtered out.

Creekmore rode to Tahlequah and telegraphed Fort Smith for help. Thirty men showed up. Christie's fort came under heavy fire, but nothing the posse threw at it had any effect. At last, their tempers frayed, their ears ringing, and their ammunition and morale depleted, the lawmen called off their attack, retreating to the weird turkey gobbling of the Cherokee death call.

After this humiliating debacle, Deputy Marshal Paden Tolbert was ordered to put an end to Christie. He contacted some of the foremost lawmen in the area, all of whom eagerly signed on. As they traveled by train and horseback to Tahlequah they were joined by others until there were 25, including G.S. White, Dave Rusk, Bill Ellis, Bill Smith, Frank

Polk, Wess Bowman, Charley Copeland, Harry Clayland, and Sam Maples. They came better armed than any previous group, bringing not only rifles, shotguns, revolvers, and dynamite but also a three-pounder cannon with 40 rounds. Originally built for Fourth of July celebrations, it was an ungainly thing, set on a wheelless carriage, and they had to laboriously haul it by wagon over the rocky, wooded hills.

Before dawn on November 2, the deputies surreptitiously encircled Ned's fort, taking whatever cover they could find. The sun had not yet risen when the fort's door opened and Arch Wolfe stepped out, heading for the spring. The lawmen ordered him to surrender. Arch fired a shot toward the sound of their voices and then ran back to the fort. He was wounded in the leg and arm but managed to back inside as Christie provided covering fire. There was a brief truce as Jim, Nancy, Christie's daughter Mary, and his baby granddaughter left the fort, and then the fight resumed.

From behind rocks and fallen trees, the lawmen fired at the slits in the fort, quickly ducking after each shot. The return fire left nearly every man with a bullet hole in his clothes—Rusk got three more rounds through his hat—but none was wounded, and perhaps this was intentional. In the course of the siege, the lawmen fired more than 2,000 rounds. One of them made up some flaming arrows, slender sticks tipped with oil-soaked rags, which he launched with an old .45-70 Springfield. The deputies cheered when one stuck in the fort's wall, but its flame was too feeble to ignite the logs.

It was time to break out the artillery; for the first time in American history, a cannon would be employed in the arrest of a single individual. Maneuvering it was backbreaking work, and its aim had to be adjusted by shifting its carriage with a crowbar. At last it was positioned, loaded, and touched off. The cannonball slammed into the fort with a resounding thwack and bounced off, having gouged a groove in one of the logs above the door but otherwise doing no damage. Ned's fort withstood the pounding of 36 more shots. When the frustrated lawmen gave the cannon an extra measure of powder, its breech split.

Meanwhile, the siege had attracted a crowd of local Cherokees, including Nancy, Mary, Jim, and Watt. Mary and Jim tried to get back into the fort but were held at gunpoint when the lawmen searched them and found they were carrying ammunition. Watt was asked to try to persuade Ned to surrender, but he refused.

As night fell, the lawmen pulled back into the woods to decide their next move. They came across the charred remains of Christie's lumber wagon, its wheels and rear axle still serviceable. Using oak planks from Christie's sawmill, they built a movable shield on it, finishing shortly after midnight. Tolbert, White, Smith, Ellis, and Copeland got behind the shield and began pushing it toward Christie's fort, as others provided covering fire from positions around the clearing. Copeland carried the bundle of dynamite, equipped with a long fuse. Bullets hit the thick oaken shield but couldn't penetrate it. Between shots the lawmen could hear the eerie death call. As they neared the fort's south wall, they kept up a steady fire at the slits on the second floor. Copeland lit the fuse on the dynamite, ran to the wall, jammed it under the bottom log, and ran back to the shield.

The lawmen managed to roll their shield back to the edge of the clearing by the time the dynamite went off. The blast lit up the night sky and debris rained down. As the smoke cleared, a small fire could be seen burning inside the fort through a gaping hole in the wall.

Christie burst out of the root-cellar under cover of the smoke. He ran toward the spring, where the lawmen had tethered their horses, firing his Winchester until he ran out of ammunition. He kept turning and pointing his rifle as bullets cracked and whistled around him. A young white man, no more than 14 years old, fired from amid the horses and hit Christie in the back. Christie fell forward, dead. Then, in a crude act of vengeance, Sam Maples, son of the marshal Christie was accused of killing, ran up and emptied both of his revolvers into Christie. "I have been waiting five years to drill that killer," he told the others.

There was weeping and wailing among the crowd of Cherokees that had gathered to watch the siege, but Watt stood stoically.

Christie's five-and-a-half-year resistance was over. He was loaded onto the lawmen's supply wagon and taken to Fayetteville, where he was officially pronounced dead. His body was then taken by train to Judge Isaac Parker's federal building in Fort Smith and displayed on the porch for an afternoon, his Winchester stuck in his stiffened arms. Photographs were taken. Schoolchildren were paraded by to get a look at "the worst outlaw in the history of the Cherokee Nation." To many of his people, Christie represented something else entirely—a hero, the last of their tribe to make a determined stand against the overwhelming might of the U.S. government.

8 Winston S. Churchill

Nothing in life is so exhila-
rating as to be shot at with-
out result.

—Winston Churchill

As a boy, Winston Churchill owned a collection of nearly 1,500 tin soldiers and spent hours arranging them
into battle scenes. His father, inspecting one such
tableau, asked him if he would like to go into the army. He
responded enthusiastically, and his future was set. He believed
that his father had detected in him a budding military genius,
and only later learned that his lackadaisical performance at
school had led his father to conclude that he was not bright
enough to do anything else.

Churchill failed the admissions examination for Sandhurst,
the British military academy, on his first two attempts, but succeeded on his third. He was graduated with his commission in
December 1894, and joined the 4th Hussars cavalry regiment.
Such was his confidence in modernity that he feared he would

not see active service, that Europe was doomed to languish in peace. However, there was some adventure to be found in Cuba, where the Spanish were putting down a revolt. Churchill wangled an invitation to accompany the Spanish as an observer. As he caught his first glimpse of Cuba's shoreline, he felt like Long John Silver gazing upon Treasure Island. As he wrote in *My Early Life*, "Here was a place where real things were going on. . . . Here was a place where something certainly would happen. Here I might leave my bones." He attempted to explain his eagerness: "It seemed to my youthful mind that it must be a thrilling and immense experience to hear the whistle of bullets all around and to play at hazard from moment to moment with death and wounds." It was on his 21st birthday, November 30, 1895, that he first heard shots fired in anger. In the days that followed, he came under fire many times and found that bullets not only whistled, they sometimes sighed, whizzed, or even buzzed like "an offended hornet." It made him a bit nervous to sleep in a hammock in a thatched hut after one shot passed through its walls, but he took comfort in the fact that the Spanish officer slung between him and the enemy "was a man of substantial physique; indeed, one might almost have called him fat. . . . I have never been prejudiced against fat men. At any rate, I did not grudge this one his meals."

Churchill left the island with his appetite for adventure whetted and a taste for Cuban cigars and afternoon siestas.

The next year, Churchill went with his regiment to India. While disembarking from a landing boat in rough seas he dislocated his right shoulder, an injury from which he never fully recovered. Churchill's regiment was stationed in Bangalore, near the bottom of the subcontinent, but all of the action was taking place 2,000 miles to the north at the Malakand Pass, where there was a tribal uprising. Pulling a few strings, he got himself transferred there.

In his account of the campaign, *The Malakand Field Force*, he described the tribesmen as dangerous foes:

·KIRCHNER·

> To the ferocity of the Zulu are added the
> craft of the Redskin and the marksmanship of
> the Boer. . . . At a thousand yards the traveller
> falls wounded by the well-aimed bullet of a
> breech-loading rifle. His assailant, approaching,
> hacks him to death with the ferocity of a South-
> Sea Islander. The weapons of the 19th century
> are in the hands of the savages of the Stone Age.

On Churchill's first operation, he was climbing a mountain ridge with a small party of Sikh infantry when his superior officer realized that they had gotten too far ahead of the main body and ordered them to pull back. Churchill and a few others covered the retreat, coming under heavy fire from the large number of tribesmen in the rocks above them. Taking a single-shot .577-450 Martini-Henry rifle from one of the soldiers, he returned fire while the Sikh handed him cartridges. Churchill made his way down the ridge, helping to carry the wounded, as the tribesmen drew ever nearer and became bolder. When he witnessed one of them hacking at a fallen British officer, he "forgot everything else at this moment except a desire to kill this man" and, as the proud winner of his school's fencing medal, resolved to engage him in personal combat. As he advanced, sword in hand, he noticed that his opponent was amply backed up. Churchill thought better of his initial plan and, in the manner of Indiana Jones, pulled out his .455 Webley pistol and shot at him.

Surrounded by the enemy, with bullets everywhere, Churchill was delivered unscathed back to his own lines only by Providence. He did note a few new tunes in the bullets' repertoire: they made a sucking noise almost like a kiss as they passed close by, and "a strange, curious sound" as they cut into the deep mud near his feet.

While in India, Churchill further broadened his horizons. "Wishing to fit myself for active-service conditions, I managed to overcome my repugnance to the taste of whisky. Nor was this a momentary acquirement. On the contrary the ground I gained in those days I have firmly entrenched, and held throughout my life."

When conflict erupted with the Mahdi's Dervishes in the Sudan, Churchill was eager to get in on the action. There was not enough combat to go around, and some of his fellow officers began to feel that he was taking more than his fair share. But through energetic lobbying, coupled with the stature he enjoyed because of his book on Malakand, he managed to get himself posted to the 21st Lancers. His shoulder injury limited his facility with the sword, so before leaving London he purchased a Model 1896 7.63mm Mauser automatic pistol, dubbed the "Broomhandle" for the shape of its grip. Its nondetachable 10-round magazine was fed by stripper clips, and it came with a wooden holster that, when attached to the grip, served as a shoulder stock.

The 20,000-man British and Egyptian force engaged the 60,000-man dervish army outside Omdurman on September 2, 1898. This was war the way Churchill had envisioned it as a boy—infantry and cavalry armed with spear, sword, and rifle, arrayed in ranks across a great flat plain. He wrote: "Nothing like the Battle of Omdurman will ever be seen again. It was the last link in the long chain of those spectacular conflicts whose vivid and majestic splendor has done so much to invest war with glamour." He commanded a troop of 25 lancers in one of the British Army's last great cavalry charges.

As he closed, two of the dervishes fired upon him. They missed but killed the trooper behind him. As he plunged into the melee, he saw a dervish in front of him dive to the ground.

> My first idea . . . was that the man was ter-
> rified. But simultaneously I saw the gleam of his
> curved sword as he drew it back for a ham-
> stringing cut. I had room and time enough to
> turn my pony out of his reach, and leaning over
> on the off side I fired two shots into him at about
> three yards. As I straightened myself in the sad-

dle, I saw before me another figure with uplifted sword. I raised my pistol and fired. So close were we that the pistol itself actually struck him. Man and sword disappeared below and behind me. On my left, 10 yards away, was an Arab horseman in a bright-colored tunic and steel helmet, with chain-mail hangings. I fired at him. He turned aside. I pulled my horse into a walk and looked around again.

As Churchill rejoined his troop, a Mahdist suddenly leapt out of a hidey-hole waving a spear. The troopers slashed at him with their swords, but he dodged most of the blows. As he staggered toward Churchill, his spear upraised, Churchill shot him dead at less than a yard. The slide on Churchill's Mauser locked back, its magazine empty; those 10 rounds had served him well.

As he looked around at his troopers, he saw that three or four were dead or missing, and, of those in the saddle, six bled from spear thrusts or sword cuts. Half the horses bore similar wounds. He asked his second sergeant if he'd enjoyed himself. "Well, I don't exactly say I enjoyed it, sir, but I think I'll get more used to it next time," the sergeant answered, to general laughter.

"It was I suppose the most dangerous two minutes I shall live to see," Churchill wrote to a friend. He reported he had killed "three for certain—two doubtful—one very doubtful."

Three days after the battle, the Mahdi's dervishes were defeated and Churchill headed home to leave the army and run unsuccessfully for political office. He wrote an account of the campaign, *The River War*, which also became a best-seller.

When the Boer War broke out in October 1899, Churchill got an assignment as a war correspondent. Shortly after his arrival in South Africa, he boarded an armored troop train bound for Ladysmith. Although correspondents were supposed to be unarmed in order not to be considered spies, he wore his Mauser pistol. About 15 miles into the journey the train was ambushed by a large, well-equipped Boer force. Several cars were derailed. Churchill took control of the situation and, in the midst of heavy fire, organized men to clear the track. Thanks to his efforts, the locomotive and tender were able to escape with a large number of wounded. He was trying to rejoin his compatriots when he found himself surrounded by the enemy. He ran, but was called to a halt by a mounted rifleman.[7] He thought he could kill the man and reached for his Mauser, but it was missing—he had taken it off while working to clear the track. Drawing comfort from Napoleon's dictum that "when one is alone and unarmed a surrender may be pardoned," Churchill raised his hands. He worried about being shot as a spy, for he still had two clips of ammunition in his pocket. He discarded one surreptitiously, but as he attempted to lose the other his captor noticed and demanded to know what he had in his hand. Feigning innocence, Churchill offered it to him, saying, "What is it? I picked it up."

Churchill was taken to a prisoner of war (POW) camp in Pretoria, 300 miles from the nearest British forces. Life as a POW was not to Churchill's liking. Not only did he resent being under the control of his enemy, but also, as he wrote, "the war is going on, great events are in progress, fine opportunities for action and adventure are slipping away." He resolved to escape and, along with a few others, formed a plan. They decided that under cover of darkness it might be possible to hoist themselves over the wall without being noticed by the guards. On the appointed evening Churchill was the first to go, but the others became afraid and wouldn't follow. He proceeded on his own. A free man for the first time in a month, he intended to enjoy it as long as he could. With an air of nonchalance he strolled through the crowded streets of the enemy capital. Once beyond the city, he sat down and soberly considered his prospects. His

---

7. According to Churchill's account, the mounted Boer was Louis Botha, destined to become the first prime minister of the Republic of South Africa and, later, a close personal friend. This remarkable claim is regarded skeptically by most historians.

escape would be discovered at dawn, and he had hundreds of miles of heavily patrolled territory to traverse. In his pockets he had chocolate and some money, but no map, no compass, no knowledge of the Afrikaans language and no one to help him. His situation seemed hopeless. Yet, as he put it, "when hope had departed, fear had gone as well." He followed a railroad line that headed east, bypassing the sentries that were posted at bridges. He hopped aboard a train and slept through the night in a freight car; before dawn he jumped off and hid all day. The following night no train passed, and Churchill decided that he must risk approaching one of the isolated dwellings whose lights he could see in the distance. He knew that there were English mine owners who had been allowed to remain in Boer territories but who might be sympathetic to him. He walked to a house and knocked on the door. Providence had led him to John Howard, an Englishman willing to take the enormous risk of aiding an escaped prisoner who was now the object of a nationwide manhunt. Howard hid Churchill in an abandoned mine for a few days and then smuggled him aboard a freight train bound for the Portuguese colony of Mozambique, equipped with food, drink, and a revolver. Although a pistol is always a comfort, Churchill observed that "it was not easy to see in what way it could helpfully be applied to any problem I was likely to have to solve." He took it out and fired a few rounds into the air exuberantly when he crossed the frontier.

Churchill's capture and escape had been widely reported in England, but he was rumored to have been killed. When he showed up at the British Consulate in Lourenço Marques it caused a sensation and made him a national hero, ultimately ensuring his election to parliament. But at the time, when asked what his government could do for him, Churchill had only one request: that he be allowed to return to his war correspondent's post. With his beloved Mauser back in his possession, he again placed himself where "the 'swish' and 'whirr'" of bullets filled the air.

9 Ty Cobb

Hit them first—and last—
at all times.

—Ty Cobb

He was the first player voted into the Baseball Hall of Fame, beating out Babe Ruth for that honor. His professional career ran from 1906 to 1928, most of it with the Detroit Tigers. He hit better than .300 in each one of those years and had a career average of .367, a record that remains unbroken. In two other records that he still holds, he stole home base 35 times and led the American League in batting for 12 years. Yet as famous as Ty Cobb still is as an athlete, he is equally famous as a personality—the meanest man who ever played professional baseball. Those who knew the Georgia Peach (born in Narrows, Georgia) called him a "nutter" and suggested that he was possessed by Furies. He purposely injured opposing players with spikes he had honed to razor sharpness and often challenged those who argued with him on the field to take him on after a game. Umpire Billy Evans, a former semipro boxer, was one of those foolish enough to accept Cobb's challenge. When Evans asked him how he wished to fight, Cobb replied, "No rules. I fight to kill." Indeed, he probably would have killed Evans had other players not dragged him off the battered umpire after 45 minutes.

Cobb aroused hatred among fans of rival teams but refused to be intimidated. After he spiked a player on the Philadelphia Athletics he received a number of death threats, and when he returned to Philly for the playoffs a surly mob of about 300 gathered outside his hotel. At 10 P.M., with no police nearby, Cobb walked outside alone and called to the crowd, "Now I'm going for a walk. And I just want to say that the first rotten, cowardly hound who tries to stop me is going to drop dead, right where he stands. Now get out of my way." The crowd parted as Cobb strode through it. Some 10 years later, after a game, Cobb found himself menaced by a crowd of Detroit fans after he'd beaten up one who'd jeered at him. Again he faced them, walking down the line of tough factory workers, challenging, "You want to fight? You want to settle this?" Seeing the mad, feral gleam in his eye, no one dared step forward. "If you're all cowards, then fuck you!" he called out as he walked to his car. Teammates who watched the scene, none of whom cared to back him up, couldn't help but marvel at his fearlessness.

A thief once made the mistake of stealing Cobb's car. Cobb was leaving a Cadillac Square restaurant in Detroit when he saw a man later identified as 19-year-old John Miles drive away in his Chalmers. Cobb was one of the fastest men in baseball, capable of running 100 yards in 10 seconds flat, and even as Miles hit 20 miles an hour Cobb caught up with him. He leaped into the car, grabbed Miles by the neck, and threw him from the driver's seat. The Chalmers swerved, narrowly missing a trolley car, but Cobb managed to get control of it before anyone was injured. Miles went to jail ruefully observing that had he known who owned the car, he never would have touched it.

KIRCHNER

75

On August 2, 1911, Cobb was driving to the Detroit station to catch a train to an exhibition game in Syracuse, New York. His wife accompanied him, to take the car back home. As they drove along a deserted street, three men flagged them down, then demanded money. To protect his wife, Cobb stepped out of the car. He was met by a flurry of blows, but hit back hard and effectively until the three men began circling him warily, looking for an opening. Cobb knocked one of them to the ground and, as that one struggled back to his feet, knocked down another. The third jumped on Cobb and stabbed him in the back, inflicting a 6-inch wound. Cobb pulled a semiautomatic from his pocket but it wouldn't fire, so he used it as a club, and at one point he had two of the muggers on the ground. Deciding that a strategic retreat was in order, the three men took off. Biographer Al Stump, hearing the story from Cobb years later, suggested that it must have been a relief that the men fled. "*Relief?*" Cobb roared, "Do you think they could pull that on me? I went after them!"

Cobb caught up with one mugger and "left him in a sorry condition," and then cornered another in a dead-end alley. He pistol-whipped him for 10 minutes, leaving him dying "in his own rotten blood," he recalled with satisfaction. The mugger's face was so badly torn up he couldn't be identified at the morgue.

When Cobb returned to the car, his wife was aghast to see him bleeding heavily from his knife wound. She begged him to see a doctor but he merely wadded up a handkerchief, shoved it into the wound and drove to the station, where he caught the train to Syracuse. He told none of his teammates what had happened, but after one noticed his blood-soaked jacket Cobb allowed a trainer to apply a bandage. Cobb played ball the following day, making two base hits in four turns at bat. Only afterward did he see a doctor to get properly stitched up, and missed no games due to the injury.

Ty Cobb was a wife beater and a bully, but, unlike many who vent their anger on the weak, he was no coward—he was just as ready to fight foes who were stronger, or who outnumbered him. Aristotle argued that defiance of death was not enough to qualify a man as truly courageous: he had to be acting toward some noble purpose. Cobb, to the philosopher, would exemplify mere unbridled pugnacity. Perhaps, but any man with a thimbleful of testosterone in his veins would relish unleashing such pugnacity on a hostile mob, a car thief, or a trio of muggers.

10 Hannah Duston

Being where she had not her own life secured by a law unto her, she thought she was not forbidden by a law to take away the lives of the murderers . . .

—From Cotton Mather's account

During the War of the Grand Alliance, 1689–1697 (King William's War in North America) that pitted Britain against France, the settlement of Haverhill, Massachusetts, was a frequent target of raids by the Abenaki Indians, who were allied with the French and received bounties for English scalps and prisoners. On March 15, 1697, the Abenakis struck again.

Forty-year-old Hannah Duston was in her farmhouse resting. Less than a week before, she had given birth to her 12th child (counting four who had died). A neighbor, 41-year-old Mary Neff, was caring for her while Hannah's husband, Thomas, and her seven other children were out in the fields.

When the attack came, Thomas Duston was cut off from his

wife, and he hurried his children to a nearby fortified house while holding off the Indians with his musket. Nathaniel Hawthorne later justified Thomas's leaving his wife to fend for herself by observing, "as is not improbable, he had such knowledge of the good lady's character as afforded him a comfortable hope that she would hold her own, even in a contest with a whole tribe of Indians."

The Abenakis looted Duston's house, even tearing the cloth from her loom, and set the house on fire. They hustled the women into the forest, Duston carrying her baby. As soon as it began to cry, an Indian grabbed it by the feet and smashed its head against a tree. All in all, the Abenakis killed 27 settlers that day, took 13 captives, and burned nine homes.

At last they reached a rendezvous point, a clearing in the woods. There were a number of captives. Some were killed on the spot, and the rest were divided up to be taken to Canada by different parties of warriors. Duston and Neff were given to a group who had another captive, a 14-year-old boy named Samuel Lennardson, whom the Abenakis had held for 18 months. For the next two weeks, they traveled about 100 miles through the untracked wilderness, across icy streams, and through mud and winter snows. Despite being poorly dressed and having lost one of her shoes, Duston managed to keep up. The captives were given heavy loads to carry and were told that when they reached Canada they would be sold to the French as slaves or else stripped naked and made to run the gauntlet until they died. They prayed desperately. Oddly enough, the Abenakis, who had been converted by French missionaries, communed regularly with God as well, pausing twice daily to pray a rosary. According to Duston's account, one of the Indians told her that she had nothing to worry about: if God intended for her to be delivered, she would be.

Divine intervention was much desired, but Duston intended, if possible, to see to her own deliverance. She was constantly on the alert for an opportunity to escape, and she took Lennardson

into her confidence. While the Abanakis and their prisoners
were traveling by canoe up the Merrimack River, they camped on
an island at the junction with the Contoocook River. At last the
Abenakis let down their guard, falling asleep around a campfire,

81

while Duston and Neff shivered beyond its warmth. Duston got up and quietly stole two tomahawks from the braves. She and Neff then killed the Indians in their sleep, except for an old woman and a child who woke up just before the slaughter was concluded and ran screaming into the forest.

Duston had seized her freedom, but there was still retribution to exact. In those days the British authorities paid a bounty on Indian scalps; Duston scalped each of her and Neff's 10 victims and wrapped the scalps in the cloth that had been torn from the loom. Duston, Neff, and Lennardson then scuttled all the canoes except one, which they filled with their scalps, supplies, and weapons. They traveled the river by night and hid by day until they reached Dunstable, now part of Nashua, New Hampshire, and then continued to Haverhill on foot.

Hannah Duston was joyously reunited with her husband and children. She was awarded £25, a truly princely sum then, for her scalps, while Neff and Lennardson split £25 between them. On October 4, 1698, Hannah gave birth to a baby girl, Lydia.

The raid, kidnapping, and heroic escape were the subject of a Colonial-era best-seller, Cotton Mather's *Humiliations Follow'd with Deliverances* (1697). The governor of Maryland sent her a set of pewter plates, and the Great and General Court of Massachusetts presented her with a pewter tankard, all of which are on display at a museum in Haverhill. In 1879 the town erected a monument to Duston, the first such in the United States to commemorate a woman's courage.

11 Nathan Bedford Forrest

> *War means fightin', and fightin' means killing.*
> —Nathan Bedford Forrest

In four years of fighting for the Confederacy, Nathan Bedford Forrest was wounded four times, had 29 horses shot out from under him, and killed 30 men. "I doubt if any commander since the days of the lion-hearted Richard killed as many enemies with his own hand as Forrest," wrote Gen. Richard Taylor in *Destruction and Reconstruction*. Despite a complete lack of formal military training, Forrest was one of the Civil War's most successful generals, an audacious innovator whose tactical insights are still studied in the world's military academies. What Forrest did, like no other, was attack: unexpectedly, ferociously, and relentlessly.

Forrest was born in 1821 in rural Tennessee, the most violent part of the violent Old South. As a young man he had his share of fights, and he is first known to have killed a man at age 24 on March 21, 1845. His uncle Jonathan had had an ongoing dispute with the Matlocks, a family of planters, and on that day three members of the Matlock family, along with their overseer, confronted Jonathan in the Hernando, Mississippi, town square. Forrest intervened, telling the Matlocks that he would not permit them to malign or mistreat his uncle while they so outnumbered him. Forrest had hardly finished speaking when one of them drew a pistol and fired at him, missing. The others went for their guns as well, wounding Forrest slightly and killing his uncle. Forrest shot two of his assailants, killing one. Seeing that Forrest was outnumbered and out of ammunition, a bystander handed him a knife, with which he drove off the others. This was the kind of performance that made a man's reputation in the South.

A few months after the Hernando incident, while traveling, Forrest and a companion were waylaid by a planter named Dyson. Dyson shot Forrest's companion, but when he turned his double-barreled weapon toward Forrest he found himself looking down the barrel of a cocked revolver. Forrest told Dyson he had better shoot straight because this was now a game at which two could play. Under Forrest's cold stare, Dyson lowered his weapon. Later he explained that his second barrel was loaded with buckshot and he feared that might not suffice for Forrest.

Within the month, while out riding Forrest came across a widow and her 18-year-old daughter whose carriage was mired in the middle of a stream. The driver, a slave, attempted to free it while the daughter's two suitors waited on the bank on horseback, unwilling to ruin their clothing by helping. Forrest dismounted, waded into the stream, and asked the women's permission to carry them to dry ground. After he did so he waded back into the water and helped the driver free their carriage. He asked the women for their names, and if he might pay a call on them the following day. Under the circumstances, the wealthy widow Elizabeth Montgomery and her daughter Mary Anne felt

National Archives

they could not refuse. When Forrest showed up, he encountered the two fastidious suitors from the previous day and threatened them with bodily harm if they didn't leave at once. Proceeding as relentlessly as he would on the battlefield, Forrest then proposed to Mary Anne, warning her that if she were to marry one of the other men, she would have many occasions in life in which she would find herself as helpless and unprotected as she had been the previous day. She accepted, pending the consent of her guardian, a minister. The minister objected, telling Forrest, "You cuss and gamble, and Mary Anne is a Christian girl."

"I know it," replied Forrest, "and that's just why I want her."

They married and settled in Memphis, where Forrest dealt in farm supplies, including that most notorious farm supply of the Old South, slaves. He became a prominent and respected member of the community and was elected to the board of aldermen.

On June 14, 1861, six days after Tennessee seceded from the Union, Forrest enlisted as a private in the cavalry. His capabilities were well known, and within a month he had been promoted to lieutenant colonel. He raised a cavalry battalion and spent his own money to equip it.

Forrest's success began at Sacramento, Kentucky, on December 28, 1861. Five hundred Union troops had been sent to wipe out his 200 raiders, who had been stripping the countryside of livestock and materiel. Rather than try to evade them, Forrest was determined to attack. He approached the Union rear guard, which was unsure whether his battalion was friend or foe. To clarify the situation, Forrest grabbed a Maynard rifle and shot one of them. As the Union troops formed their battle line, Forrest threw forward a small number of skirmishers to engage them and hold their attention. He then split his men into three sections, keeping the main one with himself while sending two smaller sections to flank the Union line. As his maneuvers were completed, his men began to fire on the Union flanks and rear as well as their front, a situation guaranteed to provoke panic. At that moment, Forrest stood in his stirrups and, waving his saber in his left hand, thundered, "Charge!"

The bluecoats broke and ran. Forrest was in the thick of the action; one of his troops claimed there must have been 50 shots fired at him in five minutes, one of which hit his horse in the head but did not kill it. A cavalryman, Adam R. Johnson, described his commander's wielding his saber against a man as large and muscular as himself, while another tried to run him through the back. The latter was shot by one of Forrest's troops, after which Forrest "hewed the big man to the ground by a mighty stroke." Almost immediately, Forrest found himself fighting a running battle with three of the enemy at once. He shot one and ducked as the others slashed at him, so that their weapons only grazed his shoulder. Reining in his horse a short distance away, he shot one antagonist who galloped up, and then he thrust his saber through the other. Accounts credit Forrest with as many as nine kills in this engagement.

At 6 feet 1 1/2 inches and 180 pounds, Forrest was always an intimidating physical presence, but in combat he seemed to be infused with demonic power. According to *The Campaigns of Lt. Gen. N.B. Forrest and of Forrest's Cavalry*, after the Battle of Sacramento, one of his officers, Capt. David C. Kelley, noted that it was

> the first time I had seen the Colonel in the face of the enemy, and, when he rode up to me in the thick of the action, I could scarcely believe him to be the man I had known for several months. . . . Forrest seemed in a desperate mood and very much excited. His face was flushed till it looked like a painted warrior, and his eyes, usually mild in their expression, glared like those of a panther about to spring upon its prey. He looked as little like the Forrest of the mess table as the storm of December resembles the quiet of June.

In February 1862, Forrest's troops were ordered to join a Confederate force at Fort Donelson on the Cumberland River in northern Tennessee. There he led several forays against a large federal army under the command of Ulysses S. Grant. In the course of one battle, Forrest's horse dropped dead after sustaining seven bullet wounds. He mounted another horse, which was killed moments later by an artillery shell that struck its hindquarters just behind Forrest's leg. Extricating himself from its corpse, he rejoined his command on foot. Though unwounded, he later counted 15 bullet holes in his greatcoat.

As Grant's army was reinforced, Forrest was shocked to find the Confederate generals who commanded the fort discussing surrender. He refused to consider it, vowing that if his men would follow him he would cut his way out, even if in doing so he "saved but one man." That night, some 500 men slipped out with him into the darkness. They encountered not one enemy and suffered not one casualty. The following day, 10,000 Confederate troops surrendered needlessly, as Forrest saw it.

In April 1862, during the Battle of Shiloh, the greatest battle of the war up to that time, Forrest was assigned to guard Lick Creek against a possible Union thrust. The frustration of such duty—standing idle when he could hear the rattle of muskets and the roar of artillery in the distance—was too much for him. After requesting a change in orders and receiving no response, he rallied his men and headed where the fighting was thickest, the area later dubbed the Hornets' Nest. Getting ahead of his troops in the charge, Forrest found himself surrounded by Union soldiers. He was hit with a rifle ball just above his left hip, which passed through the muscles of his back and lodged against his spinal column, numbing his right leg. Bluecoats shouted "Kill him! Shoot him! Stick him! Knock him off his horse!" Forrest turned and with one hand hauled a slightly built Union soldier up behind him to cover his back, then rode off, shooting open a path for himself with his revolver. Although bullets whizzed by, Forrest and his improvised shield escaped injury, and the latter was no doubt relieved to be discarded once his services were no longer required. Forrest's horse had not been so lucky and died shortly after it had carried its rider back to the Confederate lines.

With fewer than 500 men, Forrest managed to capture the 1,467-man force led by Col. Abel Streight in May 1863, in what contemporary journalist George Adair called "the boldest game of bluff on record. . . . For cool audacity, it excels all history or imagination." Forrest's men harried Streight's in a running battle of several days, during which Forrest issued the order to "shoot at everything blue and keep up the skeer." After days of relentless skirmishing, he met with Streight and offered him the opportunity to surrender "to prevent the effusion of blood." Streight was reluctant to do so without ascertaining Forrest's strength. Forrest put on an elaborate display, marching men around in circles to reappear as arriving reinforcements, and having orders loudly shouted to nonexistent companies. Two artillery pieces—the only two he had—were repeatedly repositioned for Streight's benefit. Finally, the Union general cried out in consternation, "Name of God! How many guns have you got? There's 15 I've counted already!" With a studied nonchalance, Forrest replied, "I reckon that's all that has kept up."

One night Forrest rode behind federal lines to reconnoiter the enemy's strength, accompanied by Lt. Samuel Donelson. They kept away from bonfires and counted on the darkness to conceal their gray uniforms. They were making their way back to their lines when they were challenged by two federal sentries. Forrest rode directly up to the men and roared, "How dare you halt your commanding officer?" While the sentries were momentarily taken aback, he and Donelson spurred their horses to a gallop. The sentries fired at them, but Forrest claimed their bullets caused him no concern—they might have opened one of his boils, he said, which would have been a relief.

Forrest expected his men to measure up to the standard of courage he set and frequently issued an order before battle to "shoot any man who won't fight." Some eyewitnesses claimed he once shot a standard bearer who was fleeing with the colors, though others say he merely snatched up the colors and beat fleeing troops with its staff. The general also expected all his men to pitch in on onerous tasks, and was himself always the first to do so. As his forces crossed the icy, rain-swollen Hatchie River at Estenaula, Tennessee, a ferry tipped and spilled a mule team. Forrest jumped into the chest-deep water and struggled to save the animals. A large conscript watched from the safety of the bank and, unaware that his commander was in the thick of it, loudly proclaimed that no man on earth could make him take on such a task. Forrest promptly climbed out of the river and tossed the shirker in. Another time, while his forces were crossing the Tennessee, he noticed a lieutenant not helping with the oars. The lieutenant explained that he didn't think it was necessary for officers to join in as long as there were sufficient enlisted men. Forrest knocked the man out of the ferry with a blow of his hand and, after he was pulled back in, told him, "Now, damn you, get hold of the oars and go to work! If I knock you out of the boat again, I'll let you drown."

There was another incident in which Forrest struck one of his men, though he was apparently unaware that he had done so. He habitually spent hours before an engagement in deep thought, pacing back and forth as he anticipated every contingency, and did not like to be interrupted. At one such time, a trooper made the mistake of walking up to him and attempting to start a conversation. Without a word, Forrest thrust out his fist and knocked him cold. Still lost in thought he continued to pace, stepping over the man's prostrate form.

Forrest's most violent encounter with one of his own troops occurred on June 13, 1863, when he met with Lt. A. Willis Gould, who wished to protest a transfer order. Considering the order an aspersion against his honor, Gould announced that "no man can accuse me of being a coward and both of us live." Gould then drew his revolver and, just as Forrest grabbed his gun hand, shot him in the side. Forrest forced the muzzle of the gun aside while with his left hand he took out his pocketknife, opened its blade with his teeth, and stabbed Gould between the ribs. Gould broke free and fled. Forrest was hurriedly examined by a physician, who told him that the wound would probably prove fatal because of its proximity to his intestines.

Forrest stalked the street in search of Gould, bellowing to an officer who tried to stop him, "Get out of my way! No one kills me and gets away with it!" Forrest grabbed two revolvers from another Confederate officer, burst into a tailor shop in which Gould was hiding, fired at him, and missed. Gould ran outside and collapsed dead in a patch of weeds as the result of his knife wound. Forrest found him, nudged him with his foot, then walked away to attend to his own wound, which turned out not to be life threatening. His rage ebbed, and he later expressed regret at killing Gould, saying that he never wanted to kill anybody except an enemy, and then only when fighting for his country.

In the vicious hand-to-hand fighting near Plantersville in April 1865, Forrest was singled out by Union troops. *That Devil Forrest* by John Allen Wyeth contains the following account given by Confederate Lt. George L. Cowan:

> I saw General Forrest surrounded by six Federals at one time, and they were all slashing at him. One of them struck one of his pistols and knocked it from his hand. Private Phil Dodd was fortunately near and spurred his horse to the general's rescue, and shot the Federal soldier who was so close upon him, thus enabling General Forrest to draw his other pistol, with which he killed another of the group, who was still persistent in his attack upon our commander.

In the same battle, a federal captain named J. D. Taylor engaged in a 200-yard running battle with Forrest, hacking at his arm with his saber until Forrest shot him. The general later observed, "If that boy had known enough to give me the point of his saber instead of its edge, I should not have been here to tell you about it."

One of Forrest's rough-and-ready aphorisms was "Get 'em skeered, and then keep the skeer on 'em," and he put that philosophy to good effect at the Battle of Brice's Cross Roads. It was his most celebrated victory, as his cavalry drove a numerically superior force of Union cavalry for 50 miles. At one point, the road could accommodate just four riders riding abreast, and one of his lieutenants informed him that the Confederate contingent behind them numbered precisely 10. "That is enough," Forrest responded. "Ten good men can whip 1,000 in the fix we have them."

Forrest is best known for saying, "I always make it a rule to get there first with the most men" (usually quoted as "I gets there fustest with the mostest"), but he routinely defeated larger armies with his innovative tactics. These included keeping his cannon moving with the line of his troops for use as assault weapons, having his cavalry dismount once in position to more effectively find cover and use their small arms, using his entire force in an assault rather than maintaining a reserve, attacking the enemy from several sides at once, and relentlessly pursuing the enemy once its line had broken. According to Albert Goodloe's *Confederate Echoes*, it was Forrest's view that most men regarded a battlefield "with horror and consternation," and that the more terrifying he could make it, the sooner their morale would crumble. He believed in hurling "his entire force against them in the fiercest and most warlike manner possible," and, with "unabated fury," pressing the attack "by a constant repetition of blows . . . killing, capturing, and driving them with but little difficulty."

The South was slow to recognize his military genius, but certainly the North saw him as one of its most effective opponents. During the war, Sherman called him a "devil" who should be "hunted down if it costs 10,000 lives and bankrupts the treasury," but later described him as "the most remarkable man" the war produced.

When the Confederacy was defeated, Forrest returned to his

plantation to try to pick up the pieces. A millionaire before the war, he was reduced to sharecropping on land he had once owned.

On the evening of March 30, 1866 Forrest heard one of his farmhands, an ex-slave named Thomas Edwards, beating his wife and entered his cabin to demand he stop. According to biographer John Hurst, court testomony given by A. M. Henderson reported that

> Edwards replied that he would be d——d if he would not thrash his wife whenever he pleased; that he did not care a d—n for General Forrest, and would do as he pleased, at the same time assuming a threatening attitude and insulting language. The General remarked to him that he would not permit him or anybody else to insult him, and that if he persisted in using such language he would strike him. Edwards did continue to use insulting language, whereupon the General struck him over the head with a broom or its handle. Edwards immediately assaulted the General with a knife, wounding him slightly in the hand. Unfortunately for Edwards there was an ax in the cabin which the General seized, and, as Edwards was rushing upon him he received a blow on the head which was instantly fatal.

Forrest was exonerated.

Suffering from postwar disenfranchisement and economic collapse, Confederate veterans formed the Ku Klux Klan (KKK) in 1866. Forrest accepted the leadership of the so-called Invisible Empire, and his nom de guerre of Wizard of the Saddle inspired its title Grand Wizard. However, he quit the KKK within a few years, denounced its violence, and recommended its dissolution.

Forrest was a delegate to the Democratic convention in

1868. He traveled to New York in the company of some fellow
veterans, including Gen. Basil W. Duke. As they approached a
small Northern town, the train conductor warned them that a
crowd had collected at the depot, having learned Forrest was
on the train, and that the town bully was loudly proclaiming
his intention to give him a thrashing. Although he didn't think
the crowd was disposed to back the bully, the conductor was
concerned that once violence started a riot might develop and
asked Forrest to remain in the coach at all costs. As Duke
wrote in his memoirs,

> Forrest . . . received the news very calmly,
> being too much accustomed to affairs of that
> kind to become excited, and agreed to the pro-
> gram as indicated. But when the train stopped at
> the depot, the bully immediately sprang upon
> the platform and entered our coach. He was a
> very powerful man in appearance, larger than
> Forrest. . . . He called out loudly: "Where's that
> damned butcher Forrest? I want him."
>
> I never in my life witnessed such an instan-
> taneous and marvelous transformation in any-
> one's appearance as then occurred with Forrest.
> He bounded from his seat, his form erect and
> dilated, his face the color of heated bronze, and
> his eyes flaming, blazing. He strode rapidly
> down the aisle toward the approaching champi-
> on, his gait and manner evincing perfect, invin-
> cible determination. "I am Forrest," he said.
> "What do you want?"

The bully seemed to shrivel under Forrest's glare, and suddenly he made a break for it, leaping from the coach with
Forrest following on his heels, shouting for him to stop. But as
quickly as his courage had dissipated, he vanished. Forrest,

struck by the hilarity of the situation, broke into laughter, and he was soon joined in his merriment by a sympathetic and congenial crowd.

In his last years Forrest accepted the Christian faith. Hurst's 1993 biography of Forrest describes the remarkable transformation in the face of the once-demonic warrior through the eyes of General Wheeler, a comrade in arms who saw Forrest near death at age 56, a dozen years after the war's end: "Every line or suggestion of harshness had disappeared, and he seemed to possess in these last days the gentleness of expression, the voice and manner of a woman."

12 Peter Francisco

> *Without him we would have lost two crucial battles, perhaps the War, and with it our freedom. He was truly a One-Man Army.*
>
> —George Washington

On June 23, 1765, at 5 years old, he was found abandoned on the wharf at City Point (now a part of Hopewell), Virginia. He was richly dressed, with silver buckles on his shoes, one was engraved with a "P," the other with an "F." He didn't speak English but gave his name as Pedro Francisco. It is now believed he was dropped off from a ship after being kidnapped from the island of Terceira in the Azores.

Francisco was taken in by Judge Anthony Wilson and raised as something between an indentured servant and a member of the family. As Francisco outgrew his shoes, he transferred their silver buckles to his knee britches; they were his only link with his background. By the time he was 15 he stood 6 feet, 6 inches and weighed over 250 pounds, making him a giant in a day when the average height was nearly a foot shorter. Some called him the strongest man in America—he was able to lift two grown men over his head, one seated in the palm of each hand.

Patrick Henry was a frequent guest at Judge Wilson's home, and his conversation imbued young Francisco with revolutionary fervor. In the autumn of 1776, at 16 years of age, Francisco enlisted in the 10th Virginia Regiment in the Continental Army. At the Battle of Brandywine, on September 11, 1777, he was at Chad's Ford, where both Washington and Lafayette took note of his enormous size.

As the British charged, Francisco fired his musket but was not sure his shot hit home. He reloaded and fired again as they closed. Eighty yards was about the maximum range at which one could hit a man with a smoothbore musket, and reloading was so slow that it was difficult to get off more than two shots before the lines closed. But hand-to-hand fighting was Francisco's forte, and when the redcoats were near enough he ran forward and bayoneted three or four. He was struck in the leg by a bullet but kept fighting.

Francisco was quartered in a local farmer's home while he recovered, and in a bed nearby was Lafayette, also wounded in the leg. The marquis was only two years older than the Portuguese giant, and they struck up a friendship that would last a lifetime. At their parting, Lafayette asked if there was anything he could do for Francisco. Francisco jokingly replied that he would like a sword to suit his stature—one about 5 feet long. "I could make it sing!" he said. Delighted by the idea, Lafayette promised to relay it to Washington.

Francisco fought at Germantown and endured the brutal winter at Valley Forge. Selected to serve with the elite Continental light infantry, he took part in the defense of Mud Island and was wounded in the thigh by a musket ball at Monmouth. He also participated in Gen. "Mad" Anthony Wayne's surprise night attack on the British bastion at Stony Point, north of New York City. Francisco was in one of two 20-

·KIRCHNER·

man assault units, dubbed the Forlorn Hopes, that spearheaded the attack. So that an accidental discharge would not give them away, they didn't load their muskets; all fighting would be with fixed bayonets. Francisco was the second man over the wall and headed for the flagpole to lower the Union Jack. A sentry tried to stop him, inflicting a 9-inch bayonet wound across his abdomen. Francisco turned and killed him, as well as two grenadiers. The Forlorn Hopes sustained so many casualties that Francisco was one of only two men in his unit to reach his objective. Fortunately, the main American force was right behind them and the fort was taken.

In 1799, his enlistment up, Francisco returned home as a popular hero, but he was not content to rest on his laurels. He reenlisted within a year, this time as part of the Virginia militia, which included many raw recruits. At the Battle of Camden, on August 16, 1780, these inexperienced troops broke and ran as the British charged and inflicted one of the worst defeats of the war. Francisco stayed alongside his commander, Colonel Mayo, guarding him as they retreated. He shot a grenadier who attacked the colonel, and he bayoneted a charging cavalryman clear out of his saddle. He gave the cavalryman's horse to the colonel to help him make his escape. In gratitude, the colonel later presented Francisco with his dress sword and in his will left him 1,000 acres in Kentucky. (The bequest was never honored, as Mayo's heirs contested it and Francisco would not stoop to fight for it in court.)

It was in the course of the Camden retreat that Francisco performed his most famous feat of strength. Mayo was appalled that the troops were abandoning their two fieldpieces to the enemy, so Francisco, coming across one gun carriage mired in the mud, freed the 1,100-pound cannon and dragged it to the rear on his back. (The story had at least enough credibility to be commemorated on a U.S. stamp in 1975.)

Francisco's greatest day in action was at the Battle of Guilford Courthouse on March 15, 1781. A few days earlier a shipment of supplies had arrived, and along with the food and clothing was a 5-foot broadsword earmarked for him.

Early in the battle a royal guardsman bayoneted Francisco in the leg, pinning his calf to his horse. As the guardsman withdrew his bayonet, Francisco wheeled on his horse and brought down his oversized sword. Lt. Philemon Holcombe, an eyewitness, described what followed: "Francisco's sword hit the soldier squarely on the head with such force that his head was cleft in two, a half falling on each shoulder. Those standing nearby exclaimed, 'Did you ever see the like?' and no one ever had." Despite his wound, Francisco continued to rage among the guards' 2d battalion, hewing down 11 men, but as he charged, a British bayonet caught him just above the knee and penetrated all the way to his hip bone. Francisco was thrown from his horse and fought off unconsciousness only long enough to drag himself to the shelter of some trees.

The Battle of Guilford Courthouse was technically a British victory, but it exacted such a toll on them that it is considered, along with Saratoga, one of the turning points of the war. For his gallantry, Francisco was offered a commission. Since he could neither read nor write, and thus felt he could not perform the duties of an officer, he turned it down.

Francisco had one more spectacular encounter with the British in the summer of that year. While recuperating from his wounds at home, he happened to be inside the tavern of Ben Ward when nine green-jacketed members of Lt. Col. Banastre Tarleton's legion rode up. Tarleton and his men had a reputation for brutality, and Tarleton himself was known as the Butcher. "Tarleton's quarter" was a synonym for no quarter given to a surrendering enemy. (He was the inspiration for Colonel Tavington in the movie *The Patriot*.) Francisco tried to leave by a side door, but it was guarded by a trooper with drawn sword. Unarmed and in civilian clothing, Francisco threw up his hands in surrender. As the other dragoons began looting the tavern, the one guarding Francisco asked if he had any valuables, perhaps a watch. Francisco turned over what he had, but when the trooper demanded the silver buckles at the knees of his britches, Francisco told him that the buckles had sentimental value and if he wanted them he would have to remove them himself. The dragoon put his sword under his arm and bent to the task. With a sudden move, Francisco grabbed the sword, swung it round, and buried it in the man's head.

The other dragoons scrambled through the doorway. One fired a pistol, grazing Francisco in the side, his sixth wound of the war. Francisco lopped off his hand. Thinking they had been ambushed by a larger force, several of the dragoons rushed for their horses. One of the mounted dragoons tried to shoot Francisco but his musket misfired. Francisco lifted him off his horse with a thrust. Mounting the horse, Francisco began yelling to nonexistent cohorts, "Finish them off, men! Now's our chance!"

The survivors, all of them wounded to varying degrees and only one of whom had managed to mount his horse, ran to rejoin the main force of Tarleton's Legion a quarter of a mile away, shouting warnings of ambush. As Tarleton halted his troops, Francisco rounded up the eight mounts they had left behind and headed them down a side road. He later sold them for a handsome profit, except for a fine white horse he kept for himself, which he mischievously named Tarleton.

Tarleton, enraged that his army of 400 had been held up by a single man, put a price on the giant's head, which no one had the temerity to try to collect.

The fight at the tavern is depicted in a painting that hangs in Philadelphia's Independence Hall.

Francisco rejoined Lafayette at the siege of Yorktown, where he served as the marquis' personal bodyguard and observed the British surrender.

In 1910 a 30-foot obelisk was erected to memorialize the Battle of Guilford Courthouse. Known as the Francisco Monument, one side is inscribed as follows:

TO PETER FRANCISCO A GIANT IN STATURE MIGHT AND COURAGE—WHO SLEW IN THIS ENGAGEMENT ELEVEN OF THE ENEMY WITH HIS OWN BROADSWORD RENDERING HIMSELF THEREBY PERHAPS THE MOST FAMOUS PRIVATE SOLDIER OF THE REVOLUTIONARY WAR.

In 1824, when Lafayette returned to America he invited Francisco to participate in the festivities. At an event in Richmond's Capitol Square, at the general's request the 64-year-old Francisco gave a demonstration of his still remarkable strength, lifting two men seated in the palms of his hands to the height of his shoulders.

He died on January 16, 1831.

13 Geronimo

Geronimo was born into the tribe of Chiricahua Apache around 1829, though he didn't receive the name we know him by until he was almost 30 years old. Until then he was called Goyahkla, "One Who Yawns." Like all Apache males, he was trained as a warrior from boyhood, practicing with toy bows and arrows for hours daily, stalking and shooting small game. "To me this was never work," he recalled. He was trained to "creep and freeze," to stand immobile for so long that he seemed to disappear into the landscape, and to run as much as four miles with a mouthful of water he was not allowed to swallow in order to build his endurance. He learned horsemanship: jumping barriers, riding down steep slopes, and snatching objects off the ground while hanging off the side of his mount. He was schooled in inflicting pain, and when he tortured live animals or birds his ingenuity was rewarded. He had to learn to endure pain as well; sage grass would be put on his skin and set on fire, and he had to let it burn to ashes without flinching. To become a warrior, a young man had to perform well in four battles (four being the Apaches' sacred number), showing no cowardice, not speaking unless spoken to, and bearing all burdens without complaint. Having achieved warrior status by the time he was 17, Goyahkla married and fathered three children.

At the time, the Chiricahua Apaches' main enemy, outside of rival tribes, was Mexico. The Chiricahua regularly raided Mexican settlements, and Mexico launched punitive raids in response. The northwestern states of Sonora and Chihuahua paid bounties for Apache scalps—ironically, the Apaches were more often the victims than the perpetrators of scalping.

Despite the mutual animosity, there were sanctuaries where the Apaches could camp and trade, such as the fort at Janos. In the early 1850s, after leaving his family in the Indian camp outside Janos, Goyahkla joined other tribesmen going into town. While they were there, 400 troops attacked the camp and killed everyone, including his wife, children, and aged mother. The Apaches in town were warned of the massacre and had to flee, leaving behind their dead. As the wretched band made its way back to Arizona, Goyahkla was mute with grief, and when he returned home, he burned his dwellings and everything in them, including his children's toys and his wife's beadwork. "None lost as I had," he said, "for I had lost all." For the rest of his life, he told his biographer, "my heart would ache for revenge upon Mexico."

While he was grieving, Goyahkla received his first indication that he had what the Apaches called power. He heard a spirit voice call his name four times. It told him: "No gun can ever kill you. I will take the bullets from the guns of the Mexicans, so they will have nothing but powder. And I will guide your arrows."

A year after the Janos massacre, Goyahkla led the Chiricahua reprisal. Two hundred warriors traveled into Mexico on foot, covering 40 to 45 miles a day. Many were armed with rifles, though Goyahkla was not. When they camped near the Sonoran town of Arizpe, eight Mexicans came out to talk under a flag of truce. The Apaches killed them, in order to draw out the troops. The following day, 100 Mexican troops, two companies of cavalry, and two of infantry, engaged them in one of the few pitched battles the Apaches ever fought. According to S.M. Barrett's *Geronimo: His Own Story,* Goyahkla was convinced that these were the same troops who had slaughtered his family, though there is no way he could have known. "In all the battle, I thought of my murdered mother, wife, and babies—of . . . my vow of vengeance, and I fought with fury. Many fell by my hand."

An eyewitness described Goyahkla fighting like a man possessed: "He was not content to fight according to the Apache custom, from behind rocks and greasewood bushes. Instead, he rushed into the open many times, running zigzag and dodging so that bullets from the *rurales'* [soldiers'] rifles did not hit him. Each time he ran out this way, he killed a *rurale* with his hunting knife, took the *rurale's* rifle and cartridges, and ran zigzag back again to his people. Goyahkla did not know how to use the rifles, so he gave them to other Apache warriors."

It was during this battle that he received the name by which we know him. The Mexicans, overwhelmed by this berserker performance, began to cry out, "*Cuidado!* [Watch out!] *Geronimo!*" This is usually explained as a reference to St. Jerome, but why the soldiers would have chosen to implore St. Jerome remains a mystery. In any case, the name stuck and Goyahkla became Geronimo.

At one point, after two hours of fighting, Geronimo and three Chiricahua, all of whom had used up their arrows and spears, were confronted by two armed Mexicans. Two of the Chiricahua were immediately shot dead. Geronimo and the other one ran back toward their line. The Mexicans pursued them and cut down Geronimo's comrade with a sword. Reaching the Apache line, Geronimo grabbed a spear and whirled, just as the soldier behind him took aim at him and fired. The soldier missed, and Geronimo speared him, then grabbed his sword and used it to fend off the other soldier. As they grappled, Geronimo dropped the sword, pulled his knife, and killed the Mexican. Geronimo leaped to his feet and looked around for other Mexicans to kill, but they had all fled. "Still covered with the blood of my enemies, still holding my conquering weapon, still hot with the joy of battle, victory, and vengeance, I was surrounded by the Apache braves and made war chief of all the Apaches," he later recalled.

The Apaches had won their greatest victory. By their own count, the Mexicans had suffered 26 dead and 46 wounded. When troops sent after the Apaches came upon the scene of the battle, they were so horrified by the carnage that they refused to continue the pursuit.

Others of his tribe were satisfied, but not Geronimo. He soon led two warriors on another raid. As they approached a Mexican village they came under fire, and Geronimo's two friends were killed. He had to fight his way out alone against a large force of Mexicans, some mounted and some on foot. "Three times that day I was surrounded, but I kept fighting, dodging and hiding," Geronimo recalled. Although the Mexicans hunted him with rifles and he had only his bow and arrows, he killed several of them. After he ran out of arrows, he traveled for two days without food or rest until he had shaken his pursuers.

That raid was deemed a disgrace, but Geronimo was undeterred. He returned to Mexico again and again, leading parties of as few as three or four, or as many as 30. Sometimes the Mexican army repelled the Apaches and attacked their villages in reprisal, but Geronimo's raids often brought back rich hauls of horses, cattle, and other booty.

During one attack in about 1868, Mexican troops captured

all of the tribe's horses and mules and drove them off. With a band of 20 warriors, Geronimo tracked them on foot to a cattle ranch in Sonora. Geronimo and his men fought the troops, killing two, and took back their stock and more. As the Apaches made their way north, they discovered that they were being trailed by nine mounted troopers. Geronimo, with three other warriors, stayed back to intercept them. After the Mexicans bedded down for the night, Geronimo and his men stole into their camp and stole their horses as they slept. This was considered a rather good trick.

Another time, when Geronimo's group came under fire from Mexican troops, it took cover in an arroyo and from there killed many of the Mexicans. Geronimo observed a discussion between the officers and their general and took advantage of a ditch to creep closer. "The wind was blowing in my direction, so that I could hear all [the general] said," recalled Geronimo. According to *Geronimo: His Own Story,* this is about what he told them:

> Officers, yonder in those ditches is the red devil Geronimo and his hated band. This must be his last day. Ride on him from both sides of the ditches; kill men, women, and children; take no prisoners; dead Indians are what we want. Do not spare your own men; exterminate this band at any cost; I will post the wounded to shoot all deserters; go back to your companies and advance.

As the general finished speaking, Geronimo took careful aim with his single-shot Springfield rifle and killed him.

There followed a savage battle, with charge after charge beaten back by the Apaches. After dark, the Indians crept out from cover, set fire to the prairie grass behind the Mexicans, and then escaped in the confusion.

In November 1882, Geronimo was part of a Chiricahua force that attacked a 23-man Mexican cavalry patrol. The patrol took a defensive position atop a small conical hill. Under covering fire from the others, a group of Apaches made their way up the hill crawling on their bellies and rolling stones ahead of them as shields. When they neared the crest they rose to their feet and slaughtered the Mexicans. One escaped, but Geronimo forbade anyone from chasing him, saying, "Let him go! He will tell the rest of the soldiers what has happened and they will come to the rescue. Then we can destroy more soldiers."

In *Geronimo: His Own Story,* he recounted his many battles with Mexicans:

> I received seven wounds, as follows: shot in the right leg above the knee, and still carry the bullet; shot through the left forearm; wounded in the right leg below the knee with a saber; wounded on top of the head with the butt of a musket; shot just below the outer corner of the left eye; shot in left side; shot in the back. I have killed many Mexicans; I do not know how many, for frequently I did not count them. Some of them were not worth counting.

With the increased settlement in the West following the Civil War, the United States became actively involved in the Apache war. Geronimo surrendered to U.S. forces twice, agreeing to live on the reservation, only to break out later after some provocation. The government repeatedly double-crossed the Apaches and broke promises made to them, but uprisings could also be sparked by its refusal to let Apache men beat their wives or cut off their noses as a punishment for adultery.

Geronimo's final breakout was in 1886, when he led the last band of free Indians to wage war against the United States. With only 18 warriors, traveling with 19 women and children,

Courtesy of the Arizona Historial Society/Tucson

Geronimo ran ragged a force of 5,000 cavalry and infantry—
one- quarter of the U.S. Army of the time— prompting one officer to observe that hunting the Apaches with regular troops was
like "chasing deer with a brass band." In addition to the
Americans, Geronimo was chased by 3,000 Mexican soldiers
and some 1,000 Indian scouts, *vaqueros*, and vigilantes. For
more than five months he eluded capture. His warriors raided
settlers in search of supplies and slaughtered at least 14
Americans, while Mexico claimed a death toll of between 500
and 600. As he described the rampage in *Geronimo: His Own
Story*, "We were reckless of our lives, because we felt that every
man's hand was against us. If we returned to the reservation we
would be put in prison and killed; if we stayed in Mexico they
would continue to send soldiers to fight us; so we gave no quarter to anyone and asked no favors."

At last, with his people losing heart under the unrelenting
pressure, Geronimo consented to negotiate. He learned, to his
horror, that Chiricahua families were being moved from the
Arizona reservation to an unknown place called Florida. Many
of the warriors said they were willing to return to the reservation if it meant they would be reunited with their wives and
children. Believing promises that ultimately would not be kept,
Geronimo again surrendered to the United States government.

He spent the rest of his life in captivity, shuttled between
military bases and sometimes publicly paraded as a curiosity.
He rode in an open car at Theodore Roosevelt's presidential
inauguration, appeared at the St. Louis Exposition, and made
money selling autographed photos of himself. He was never
allowed to return to his homeland. He bitterly regretted that he
had surrendered, wishing that he and his band of warriors had
fought to the last man. At the same time, he confessed that he
was haunted by the innocents he had killed, particularly babies
he had stabbed in their cradles. "I wake up groaning and very
sad at night when I remember the helpless children," he said.

In 1898, an artist named E. A. Burbank visited Geronimo at

Fort Sill, Oklahoma, to paint his portrait. Burbank had a .22 rifle, and the old Apache challenged him to a shooting contest, the target a small scrap of paper pinned to a tree some distance away. Geronimo proposed a wager of $10 per shot, but Burbank, not wanting to take advantage of Geronimo's "bleary eyes," suggested they just shoot for fun. It turned out to be a wise decision, for Geronimo, who had long since mastered the rifle, never missed.

Geronimo told Burbank that no man could kill him, and to prove his point pulled off his shirt. As the artist recounted in *Burbank Among the Indians,*

> I was dumbfounded to see the number of bullet holes in his body. . . . I had never heard of anyone living with at least 50 bullet wounds. . . . Geronimo had that many scars.
>
> Some of these bullet holes were large enough to hold small pebbles that Geronimo picked up and placed in them. Putting a pebble in a bullet wound he would make a noise like a gun, then take the pebble out and throw it on the ground. Jokingly I told him he was probably so far away that the bullets didn't penetrate him, but that if he had been nearer they probably would have killed him.
>
> "No, no!' he shouted. 'Bullets cannot kill me!"

Geronimo rode into Lawton, Oklahoma (outside Ft. Sill), on a cold February day in 1909. He sold some handmade bows and arrows to souvenir seekers and got drunk with the proceeds. On his way home he fell off his horse and lay out all night on the ground. He contracted pneumonia and died. He was 85 years old.

14 Gurkhas:
Jitbahadur Rai, Dwansing Basnet, Lachhiman Gurung

It is better to die than to be a coward.
—Motto of Britain's Gurkha Brigade

There is a story that a group of Gurkha troops, when told they would have to jump out of a plane at 600 feet, looked uncharacteristically concerned. One told his officer that he thought 300 feet might be more reasonable. The officer explained to him that at that altitude their parachutes wouldn't have time to open. "Oh, we'll have *parachutes!*" replied the Gurkha, relieved.

The tale is apocryphal, but it illustrates the fearlessness for which the Gurkhas are known. For some reason rooted in their particular culture, Gurkhas seem to make ideal soldiers. They are invariably described as cheerful, tough, hardy, disciplined, loyal, brave, and capable of incredible ferocity, especially with their ever-present *kukri* knives.

Early in the 19th century, when Britain fought to bring India into its empire, it found that the most disciplined and effective opposition came from the Gurkhas, a tribe of small, wiry Nepalese hill people. For their part, the Gurkhas said, "The English are as brave as lions; they are splendid sepoys [soldiers] and very nearly the equal of us." In 1816, after finally conquering them, the British formed special Gurkha regiments, and since then the Gurkhas have served in all of Britain's wars. Although they earn far more in the British service than they could in their homeland, it is evidently not only money that attracts them. It is not ideology either; they know little of political freedom in their own nation. Travel and adventure are a lure, but most of all they seek the opportunity to fight. In combat against the Turks in 1916, a British officer described them as "happy and keen and busy as ferrets." One who commanded Gurkhas in North Africa in World War II noted that a peculiar sound arose from them as they first came under enemy machine-gun fire, "an excited whimper not unlike hounds finding the scent."

There is a story of a recruiter who visited a Gurkha battalion to encourage them to volunteer for the paratroops. He thought he had brought a training film extolling the excitement and glamour of the airborne service, but when it was played he discovered that he had the wrong film—this one demonstrated how to *kill* paratroops. It opened with scenes of a massive parachute drop, while the narrator intoned, "Now, if you do your job well, there is no reason why 95 percent of these men should ever reach the ground alive." The paratroops were machine-gunned in the air and those surviving were slaughtered as they landed. The recruiter thought he would have to write off his mission as a total flop, but to his surprise, he found that every Gurkha present wished to sign up. All that had registered on them was that the paratroop service offered plenty of fighting, and no one wanted to miss out.

Tales abound of the physical toughness of the Gurkhas. While fighting in northwest India in 1891, Gurkha Gorey Thapa was struck in the head by a bullet without ill effect, to himself or anyone else. This was fortunate: the year before a bullet had ricocheted off his head and killed a British officer, Lieutenant Swinton. In 1931 a Gurkha of the 2d Battalion, 4th Gurkha Regiment was kicked in the head by a mule. He complained of a headache; the mule went lame. In

·KIRCHNER·

117

World War II Burma, Manbahadur Limbu, a Havildar (NCO) in the 7th Gurkhas, was shot through the spleen. To finish him off, a Japanese officer sliced open the back of his head with his sword. After resting a few hours, Manbahadur got to his feet and walked 60 miles to rejoin his unit. A doctor told him he needed time to recuperate, but Manbahadur brushed off the advice, explaining that he was concerned that his men might grow slack in his absence.

Manbahadur was by no means exceptional. Captured Gurkhas have always shown determination to escape and rejoin their regiments, fearful that they might "miss the war." In World War II one Gurkha escaped from the Germans three times, finally joining up with the French resistance. A Gurkha who managed to escape from a Japanese POW camp wandered around Burma for two years, disguised as a Burmese, until he was able to connect with the U.S. Army's Merrill's Marauders. Another was captured and escaped twice and, aided by sympathetic tribesmen, traveled 1,500 miles on foot to his unit. Havildar Manbahadur Rai of the 1st Battalion, 7th Gurkha Regiment escaped from a Japanese prison camp and walked 600 miles in five months to return to British lines, navigating with a map he had purchased from a British soldier before his capture. (The British officers he showed it to upon his arrival were dumbfounded: it was a street map of London.)

If the Gurkha has a limitation as a soldier, it is his tendency to follow orders a bit too literally, as in this account from the history of the 1st Battalion, 5th Gurkha Regiment:

> Major Morlan-Hughes selected a house for his headquarters and gave orders for the removal and burial of nine German bodies lying in the cellar. A party of Gurkhas carried these on a ladder and dumped them into a shell-hole. They had disposed of eight and were carrying up the ninth when the "corpse" leaped to his feet with

a scream of terror. Kukris were drawn and the helpless German was about to be dispatched when some British antiaircraft gunners standing near intervened, saying: "Hey, Johnny, you can't kill him like that!" The reply, a typical example of remorseless Gurkha logic, was: "But we were ordered to bury nine dead Germans. Surely you don't expect us to bury one of them alive!"

The Gurkhas' traditional knife, the *kukri*, is designed for the cut, not the thrust. It's a marvel or ergonomics with enormous shearing power for a weapon of its size, its boomerang shape always positioning its edge at a leading angle to the target. Its foot-long blade is also heaviest near its tip, adding momentum to a blow. With their *kukris,* Gurkhas pride themselves on being able to decapitate a man with one stroke, which, more than anything else, explains why their battle cry *Ayo Gurkhali!* (The Gurkhas are here!) chills their enemies' blood.

The knives proved particularly useful on nighttime raids: Gurkhas would sometimes sneak into German encampments, behead every third person, and set each severed head on the chest of its body. The resulting tableau was understandably demoralizing for those who awoke to it. The *kukri* was also ideal for hand-to-hand fighting. In Italy in World War II, a number of Gurkhas were honored for single-handedly chopping down clusters of the enemy, and there are two accounts of Gurkha units capturing tanks intact by diving inside them and scraping them clean of Germans with their knives. In the Arno Valley in July 1944, C Company of the 2d Battalion, 7th Gurkhas was pinned down by machine-gun fire. When tracers ignited the grass in front of him, Jitbahadur Rai took advantage of the obscuring smoke to charge the German position. With two swipes of his *kukri*, Jitbahadur killed two of the gunners, who collapsed on top of him. He was immobilized under about 350 pounds of dead Kraut when the third came at him. Jitbahadur managed to free his arm and, with a wild slash, nearly severed the man's arm above the elbow. Later, as the German was carried away on a stretcher, Jitbahadur walked beside him and, in an attempt to comfort him, patted his shoulder and repeatedly assured him that he had no intention of finishing the job. His intentions were lost on the terrified German; the hand not doing the patting was still clutching a bloody *kukri*, and his reassurances were being delivered in Gurkhali.

Jemadar Dwansing Basnet demonstrated his proficiency with the *kukri* in Tunisia, and his account is recorded in the regimental history of the 1st Battalion, 9th Gurkhas. While reconnoitering ahead of his platoon at night, he was challenged in a foreign language. As Dwansing recalled:

> To make quite sure I crept up and found myself looking into the face of a German. I recognized him by his helmet. He was fumbling with his weapon, so I cut off his head with my *kukri*. Another appeared from a slit trench, and I cut him down also. I was able to do the same with two others, but one made a great deal of noise, which raised the alarm. I had cut at the fifth, but I am afraid I only wounded him. Yet perhaps the wound was severe, for I struck him between the neck and the shoulders.
>
> I was now involved in a struggle with a number of Germans, and eventually, after my hands had become cut and slippery with blood, they managed to wrest my *kukri* from me. One German beat me over the head with it, inflicting a number of wounds. He was not very skillful, however, sometimes striking me with the sharp edge but oftener with the blunt.

Beaten to the ground, Dwansing lay there feigning death

until the Germans retreated to their trenches. Wiping the blood from his eyes, he spotted an enemy machine gun nearby. As he lay there thinking about how he might get to the gun, his platoon advanced and began showering the Germans with grenades. Fearing that he would be killed, he struggled to his feet and ran toward his men, who, mistaking him for the enemy, nearly shot him. Having thus escaped the threat of friendly fire, he was determined to retake command of his plattoon and resume fighting. His company commander had different ideas, however, and firmly ordered Dwansing to the regimental aid post.

On the night of May 12, 1945, C Company of the 4th Battalion, 8th Gurkhas in Burma came under attack by some 200 Japanese. A grenade fell on the edge of the trench held by Rifleman Lachhiman Gurung and two other Gurkhas. Lachhiman threw it back. A second grenade landed in the trench, and he threw that one back too. He wasn't so lucky with the third, which blew off his right hand and severely wounded his comrades. At this point, the Japanese launched their assault. Lachhiman managed to fire and reload his rifle with his left hand, calling out, "Come and fight! Come and fight! While I live I will kill you!" Time after time, the Japanese attacked and fell back under the determined resistance. When dawn arrived, 87 dead Japanese were found in front of C Company's position; 31 of these lay in front of the trench occupied by Lachhiman Gurung. When he was awarded the Victoria Cross, he thought there must have been some mistake. He denied that he or his people were especially brave. "It is only that we have such bad tempers when something makes us angry," he explained.

During the Falklands War, Argentine troops, knowing the Gurkhas' reputation, frequently surrendered to other units rather than face them. One of the British officers commanding a Gurkha regiment observed that "it was desperately frustrating and exasperating for us to find no enemy on an objective, but when all is said and done, if we can win by reputation, who wants to kill people?"

An admirable sentiment, but would the Gurkhas agree?

15 Frank Hamer

*He is absolutely void of fear,
and while he is not an edu-
cated man, he is bright and
intelligent, very industrious
and a splendid detective. . . .
The harder the criminal and
the more dangerous and
hazardous the work, the better he likes it . . . the lawless
element stand in awe of him
wherever he has worked.*
—Capt. John H. Rogers,
Texas Ranger

In 1940, when the New York Yankees were playing an exhibition game in Houston, Joe DiMaggio was in a restaurant when someone told him that Frank Hamer, the most famous Texas Ranger alive, was at a nearby table. After DiMaggio introduced himself to the tall, black-suited lawman and asked for his autograph, Hamer invited the Yankee Clipper to sit down. In the course of their conversation, DiMaggio asked a rude question, but one to which many people would have liked an answer: how many men Hamer had killed. "They tell me you've killed between 45 and 50," he prompted.

Hamer replied genially:

> No, no, but now that I think of it, there was
> one time when we were out moving some cattle

across New Mexico and we got caught in a snowstorm. I was sleeping with an old boy, and when it came time for me to get up and go on night herd, I failed to pull the saddle blanket back up over him and he froze to death. Near as I can recollect, that's the only man I've ever killed in my whole life.

After a few seconds of bewildered silence, DiMaggio caught on and burst out laughing.

During his three decades in law enforcement, Hamer participated in 52 gunfights, was ambushed four times, wounded by bullets 23 times, and left for dead twice. But he would never discuss how many lives he had taken, which he regarded as a distasteful aspect of his duty.

Hamer killed his first man in 1900 when he was 16 years old. He and his younger brother Harrison were sharecropping in San Saba County, Texas, and Dan McSwain, the landowner, noticed Frank's proficiency with the pistol, shotgun, and rifle. McSwain approached him one day and asked him how he would like to earn $150.

"Who do I have to kill?" joked Frank, and was shocked to learn that that was in fact the nature of the deal; there was a neighboring rancher that McSwain wanted dead. Angrily refusing, Frank told McSwain that he intended to warn the rancher, and did so that evening. Two days later, when the boys were plowing, McSwain came after them with a shotgun. Frank was wounded with a blast of buckshot, but he pulled a small pistol and drove McSwain off. McSwain went home to get his rifle and returned on horseback to search for the boys. They hid until he passed, then fled. Hamer moved out of the area to convalesce. When he had recovered he returned to McSwain's house and called him out. Both went for their pistols. McSwain came in second.

Hamer worked as a cowboy during the next few years, and on two occasions captured horse thieves at gunpoint. Impressed, the local sheriff recommended him for the Texas Rangers. On April 21, 1906, at 22 years of age, he was sworn in. Before the year was out he was one of five rangers sent to capture a murderer, Ed Putnam, who had barricaded himself in a farmhouse. After a lengthy gun battle, Hamer noticed a slight movement at a curtain, which Putnam was pushing aside with the muzzle of his pistol in order to take a shot. Even though he couldn't see Putnam, Hamer figured out where he had to be standing and killed him with one shot from his Winchester rifle.

Two years later, Hamer left active duty with the Texas Rangers to accept the post of city marshal in Navasota. The entrenched White Citizens Council, which openly flouted the law and ran roughshod over local blacks and sharecroppers, hired Hamer under the misapprehension that the young man would be easily cowed. After one leading citizen got drunk and shot up the town, Hamer marched into a busy saloon and collared him. As a hostile crowd clustered around, Hamer slowly surveyed their faces, smiled slightly, and said, "I understand you don't allow 'your kind' to be arrested." When no one responded to the challenge, Hamer marched his prisoner off to jail.

In the course of bringing the town under control, Hamer had to fight a number of times. He rarely used his fists, preferring an open-handed smack against the side of a man's head. Hamer was 6 feet 3 inches tall and weighed 200 pounds; his grizzly-bear-like swats never failed to drop an opponent. He also learned the efficacy of his boots against shins, knees, and groins. Historian Walter Prescott Webb wrote that, while Hamer killed no one in Navasota, "some [were] pretty well marked for future identification." In 1910, his mission accomplished, Hamer moved on.

In 1916, as the state's expert witness against a killer in a bitter land feud, Hamer became a marked man, with a $4,000 price on his head. On October 1, 1917, as he was heading for a court appearance, he was warned that some hired guns lay in wait for him in Sweetwater, a town through which he had to pass. Hamer wouldn't change his route, but took the precaution of strapping on an extra revolver, a Smith & Wesson Triple-Lock .44, to augment his single-action Colt .45, "Old Lucky."

Just outside of Sweetwater, Hamer got a flat tire (one wonders whether the tire wasn't shot out) and he pulled into the town's service station. With him were his wife Gladys, his brother Harrison, and a party to the case, Emmett Johnson. As his brother and Johnson went to the toilet, Hamer walked into the office. Gladys remained in the car.

As Hamer left the office one of the assassins, a former sheriff and Texas Ranger named Gee McMeans, stepped out from behind a door about four feet away, a .45 automatic in his hand. Shouting, "I've got you now, God damn you!" he shot Hamer in his left shoulder. Hamer grabbed for the pistol and managed to push it down before McMeans shot again. Even as the second bullet tore into his leg, Hamer noticed that he did not hear an ejected casing hit the wooden sidewalk; by grabbing the automatic he had caused it to jam. Hamer wrenched the pistol away and began cuffing McMeans with his open hand.

Meanwhile McMeans' associate, H. E. Phillips, attempted to sneak up on Hamer with an automatic shotgun. From the car, Gladys Hamer began shooting at him with a small-caliber semiautomatic, forcing him to duck for cover, but when her gun ran dry Phillips ran up behind Hamer and fired from about three feet away.

"I got him! I got him!" shouted Phillips as Hamer went to his knees. But Hamer shook off the effect of the concussion and stood back up. Phillips' blast had gone astray, merely tearing the brim from the lawman's hat. Phillips and McMeans ran for their car as Hamer went after them. McMeans pulled a pump shotgun from his car, but Hamer raised his .44 and shot him through the heart, killing him. Hamer then turned on the cowering Phillips and invited him to fight face to face, but Phillips had had enough and ran away, shotgun in hand. Hamer shouted at him to turn around, but he kept running.

·KIRCHNER·

Harrison, caught with his pants down during the shooting, now arrived and aimed a rifle at the retreating Phillips. As he squeezed the trigger, Frank pushed the barrel up. He didn't want his brother to shoot a man in the back, even one who had just tried to kill him. Phillips was soon arrested.

A few hours later, a certain Bob Higgdon blew into town. Described by some as "the deadliest gunman in the Southwest," he was one of the men hired to kill Hamer; he'd even had a special quick-draw holster made up for the occasion. He saw a shrouded body being carted off to the funeral parlor and, assuming it was Hamer, loudly proclaimed his disappointment at having arrived too late to do the job himself. When he was informed that the dead man was McMeans and that Hamer was still in town, Higgdon muttered something about how it wouldn't be right to take on a wounded man, not right at all, and left on the next train.

Hamer took a year off to recover from his wounds and traveled with his wife to Los Angeles, where he met and formed a strong friendship with cowboy movie actor Tom Mix. Mix, impressed by

Hamer's riding ability and skill with the pistol, thought the latter could be a star in Westerns, but the lawman dismissed the notion as absurd. He returned to Texas and reenlisted with the Rangers at Brownsville on October 1, 1918. Three days later he and several other Rangers got into a fierce nighttime gun battle with Mexican bootleggers. Sighting in on a single muzzle flash from the bandit leader's pistol, Hamer opened up with his semi-automatic .25 Remington, firing so fast his men likened the rifle to a pear burner, a small flamethrower used to burn the thorns off prickly pears. Hamer hit the bandit three times, killing him.

In 1921, when Hamer took over the Ranger company stationed at Del Rio, a band of outlaws led by Ralph "Red" Lopez was smuggling drugs, bootlegging whisky, rustling cattle, and committing numerous robberies in the area. Lopez, a former rodeo rider, had been wanted for murder since 1913. He was a crack shot with a rifle, which he fired from the hip; a 30-man posse that once chased him had lost six of its members to his devastating marksmanship. After Red Lopez' gang killed 19 American citizens while robbing a train near the border, stopping him rose to the top of Hamer's list.

Eventually, an informer offered to set Lopez up, so Hamer led his company to the isolated area where the meeting was to take place. This informer told Hamer that if he and his men got into a nearby irrigation ditch, they would be in an excellent position to ambush Lopez when he arrived. Hamer pretended to go along with this suggestion, but as soon as the informer had left Hamer moved his men behind a small rise some yards away. Just after dark, they saw 20 heavily armed Mexicans creep up on the ditch they had vacated. From his position behind them, Hamer shouted in Spanish, "Halt! We're officers of the law."

A furious gun battle erupted and lasted half an hour, after which the surviving bandits fled, leaving 11 dead. Hamer was bleeding from a cut across his cheek where a bullet had grazed him, but Red Lopez was dead. Hamer's shot had hit the bandit in his upper vest pocket and pierced a gold watch he carried there. For years the perforated timepiece was displayed at the customs house in Laredo.

After busting the speakeasies in the wide-open boomtown of Mexia in 1922, Hamer gave an impromptu shooting demonstration with his .25 Remington rifle, consecutively breaking more than 100 three-inch butter dishes thrown into the air. A film of the stunt was sent to the executives at Remington, who were so impressed that they made up a special .30-caliber model 8F autoloader for Hamer, inlaid with gold and engraved with scenes from his career. It became Hamer's favorite deer rifle.

As handy as he was with a rifle, Hamer was even better with a pistol. He was once challenged to a pistol-shooting contest by a sheriff famed as a crack shot. While the targets were being set up, Hamer pointed out a shiny rock about 100 yards away. Using his right hand to steady his left (he was left-handed), he aimed high to compensate for the bullet drop and hit his target with his first shot. The sheriff groused, "I said a *pistol* match. Forty yard limits! Anything over that is rifle range."

According to one friend, while driving along an unpaved road Hamer would occasionally stick his pistol out the window and fire at a rock ahead of him, keeping it tumbling until his revolver ran dry.

Hamer didn't believe in shooting from the hip, which he described as "a lot of damned Hollywood nonsense," although he admitted to having done so on those occasions when the men he was shooting at were so close he didn't have room to aim properly. He rarely wore a cartridge belt, declaring that any man who needed all those extra rounds was "just plain guilty of sloppy peace-officering."

Gifted with excellent eyesight, Hamer could actually see his bullets after they left the barrel—he said they looked like bees, enveloped in a tiny cloud of heat waves as they passed through the air. He likened the blast of pellets from a shotgun to a swarm of angry hornets. On a rifle range, Hamer could call shots before they hit the target. As remarkable as it sounds, many experienced shooters have described the same phenomenon.

One of the most famous stories associated with the Texas Rangers concerned a town, beset by a rampaging mob, which put out a call for a company of rangers to restore order. When only one ranger showed up, the citizens' committee asked why. He responded, "Well, you ain't got but one mob, have you?" Many times in his career, Hamer demonstrated that he was more than a match for "one mob." In June 1922, a vicious struggle broke out in Corpus Christi between a corrupt local political machine and citizens seeking reform. The sheriff brutally beat one of the reform leaders and then, along with his deputy and constable, shot down Fred Roberts, a man who came to the reformer's aid. The governor sent Hamer and a group of rangers to investigate. When Hamer arrived, he learned that the killers were barricaded in the courthouse, along with 30 or 40 supporters. Telling the others to stay back, Hamer walked up the courthouse steps and kicked open the double doors. Inside, a dozen rifles, shotguns, and pistols were pointed at him.

"I'm Frank Hamer, Texas Ranger," he announced to the mob, sweeping them with a gaze that could induce frostbite. "I have a warrant for the arrest of the men involved in the murder of Fred Roberts. The rest of you put up those guns and get the hell out of here."

He then walked up to the accused and began reading them the murder warrant, ignoring the armed men around him. Like a grade school class that had been dismissed, they sheepishly turned and left. We hear a lot today about the value of a show of force in law enforcement, of confronting armed suspects with so many officers that they see the futility of resistance, but such was the force of Hamer's personality that he alone had the same effect. Had he been less strong, Hamer would have had to have been more violent. So confident was he in his ability to dominate any situation that he used only the force necessary.

The grateful citizens of Corpus Christi presented him with an engraved nickel-plated single-action Colt.

At the end of the year, on Christmas Eve, Hamer was at home decorating the tree with his wife when there was a knock at the door. Gladys opened it to find a tall stranger there, asking for her husband. When Hamer went to greet him, the man hemmed and hawed for a moment, then drew a 9mm pistol. Before he could shoot, Hamer hit him on the side of the head, knocking him off the porch and down the steep front steps. Dropping his weapon, the man scrambled to his feet and ran away. Rather than shoot him, Hamer picked up an empty milk bottle to heave after him, then thought better of it.

Hamer had no idea who had dispatched the inept assassin; there were so many mobsters, bootleggers, corrupt politicians, and run-of-the-mill miscreants that had it in for him, it would have been impossible to guess.

In 1933, Hamer left the Texas Rangers to work as a special investigator for a Houston oil company at almost three times his former pay. A year later he was asked to come back for a special assignment: to track down the notorious Bonnie Parker and Clyde Barrow, the psychopathic pair John Dillinger himself had described as "giving bank robbery a bad name." They had been rampaging through the central states for a year and a half, killing so many who stood in their way, including nine law officers. Regarded as the best man for the job, Hamer considered it his duty to accept.

After several months of investigating, Hamer got a tip that the couple would be visiting a secret mail drop in rural Louisiana. On May 22, 1934, backed by five lawmen, Hamer set up an ambush. He was armed with a Colt semiautomatic pistol and a .35 Remington autoloader fitted with a large-capacity magazine.[8]

The lawmen waited in hiding from the middle of the night

---

8. The rifle was specially modified by the Peace Officer's Equipment Co. in St. Joseph, Missouri. It had a 15-round single-column magazine (often erroneously identified as holding 20 rounds). Hamer's pistol, usually identified as .45 caliber, was according to his son a .38 Super, chosen for its superior penetration of steel car bodies and bullet-proof vests.

through the next morning. Shortly after 9 A.M., they heard a powerful Ford sedan approaching at high speed. As Barrow brought the car to a halt in front of the ambush, Hamer stepped into the road and said, "Stick 'em up! We're lawmen!"

At least that's the way he recalled it. Ted Hinton, who was part of the ambush squad, remembers that Hamer simply ordered, "Shoot," in a voice audible only to those around him. Hinton's version seems more plausible, because Clyde Barrow had declared he would not be taken alive and had proven it on several occasions.

Bonnie Parker raised the sawed-off shotgun she was holding, and Hamer opened fire. "I hated to bust the cap on a woman, especially when she was sitting down; however if it wouldn't have been her, it would have been us," he said.

The other lawmen poured out a fusillade, killing Barrow before he could get the shotgun on his lap into play.[9] As she was struck by about two dozen bullets, Bonnie "screamed like a panther," according to one witness.

The news that Bonnie and Clyde had been killed provoked a mania. Crowds converged on the undertaker's parlor in Arcadia, Louisiana, to catch a glimpse of their bloody bodies and tear off pieces of their bullet-riddled car as souvenirs. The spectacle disgusted Hamer, who was also uncomfortable with his sudden celebrity. NBC called that night offering him $1,000 for a short radio interview; "Hell, no! I won't do it," he shouted and hung up the phone. A testimonial dinner was organized, but when he was told of it he muttered, "I have a date with a man

---

9. Bonnie and Clyde's 1934 Ford was a rolling arsenal. On his lap, Clyde Barrow had a 10-gauge sawed-off Winchester model 87 lever action shotgun (the model Schwarzenegger carried in *Terminator 2: Judgment Day*), and Bonnie Parker was holding a 20-gauge Remington model 11 auto-loading shotgun, its barrel sawed off to 15 inches and its stock cut down to a pistol grip. The car also contained three Browning Automatic Rifles stolen from a National Guard armory, along with 100 loaded 20-round magazines. There was a government-issue Colt .45 jammed under each of Clyde's thighs, as well as five more in the trunk (two of these were Colt .38 Supers according to Hinton); two pocket Colt automatics in .32 and .380, and a Colt .45 revolver. Scattered around the car were some 3,000 rounds of ammunition.

downtown that evening," his all-purpose excuse whenever he wanted to beg off a social engagement. (The dinner was canceled.) Near the end of the year, he came upon a traveling show that featured Bonnie and Clyde's "death car." The promoter delivered a lurid account of Hamer's role in their deaths. Enraged, Hamer leaped on the stage and smacked the man down. "Don't ever use my name again in public," he commanded.

For years Hamer was beseeched by friends in Hollywood to release the movie rights to his story, but he refused. One of them noted that he seemed to disdain publicity as much as most law enforcement officers craved it. There was one emolument, a tribute befitting a warrior, that Hamer accepted. Because of the pay cut he had taken to pursue Bonnie and Clyde, a grateful Texas legislature awarded him their guns. The shotguns, still stained with the couple's blood, are now on exhibit at the Texas Ranger Hall of Fame and Museum at Waco.

Frank Hamer died peacefully in his sleep on July 10, 1955, at the age of 71.

16 Nancy Hart

*A woman entirely unedu-
cated and ignorant of all the
conventional civilities of
life, but a zealous lover of
liberty [and] a tigress to the
enemies of her country.*
—Elizabeth Ellet

Nancy Hart never achieved the renown of her cousin Daniel Boone, but she certainly rivaled him in resourcefulness and audacity. She was born in about 1735 and married Benjamin Hart while in her teens. They had eight children and lived in the settlement on the Broad River in northern Georgia. Benjamin didn't worry when he left Nancy alone at home with the children—she was 6 feet tall, muscular, hot tempered, and an excellent shot, who covered one wall of their log cabin with the antlers of deer she had shot. She also smoked a pipe and was cross-eyed. The Cherokee who lived nearby had a nickname for her: *Wahatchee*, or War Woman.

Benjamin joined the Georgia militia when the American Revolution broke out in 1776. Nancy served as well. She once

crossed the Savannah River on a homemade raft to infiltrate the British garrison at Augusta, and, posing as a half-wit, gathered valuable intelligence concerning troop strength and dispositions. She also spied on British camps under the pretext of selling eggs. Her activities aroused some suspicion, and a Tory informant crept up to her cabin to spy on her. When her son told her that a man was looking in the window, she quickly turned from her stove and tossed a ladleful of hot lye into the man's face, then tied him up and turned him over to patriot forces.

One day, while her husband was away and she had only her 12-year-old daughter Sara with her, six Loyalists, or "Tories" came to her cabin demanding food. Previous raids had stripped the farm of its livestock, but these soldiers shot her one remaining turkey and ordered her to cook it. As Hart grudgingly prepared the meal, the Tories leaned their Brown Bess muskets against the wall and sat at the table. They were in a good humor, boasting that they had just killed Col. John Dooley, the Harts' nearest neighbor and a good friend. Containing her rage, Nancy quickly planned her vengeance. She sent Sara to the spring to get water, whispering to her to blow an alarm on the conch shell that was kept there for emergencies. Hart then put on her most hospitable manner and made sure her visitors were well supplied with corn whiskey. They grew increasingly relaxed.

While the soldiers were distracted, Hart knocked some of the mud chinking from between the logs in the wall. Then, as she returned to the kitchen area after pouring a round of drinks, she surreptitiously picked up one of the muskets and slipped it through the hole. She did this four times, so that there were only two muskets left in the house by the time one of the Tories realized what she was doing. As he lunged toward her, Hart snatched up a musket and shot him, and then picked up the other and held it on the group. Because she was cross-eyed the soldiers were confused about whom she was looking at.

"She can't get all of us with one shot. Rush her!" ordered the leader. Hart dropped him. As the others hesitated for a moment, Sara rushed in and handed her mother one of the muskets that had been thrust out through the wall. Hart covered the men until her husband came back with several members of the local militia. He suggested shooting them all, but she responded that shooting was too good for them. She insisted they be hanged.

Because the British still controlled that part of Georgia, Hart's deed was kept a secret until after the war, and most historians considered it only a legend. It was not given credence until 1912, when workers constructing the Elberton & Eastern Railroad line discovered an unmarked grave in the vicinity of the old Hart cabin containing the remains of six men.

Nancy Hart died in Kentucky in 1830 at 95. In 1954, the Georgia legislature named the county in which she had lived in her honor.

17 Erich Hartmann & Hans-Joachim Marseille

> *He was the unrivaled virtuoso among the fighter pilots of the Second World War. His achievements were previously thought to have been impossible.*
>
> —Adolf Galland, writing of Marseille

The top U.S. Army Air Corps ace in the European theater in World War II was Francis S. Grabeski, with 31 victories; the top British ace, James Johnson, had 38; the top Allied ace, a Russian, Ivan Kozhedub, had 62. The top German, Erich Hartmann, scored 352.

To understand this astonishing discrepancy, we must consider that German pilots would fly 500 to 1,000 missions, 10 times as many as their Allied counterparts, and were nearly always outnumbered by their foes. It was a target-rich environment, and those who survived developed an almost insuperable level of skill. The Luftwaffe also practiced a different style of combat than did the Allies. Once a pilot was recognized as an *experte*, his squadron mates let him take the lead in attacks while they protected his tail. The designation of "ace," earned with five kills, did not exist in the Luftwaffe, but if it had Germany could have claimed more than 3,000. It had more than 100 *experten* with 100 kills (90 percent of them on the Eastern Front). Between them, the top five German pilots accounted for 1,453 aircraft.

Hartmann, at the head of the list with 51 more than the next man, flew with Jagdgruppe (JG) 52, the Luftwaffe's most successful fighter unit. In two and a half years, he flew 1,425 missions and was in 800 "rhubarbs," or aerial combats. Almost all of his victories were against Soviet Pilots, but when he encountered U.S. Pilots over Romania he shot down seven, despite the superiority of their P-51s.

We don't know the name of the top German infantryman of World War II, the one who killed the most men on the Allied side, and if we did we wouldn't feel inclined to celebrate him, but somehow the fighter airplane war is different. It seemed to have a purity, inspiring comparisons to knightly combat in the Age of Chivalry. It involved no civilians or reluctant warriors; no one flew a fighter against his wishes. Often battles did not result in death—the "kill" refers to a plane destroyed, not a man. Pilots regarded even their enemies as brothers in a unique fraternity, and, in most cases, once an opponent had parachuted from his plane he was no longer a target. Hartmann was shot down no less than 16 times, adding kills to the tallies of other pilots even as he lived to fight another day.

He first saw combat in October 1942 and hardly distinguished himself—in fact, he got his knickers in a severe twist. An after-action report scorched him for separating from his leader without permission, losing his orientation, flying into his leader's firing position, failing to follow his leader's order to rejoin the formation, fleeing his leader (whom he mistook for an enemy), and crash-landing his plane without having inflicted any damage on the enemy.

After six months and more than 100 missions, Hartmann's score amounted to only seven.

·KIRCHNER·

Most great fighter pilots can identify a moment when they "found" themselves—when the necessary blend of skills suddenly jelled. For Hartmann, it was on July 7, 1943, a day on which he shot down seven planes. His score for July and August of that year was 78.

141

Hartmann's approach to aerial combat was similar to that of World War I's top ace, Baron Manfred von Richthofen. He always looked for the element of surprise and avoided dogfighting. Coming out of the sun or a cloud bank, he would dive on his target from its six o'clock[10] position, often closing to less than 100 feet to ensure a devastating hit. "Only if the windshield is filled up, then pull the trigger," he told his men. Quickly breaking away to avoid debris, he would check his tail for pursuers and climb. Only after what he called a "coffee break," a pause to reflect, would he decide whether circumstances favored another attack. He described his four-step system as "See–Decide–Attack–Reverse."

Hartmann was a skilled hunter. His eyesight was so sharp he could spot enemy planes minutes before anyone else, and as he said, "The pilot that sees the other first already has half the victory." As his body of experience grew he could often anticipate the action of a foe, and the hairs on the back of his neck became highly sensitive to enemies on his tail.

Hartman's flaxen hair and sunny, boyish face earned him the nickname *Bubi* (Boy), but to the Soviets he was the Black Devil, and once they learned to recognize his Me 109 by the black tulip design on its nose they made a practice of avoiding him. As his kill rates dropped, he switched to an unmarked plane and allowed green pilots to fly his distinctively painted Messerschmitt. It was the best form of insurance he could have given them.

By October 29, 1943, Hartmann had 150 victories. By July 1, 1944, he was at 250. On August 23, he had his best day ever, downing 11 planes in two sorties and raising his score to 301— making him one of only two men ever to pass 300. Hitler had previously awarded him the Oak Leaves and Swords to his Knight's Cross; now Hartmann traveled to the Fürer's Wolf's Lair to receive the addition of the Diamonds to his medal, this

---

10. The face of a clock is used to describe angles relative to a plane, with twelve o'clock being directly in front of the pilot and six o'clock directly behind him.

making it Germany's highest award.[11] This took place a little over a month after the July 20, 1944, attempt on Hitler's life, and security was tight. When Hartmann was asked to remove his pistol before being ushered into Hitler's presence, he responded, "Please tell the Führer that I do not want to receive the Diamonds if he has no *vertrauen* [faith in the personal integrity] of his officers." Fearing Hitler's rage if Hartmann did not appear, the security officer let him retain his sidearm.

While on leave Hartmann married his childhood sweetheart, Ursula Pätsch, whose nickname, "Uschi," he had painted on his Me 109 under a broken heart. He affectionately called her his "302nd victory."

On May 8, 1945, the last day of the war, Hartmann spotted a Yak-9P performing aerobatics over Red Army troops as they marched triumphantly into the German town of Brünn. As the exuberant Soviet pilot hung inverted at the top of his loop, Hartmann gave him a burst in the belly and chalked up his final kill, number 352.

When he landed, Major Hartmann was ordered to fly to Dortmund and surrender to the British for his own protection, but he would not desert his men. His decision cost him 10 years of captivity in the Soviet Union. This was his most brutal and lonely battle, one in which his only weapons were his iron will and fighting spirit, sustained by his love for Uschi, who kept faith with him and worked tirelessly for his release.

The Soviets were pleased to have Germany's most successful fighter pilot in their hands, but when they called him such he demurred.

"But no other pilot in any air force shot down such a large number of aircraft," they insisted.

"Well, I shot down only Russians, along with a few Americans. On the Western front, we had a pilot named Marseille who shot down over 150 British aircraft. In our air

---

11. With the exception of the award designed expressly for Hans-Ulrich Rudel.

force, one British-flown aircraft was considered the equal of three Russian-flown machines. So I am not the leading pilot," explained Hartmann, provoking his captors' fury.

Most experts share Hartmann's assessment of the relative merits of Soviet and British pilots, and of his own skill compared with that of Marseille. Hartmann was awesome, but Marseille was uncanny.

Although he came from a prominent military family, Marseille was a bohemian type with a distinctly unmilitary attitude. The slightly built Berliner listened to jazz, liked swing dancing, and had a penchant for practical jokes. He joined the Luftwaffe in November 1938 and soon began piling up infractions—while still in training, he was disciplined for landing his fighter on a deserted section of an autobahn so he could take a leak—but at the same time, he was an artist in the air, capable of dazzling fellow pilots with his aerobatic stunts.

Flying with JG 52 in September 1940 during the Battle of Britain, he shot down a British plane on his very first day in combat. Before the end of the year he had shot down seven planes and earned the Iron Cross 1st Class. But he had to bail out of six planes of his own and was so reckless in the attack that he usually returned to his base with his Me 109 thoroughly shot up. His squadron leader, Johannes Steinhoff, who had him transferred out of the unit, later said,

> Marseille was remarkably handsome. He was a gifted pilot and fighter, but he was unreliable. He had girlfriends everywhere, who took up so much of his time that he was often too tired to be allowed to fly. His often irresponsible understanding of duty was the primary reason I sent him packing. But he had an irresistible charm.

In early 1941, Marseille was reassigned to JG 27 and in April was sent with it to North Africa. He drew some pay en

·KIRCHNER·

route, and as the field pay clerk was about to stamp his paybook on the page reserved for decorations, Marseille hastily stopped him. The clerk asked whether he really expected to get more than the Iron Cross 1st Class already recorded there.

"Of course," replied Marseille.

Leaving an exaggerated amount of space, the cashier mockingly told him, "Now you've got room for the Oak Leaves, Swords, and all!"

On April 23, Marseille scored JG 27's first victory in North Africa, bringing down an RAF Hurricane over Tobruk. On another sortie later that day he was forced to crash-land, his plane hitting the ground 30 times; in fact, he would have been killed by a burst that passed through the canopy had he not happened to lean forward. His group commander, Eduard Neumann, called him on the carpet. "You are only alive because you have more luck than sense," said Neumann. "But don't imagine that it will continue indefinitely. One can overstrain one's luck like one can an airplane."

Like Hartmann, Marseille was fortunate in having a commanding officer who allowed him time to develop.

Marseille had a vision of air combat beyond the usual surprise bounce and no deflection shot from astern. As he told fellow pilot Hans-Arnold Stahlschmidt:

> You've got to be able to shoot from any position. From left or right turns, out of a roll, on your back, whenever. Only this way can you develop your own particular tactics. Attack tactics that the enemy simply cannot anticipate—a series of unpredictable movements and actions. Never the same, always stemming from the situation at hand. Only then can you plunge into the middle of an enemy swarm and blow it up from the inside.

Such an approach seemed preposterous, since in a dogfight the differing speed and flight courses of the two planes made it extremely difficult to calculate the lead, or "deflection," necessary to get a hit. Nevertheless, Marseille was determined to master it and developed his own training program. When his group was returning from operations, he would break away and make dummy attacks on his comrades. Although standard procedure was to attack at the highest possible speed, he learned that he had to throttle back and even lower his flaps to decrease his radius of turn and often had to fire after his opponent had disappeared beneath his plane's nose. An innate feel for time and space, honed with practice, enabled him to perfect the art of deflection shooting to a degree that has never been equaled.

On September 24, 1941, he shot down five planes in one day. That evening he announced, "I believe I've now got it." By June 1942 he had racked up 75 victories.

When a group of fighters was attacked, a standard defensive tactic was to form a Lufberry circle, in which the fighters flew in a circular formation so that each plane could guard the rear of the plane ahead. This assumed, of course, that an attacker would have to get on his quarry's six o'clock position and thus was of little use against Marseille, to whom planes in a Lufberry circle were like revolving ducks in a shooting gallery. Attacking from whatever angle he chose, he would routinely score multiple victories in a single pass, often shooting down a second victim before the first had hit the ground. His wingman, Reiner Pöttgen, had his work cut out for him, not only guarding his leader's tail but noting his victories, their times, and positions. For his efforts Pöttgen was dubbed the Flying Adding Machine. Marseille earned the appellation of Star of Africa. His Me 109F, marked with a large yellow 14, became as famous a symbol of the Afrikakorps as Rommel's half-tracked vehicle.

On June 3, 1942, swooping in and out of a Lufberry circle, Marseille shot down six Allied P-40s in 11 minutes, three of them with his machine guns only after his cannon had stopped working. From a starting load of about 150 20mm rounds and 1,000 7.92mm rounds, his total ammunition expenditure was 10 20mm rounds and 360 7.92mm rounds. His plane was not struck by a single bullet. Several times during the course of his gyrations, he found himself looking directly into enemy gun barrels, but he knew that from that position he had nothing to fear. "Only if he pulls lead am I in danger," he observed.

In his battle report for this action, Pöttgen wrote,

Each time he fired I saw his shells strike first
the enemy plane's nose, then travel along to the
cockpit. No ammunition was wasted. . . . How
he was able to do this, hitting his mark so precisely in a hundredth of a second, he himself
couldn't even explain, and, as a result, can't
relay this secret to his comrades at arms.

Fighter pilots are predators by nature, eager for the fight,
but one wonders what went through the minds of those who
faced Marseille when they realized that against him their
attacks seemed to pose no threat, their defenses no protection.

When Marseille's score reached 91 on June 15, 1942, his
comrades organized a pool on when he would reach 100, earning him the Swords for the Knights Cross, which he had so confidently reserved a space for in his paybook. One of the men
asked him for a prediction.

"The day after tomorrow, at noon," replied Marseille.

The following day he shot down four planes, bringing his
score to 95. On the day after that, as he returned from a mission
at 12:35 P.M., the atmosphere in JG 27 was electric. Sweeping low
over the base, Marseille waggled his wings three times—98.
Then, in a second pass, he waggled them three times more—101.

After Marseille landed, his plane was mobbed by his exul-
tant squadron mates. But through the canopy they saw him sitting motionless in the cramped cockpit, staring at his instru-
ments, his face haggard and expressionless. He had been living
for combat, and the strain was taking a toll. Slowly he took off
his helmet and looked at the crowd of men cheering him. Then
he broke into a grin, his devil-may-care manner reasserting itself.

Marseille was given two months leave while he returned to
Germany to receive the Swords to his Knight's Cross.
Everywhere he went he was greeted by crowds. He met with top
Nazi officials as well as the designer of his plane, Willy
Messerschmitt, with whom he conferred at length. Afterward,

climbing into a brand-new Me 109G-10 he put on an aerobatic display for the workers and engineers at the factory. He also became engaged and traveled with his fiancée to Rome, where Mussolini presented him with Italy's highest medal for bravery. (Marseille didn't appreciate being kissed on both cheeks by Il Duce, who he said had shaved poorly.)

He returned to JG 27 on August 23, 1942. His friends had transformed his tent into a sort of bistro, with packing-crate furniture, sandbag couches, a record player, and a fully stocked bar tended by Matthias, a South African from the Transvaal who became Marseille's good friend. It was a status symbol to have partied with Marseille, and many top-ranking Axis officers made the pilgrimage. He received piles of fan mail from adoring women, who begged for everything from a lock of his hair to the opportunity to bear his children.

September 1, 1942, was the third anniversary of the outbreak of the war. Field Marshal Kesselring was visiting the base when Marseille reported to the operations HQ tent at noon, after flying two sorties, and reported that 12 enemy aircraft had been shot down so far that day.

"And how many of those did you shoot down yourself?" asked his commander.

"Twelve, sir," answered Marseille.

Kesselring shook hands with the young pilot and immediately sat down, without saying a word.

That morning Marseille was in the air at 7:30. By 8:40 A.M. he had shot down two P-40s and two Spitfires. On his second mission, he shot down eight P-40s in the space of 10 minutes. (To fully comprehend this, it is helpful to ponder the times of the kills: 10:55, 10:56, 10:58, 10:59, 11:01, 11:02, 11:03, and 11:05.) Although that may have been enough to render Kesselring speechless, Marseille had not finished for the day. After their meeting he took a nap, then went up again and shot down five more P-40s. Seventeen planes in a single day. In spite of the fact that German statistics were rigorously verified, investigators from the Western Allies were reluctant to accept this figure until a postwar analysis of aircraft losses against German claims supported it. Marseille's one-day tally was surpassed only once, and that was on the Eastern Front when Emil Lang shot down 18 hostiles.

Marseille had earned the Diamonds to his Knight's Cross, but he would not live to collect them.

On September 28, 1942, he engaged five Spitfires high over the desert. He shot down two, but as two others dived on him he noticed that his fuel was low and headed back over German lines. One tenacious RAF flyer hung on, peppering the Messerschmitt as Marseille tried to shake him with every trick he had. He had never been so harried. After nearly 15 minutes he shut his eyes and flew directly at the sun. As the enemy pilot was blinded by the glare, Marseille turned in a tight chandelle[12] and delivered a well-placed burst. It was his 158th kill, his 57th in September alone—and he alone had accounted for 12 percent of all planes shot down by the Luftwaffe in North Africa.

As he approached his landing field he didn't waggle his wings to signal the victory, and after landing he slowly climbed from his plane, ashen faced. His crew was shocked—he looked like an old man as he reached with a trembling hand for a cigarette. Describing the enemy pilot, Marseille said he was "a masterful adversary. Never before had an enemy fought like he did. I don't know how things will turn out next time."

Marseille had long had premonitions of death. He once told a comrade about a dream: "I'm flying, then suddenly it gets dark all around me. I know I'm falling, but I don't feel anything. And before I hit the ground, it's already all over for me."

On the last day of September 1942, while returning from an uneventful patrol, the engine of his new Me 109G caught fire, and his cockpit filled with smoke. His squadron mates closed around him and attempted to guide him back to the base, but

---

12. A chandelle is an abrupt climbing turn.

after they had flown back over the German lines, he radioed, "I must get out now. I can't stand it any more," inverted his plane, and bailed out. His mates watched in horror as he struck his chest on the tail fin and plummeted limply for 10,000 feet, never opening his parachute.

On the spot where he was found, face down in the desert, a rough stone pyramid was erected, inscribed "Here Lies Undefeated Hptm. Hans Marseille."

He was 22 years old.

18 Wild Bill Hickok

*That I have killed men I
admit, but never unless in
absolute self defense, or in
the performance of an official duty. I never, in all my
life, took mean advantage of
an enemy. Yet understand, I
never allowed a man to get
the drop on me.*

—James "Wild Bill"
Butler Hickok

He earned his nickname in 1861 when he single-handedly faced down a lynch mob in Independence, Missouri, prompting a woman to shout, "Good for you, Wild Bill!" He served as a scout and a spy in the Union army, where he used his sharpshooting skills against the rebels. Afterward, he scouted for Col. George Custer and became a legend in his own time when Col. George Ward Nichols wrote a laudatory profile of him in *Harper's* magazine in 1867. Hickok went on to serve as a deputy U.S. marshal, sheriff of Ellis County, Kansas, and as the town-taming marshal of Abilene in the same state. When a newspaper reporter once asked how many men he had slain, Hickok answered, "I would be willing to take my oath on the Bible tomorrow that I have killed over a hundred." In fact, Hickok depopulated the West by only seven or eight, which is still the top score of any Old West gunfighter who fought on the side of the law.

Hickok favored Colt's .36-caliber Navy or .44-caliber Army revolvers, carrying a brace of them, butts forward, in a red sash around his waist. The press dubbed him the "Prince of Pistoleers" and attributed to him shooting feats ranging from the feasible to the fantastic. One of the more credible witnesses described him throwing a tomato can into the air, drawing, and putting two shots into it before it hit the ground. He then drew his other revolver and, firing a gun with each hand, kept it rolling until his weapons were empty. Such marksmanship rarely figured in Old West shootouts, which usually occurred at arm's length, but had Hickok not been a remarkable shot he might never have survived his second affray.

In 1865, while living in Springfield, Missouri, Hickok fell afoul of Confederate veteran Dave Tutt—over a woman, among other things. During a high-stakes card game, Tutt took Hickok's prized Waltham watch off the table, claiming it as payment for a prior debt. Hickok stood up and said, "I don't want to make a row in this house. . . . You'd better put that watch back on the table."

Tutt refused and walked out with it.

The situation festered for several days. Tutt's friends told Hickok that their man planned to wear the watch on the town square the next day at noon as an open challenge. Hickok told them that Tutt had better not, unless he believed dead men could walk.

The following day was July 21, 1865. As was his daily ritual, Hickok cleaned, oiled, and carefully loaded his cap-and-ball Colts, poking through the black powder with a pin to be sure it filled the nipple that held the cap, and inspecting the inside of each cap to be sure it contained no debris. He would not chance a misfire.

At noon he walked outside. Tutt appeared at the opposite side of the large plaza, flaunting the Waltham. As a crowd

National Archives

looked on, Tutt began walking toward Hickok. Such a show-down may be a fixture of Western movies, but it rarely occurred in the real West, where a man who fought fair was considered to have a poor grasp of tactics.

At a distance usually reported as 75 yards, sometimes as 50, Hickok shouted, "Don't come any closer, Dave!"

Tutt drew his revolver, fired, and missed. Steadying his revolver on his left arm Hickok fired once, hitting Tutt in the center of the chest. Hickok did not wait to watch Tutt fall, but spun around and covered Tutt's friends as they reached for their weapons. "Aren't you satisfied, gentlemen?" asked Hickok. "Put up your shooting irons, or there'll be more dead men here."

The heart shot, which kills by oxygen starvation of the brain, is rarely instantly fatal. Tutt managed to drag himself to the courthouse before dropping dead beside one of its pillars. Perhaps, as consciousness faded, he reflected upon Hickok's astounding marksmanship. It had ensured Tutt a place in fron-tier history: he had been killed at the longest range on record for a pistol duel.

Could Hickok have repeated such a shot on demand? Probably not. In a feature for *Guns & Ammo*, an expert marks-man tested Colt revolvers of the type of Hickok used. Firing from a rest he was barely able to group six shots within a foot at 75 yards, and seven inches at 50. Hickok's shot required a large element of luck, but had he not been so good, he wouldn't have been as lucky.

Eleven years later, Hickok was shot in the back of the head as he played cards in a Deadwood, Dakota Territory, saloon, having neglected to follow his usual practice of sitting with his back to a wall.

19 Andrew Jackson

*A tall, gaunt man, of very
erect carriage, with a coun-
tenance full of stern decision
and fearless energy, but fur-
rowed with care and anxi-
ety. . . . His complexion was
sallow and unhealthy; his
hair iron gray, his body
thin and emaciated . . . but
the fierce glare of his bright
and hawk-like grey eye
betrayed a soul and spirit
that triumphed over all the
infirmities of the body.*
—J. Kilty Smith

When Andrew Jackson ran for president, one of his political enemies published a list of more than 100 fights in which he claimed the general had been involved. Based on hearsay, the number is wildly inflated, but Jackson would have been the last to dispute it. Throughout his life he was a fighter and proud of it.

As a child, Jackson was teased mercilessly for his tendency to drool. Even though he was slightly built, he would respond with his fists no matter how large his opponent or how often he was beaten. "I could throw him three times out of four," one of his classmates said, "but he would never *stay* throwed. He was dead game and would never give up." As a prank, some of his boyhood friends once handed him a musket loaded to the muz-

157

zle with powder, knowing it would knock him flat when he fired it. He fell over as expected, but the fun ended when he bounded to his feet, eyes blazing, and roared, "By God, if one of you laughs, I'll kill him."

In January 1781, when Jackson was 14, he and his older brother Robert enlisted in the Continental Army. (His oldest brother had already died in the war, of exposure.) Before they had served long, the brothers were betrayed by a Tory neighbor and captured. A British officer ordered Andrew to shine his boots, and when he refused, the officer hacked at him with his saber. Andrew tried to ward off the blow but was severely cut on his hand and forehead, resulting in scars he carried for a lifetime.

In a prisoner-of-war camp, the Jackson brothers contracted smallpox and were barely alive when released to their mother in a prisoner exchange. Robert died two days later, but after a long convalescence, Andrew recovered. His mother continued to nurse other prisoners until she became ill herself. She died in November 1781, but not before giving him advice he would live by: "Never tell a lie, nor take what is not your own, nor sue anybody for slander or assault and battery. *Always settle them cases yourself.*"

Jackson's father had died before he was born, so at 15 he was the sole surviving member of his family. Although his brothers and mother had not been killed by enemy bullets, each was in some way a victim of the war, and he had a thirst for vengeance against the British that would not be slaked for 34 years.

Jackson studied law and was admitted to the North Carolina bar in 1787. The following year, he was appointed prosecuting attorney of the Western District, which later became Tennessee. After an argument in court, Jackson challenged another lawyer, Col. Waightstill Avery, to a duel, but the dispute was settled peaceably. As reported by Gerald Johnson in *Andrew Jackson: An Epic in Homespun*, he also had some informal confrontations, such as one he told a friend about while president:

When I was a young man practicing law in Tennessee, there was a big, bullying fellow that wanted to pick a quarrel with me, and so trod on my toes. Supposing it accidental, I said nothing. Soon after he did it again, and I began to suspect his object. In a few minutes he came by a third time, pushing against me violently, and evidently meaning *fight*. He was a man of immense size, one of the very biggest men I ever saw. As quick as a flash I snatched a small rail from the top of a fence, and gave him the point of it full in his stomach. Sir, it doubled him up. He fell at my feet and I stamped on him. Soon he got up savage, and was about to fly at me like a tiger. The bystanders made as though they would interfere. Says I, "Gentlemen, stand back, give me room, that's all I ask and I'll manage him." With that I stood ready with the rail pointed. He gave me one look, and turned away, a whipped man, sir, and feeling like one. So, sir, I say to you, if any villain assaults you, give him the point in the belly.

Jackson stayed at a rooming house run by the widow Donelson and fell in love with her daughter Rachel, a great beauty and a true frontier woman who had survived a thousand-mile river journey to Nashville in the dead of winter, during which her party was attacked by Indians twice and several members were killed. She'd had a brief marriage to Lewis Robards, which had broken up. The violently jealous Robards occasionally showed up at the rooming house, but he faded under Jackson's glare, especially after Jackson ran his thumb along the edge of his hunting knife and expressed a strong desire to cut Robards' ears off.

In 1791, Jackson married Rachel under the impression that she was legally divorced. In fact, the court had only been authorized to determine whether there were sufficient grounds; the divorce itself was not granted until 1793, and then on the basis that Rachel had been living with Jackson for two years. The situation caused considerable gossip, but Jackson was a fiercely devoted husband, and those who felt there was anything untoward about his marriage were advised to keep it to themselves.

Jackson helped draft the constitution of the new state of Tennessee, served as a congressman and later a senator, and was a general in its militia. According to *The Life of Andrew Jackson*, while Jackson was heatedly debating Governor John Sevier on the steps of the Knoxville courthouse on October 1, 1803, Sevier expounded upon his many contributions to the state, to which Jackson responded, "I've performed some services myself, which I believe have met with approval."

"Services!" barked Sevier. "I know of no great service you have rendered the country, except taking a trip to Natchez with another man's wife!"

His eyes spitting blue light, Jackson roared, "Great God! Do you mention her sacred name?" He swung his cane at Sevier, who wielded a saber. Both men pulled pistols and exchanged shots. Neither bullet found its mark, though a bystander was grazed, and the men were separated before they did each other any serious damage. When Sevier subsequently proved reluctant to accept Jackson's formal challenge, Jackson sent him the following message:

> In the publick streets of Knoxville you appeared to pant for combat. You ransacked the vocabulary of vulgarity. . . . You . . . took the sacred name of a lady in your polluted lips, and dared me publickly to challenge. . . . I have spoken for a place in the paper for the following advertisement:
>
> "To all who shall see these presents Greetings.

"Know ye that I Andrew Jackson, do pro-
nounce, publish, and declare to the world, that
his excellency John Sevier . . . is a base coward
and a poltroon. He will basely insult, but has not
the courage to repair. ANDREW JACKSON."
You may prevent the insertion of the above by
meeting me in two hours after the receipt of this.

Sevier did not respond, and Jackson's notice was published.
The "posting," as such provocations were called, had its desired
effect, but when the two met for combat, Sevier's horse ran away
with his pistols. When Jackson pulled his pistol, Sevier hid
behind a tree, damning him and asking if he would fire on a
"naked" man. The seconds drew their weapons, resulting in a
standoff in which every man was covered by another's gun.
Perhaps realizing that the situation had deteriorated to a point
where no one could hope to extract any glory from it, the parties
disengaged, contenting themselves with a spirited exchange of
vilification that continued as long as they were within earshot.

Jackson fought his most famous duel with Charles
Dickinson, a wealthy young lawyer, gambler, and wastrel who
was a dozen years his junior. It had been brought to Jackson's
attention that Dickinson had made disparaging remarks about
Rachel, and he demanded an explanation. Dickinson apologized, claiming that if he had made such remarks he must have
been drunk, and the matter was shelved, though Jackson smol-
dered. Later, animosity reignited in a dispute over a horse race.
The ritual exchange of fighting words began, followed by a
request for satisfaction. The parties arranged to meet across the
state line in Kentucky on May 30, 1806.

Jackson left home before dawn on May 29, telling Rachel
only that he had to settle some trouble. In Nashville, Jackson
met his second, Dr. John Overton, as well as two other men
who would back him up, and the four rode to Kentucky.

Dickinson was considered the finest pistol shot in

Tennessee, and he and his friends rode to the site of the duel in a festive mood, with Dickinson giving exhibitions of his skill along the way. He set up a target at 24 feet, the range at which the duel was to be fought, and put four shots into it that could be covered by a silver dollar. (The short distance—eight paces— was agreed upon out of deference to Jackson's inferior marksmanship.) While stopped at a tavern, he suspended a piece of string and severed it with a shot at the same distance. "If General Jackson comes along this road, show him that!" he told the tavern owner.

Jackson's group proceeded in a more sober mood. Jackson spoke of the duel only twice, to express his hope that Dickinson would be on time and to comment on Dickinson's superior skill.

Jackson also expressed frustration that he had been too young to be of much account in the last war with England and hoped he would not be too old in the next.

"How old do you think that might be?" asked Overton.

Jackson smiled grimly. "About 100 years, if England's the enemy."

The night before the duel, Jackson's party stayed at an inn. Jackson ate a large supper, then sat on the porch smoking his pipe and conversing with other guests until 10 o'clock. He slept soundly and had to be roused at 5:00 A.M.

At 7:00 A.M., as he arrived at the field of honor, one of his friends asked how he felt about his prospects.

"Oh, all right," answered Jackson. "I'll wing him, never fear."

Twenty-four feet were paced off, and pegs were hammered into the ground where each man was to stand. The seconds drew lots. Dickinson's man won the choice of position. Overton won the right to give the firing command. The weapons were the traditional smoothbore .70-caliber flintlocks with nine-inch barrels. Jackson and Dickinson took their positions and faced Overton, pistols cocked and pointed down. Dickinson seemed relaxed and confident, while Jackson's posture was one of intense concentration.

Overton called out, "Gentlemen, are you ready?"

Both answered in the affirmative.

At the command *Fire!* Dickinson instantly turned, raised his pistol, and shot Jackson. Overton saw a puff of dust fly from the chest of Jackson's loose-fitting frock coat. Jackson pressed his left hand to his chest but remained erect.

Seeing that Jackson still stood, Dickinson exclaimed, "Great God! Have I missed him?" and stepped back from his peg.

"Back to the mark, sir!" roared Overton, pistol in hand. Dickinson, obliged to wait for Jackson's shot, averted his gaze. Jackson carefully aimed and pulled the trigger, but there was no report: the hammer had fallen to half cock. Jackson recocked and fired, and Dickinson slumped to the ground, mortally wounded.

Jackson's party left the field. After they had walked a short distance, Overton noticed that the general's boots were spilling over with blood.

"My God, General, are you hit?" he asked.

"Oh, I believe he has pinked me a little," answered Jackson, and then added, "I don't want those people to know. Let's move on." So great was Jackson's hatred for Dickinson that he wanted the satisfaction of leaving him to die thinking he had thrown his shot. In fact, Dickinson's ball had struck Jackson in the chest, missing his heart only by an inch or so. The wound troubled Jackson for years, but his conscience not for a moment. Since he would probably have been shot through the heart had the loose fit of his coat not thrown off Dickinson's aim, a chivalrous interpretation of the *code duello* would have suggested that he not deliberately kill his man, but he was determined to do so—even, he later said, "if he had shot me through the brain."

Some 70-odd friends and relatives of Dickinson requested that the next edition of Nashville's *Impartial Review* have a black border, to signify mourning. Jackson took offense at this and wrote the editor asking that the names of those who had made the request be published. This caused 26 of them to withdraw. After all, Charles Dickinson, the finest pistol shot in

Tennessee, was dead and Andrew Jackson, the man who had killed him, was very much alive.

In 1812, war brewed with Britain. Jackson received orders to march his 2,000 men 800 miles to Natchez, Mississippi, where, it turned out that the federal government had no idea what to do with them. They were ordered to return home. Despite the futile effort, it was during this campaign that Jackson acquired the nickname Old Hickory for his toughness, as he walked tirelessly beside his troops, having given up his horses for the ill to ride.

According to the 1910 *Encyclopedia Britannica*, "Up to the time of his nomination for the presidency, the biographer of Jackson finds nothing to record but military exploits in which he displayed perseverance, energy and skill of a very high order, and a succession of personal acts in which he showed himself ignorant, violent, perverse, quarrelsome and astonishingly indiscreet." The latter traits were amply displayed in his feud with Thomas Hart Benton. The two had been close (and would again reconcile within a few years), but friction arose when Jackson served as a second to a rival of Thomas' brother Jesse. It escalated through an exchange of testy letters and erupted on September 4, 1813, when Jackson, accompanied by two friends, Stockley Hays and John Coffee, ran into Benton in front of the Nashville Inn. Armed with a horsewhip as well as pistols, Jackson started toward him, shouting, "Now defend yourself, you damned rascal!" Benton reached for his pistol but Jackson drew his first. He pressed it against Benton's chest and marched him into the hotel. Stepping out of a doorway from behind Jackson, Jesse Benton shot him. Jackson fired his pistol at Thomas as he pitched forward. He missed, but his muzzle flash set fire to the sleeve of Thomas's coat. Thomas fired twice at Jackson as he fell, and Jesse drew another pistol to shoot him again, but a bystander stepped in and shielded the general's prostrate body.

A farcical donnybrook ensued. John Coffey came into the hallway shooting, missed, then reversed his grip on his pistols to use them as clubs, forcing Thomas Benton back until he fell down a flight of stairs. Hays lunged at Jesse Benton with his sword cane, but its blade snapped on a button of Jesse's coat. Jesse pressed his pistol against Hays and pulled the trigger, but it failed to fire.

Jackson was the only one seriously injured, shot in the left shoulder and arm. He was put in bed, and every doctor in Nashville labored to stanch the flow of his blood, which soaked two mattresses. Some argued for amputation but Jackson demurred, telling them, "I'll keep my arm."

Once again, Rachel had to nurse her husband back from the threshold of death. He remained in bed at his estate, The Hermitage, for a month, until news reached him that the Creeks, allied with the British, had massacred 250 settlers in Georgia and Alabama. Nothing could revitalize Jackson like the prospect of a good fight. "The health of your general is restored," he announced to his troops. "He will command in person."

It was a difficult campaign, and provisions did not come through for the volunteer troops, who were reduced to eating tripe and, occasionally, acorns. Only regular displays of Jackson's pyrotechnic temper kept the troops from deserting; on one occasion, he faced down an entire brigade that planned to march home. After scorching them with a tirade, he snatched a musket from a soldier and announced that he would kill the first man who moved. "Damned if I don't believe the old fellow will shoot!" said one of the astonished troops. The gun was later discovered to be unloaded, but it had served its purpose.

Rachel, running The Hermitage in her husband's absence, wrote him heart-wrenching letters such as this one, published in *The Life of Andrew Jackson*: "Where'er I go, where'er I turn, my thoughts, my fears, my doubts distress me. Then a little hope revives again and that keeps me alive. . . . Do not my beloved husband let love of country, fame, and honor, make you forget [me]. . . . You will say this is not the language of a patriot, but it is the language of a faithful wife. . . ." He answered her with heartfelt letters of his own but continued to fulfill his duty as he saw it.

Jackson went to New Orleans in December 1814 to organize the city's defenses against an anticipated British invasion. His chief of engineers wrote that although Jackson seemed ready to sink under the weight of sickness and fatigue, his mind never lost the energy that caused insurmountable obstacles to melt before him. This energy spread to his whole army, which felt there was nothing it was incapable of doing if he ordered it done. It didn't matter to Jackson that his ragtag force was outnumbered nearly two to one by some 8,000 battle-hardened British regulars. "I will smash them, so help me God!" he declared, and on January 8, 1815, he did, dealing the British their most humiliating defeat since Yorktown and Toulon. The Battle of New Orleans was fought two weeks after the Treaty of Ghent had been signed, which ended the war between the United States and Britain, but that didn't diminish its glory. It was America's first great victory as an independent power, and with it Jackson saved more than a city, he saved the nation's self-respect.

As Jackson was being feted in New Orleans, Rachel traveled from Nashville to join him. Blissfully unaware of the latest fashions, her skin roughened and tanned from outdoor work, she did not blend into sophisticated society. In his memoirs, Vincent Nolte, a member of the city's social elite, uncharitably described her dancing with her husband: "To see these two figures, the general a long, haggard man, with limbs like a skeleton, and Madame le Generale, a short, fat dumpling, bobbing opposite each other . . . to the wild melody of Possum Up de Gum Tree . . . was very remarkable." (Presumably, he took care that his words did not come to the general's attention.)

Along with Jackson's national prominence came political opportunities. In 1824 he was persuaded to run for

New York Public Library Picture Collection

president. He received a plurality, but the election was decided in the House of Representatives, which chose John Quincy Adams. Feeling cheated, Jackson ran again in 1828. The Eastern, pro-Adams press raked him over the coals; he was called illiterate, drunken, lewd, avaricious, a gambler, a wastrel, a liar, a homicidal maniac, a bribe taker, a shyster, a swindler, an imbecile, an atheist, and a slave trader, but he and his wife only really suffered when the circumstances of their marriage were again dragged through the mud. The distraught Rachel suffered heart trouble. Jackson won the election in a landslide, but he drew little joy from it, for Rachel died six weeks later. On her gravestone he had inscribed: "A being so gentle and yet so virtuous, vile slander might wound but could not dishonor."

Even as president Jackson could not avoid violent encounters. In 1833 he was seated behind a table aboard a steamer when Lt. Robert B. Randolph, who had been dismissed from the navy by Jackson's direct order, approached him as if to shake his hand, but instead thrust up his hand to pull Jackson's nose, the most contemptuous of assaults. "What, sir! What, sir!" shouted the 66-year-old president as he kicked the table away and leapt to his feet. He chased Randolph, with upraised cane, but the younger man escaped. One of Jackson's friends offered to pursue Randolph and kill him, but Jackson declined, saying, "I want no man to stand between me and my assailants, and none to take revenge on my account." Jackson later claimed that had he been in a better position to respond to the attack, Randolph "never would have moved with life from the tracks he stood in."

Jackson was the first president to suffer an assassination attempt, when on January 30, 1835, a deranged Englishman, Richard Lawrence, pulled a pistol on him. Its percussion cap failed to set off the charge, and he drew another. In one of those coincidences that suggests the hand of God, it misfired in the same manner. Jackson went after Lawrence with his walking stick and had to be physically restrained.

Jackson died on June 8, 1845, and was buried on the grounds of The Hermitage beside his wife.

20 Jean-Louis

The purpose of fencing is to develop a man with enough self-control so as to make him able to direct his attack with accuracy and avoid as much as possible the deadly end.

—Jean-Louis

In an age when there were no greater swordsmen on earth than the French, the greatest swordsman in France was an immigrant from Haiti.

After the 1795 insurrection on Haiti, many islanders loyal to the colonial power took advantage of an offer to resettle in France, among them a puny 11-year-old orphan of mixed race who wished to become a soldier. Despite qualms about "his brown complexion and fragile physical appearance," he was put in the 32d Regiment. His surname was dropped in his paperwork, and from then on he was known only as Jean-Louis. The 32d's colonel sent him to the regimental fencing school in order to build him up, although he had doubts that the boy would ever be fit for service.

Ignoring constant taunts about his race and size, Jean-Louis assiduously applied himself to the science of the sword, spending every available hour at the *salle d'armes* (fencing hall). Normally a novice received scant attention, but the *maître d'armes*, a Belgian nobleman named d'Erapé, was so struck by Jean-Louis' determination that he began giving him private lessons. He soon discovered that he had a prodigy on his hands. Within a few years Jean Louis, now tall and sinewy, was selected to participate in the annual fencing demonstration before the entire regiment. Still in his mid-teens, he took his examination for *maître d'armes* before a jury of the finest fencers in France and passed with honors, the youngest candidate ever to do so.

The novelist Théophile Gautier observed that

> the Frenchman is an intellectual swordsman; the basis of his art is a thorough knowledge of its mathematics. Upon this foundation he superimposes a structure of audacity. But he often falls into one error or another, for all his mental brilliancy. He may become rigidly formal in his practice, or, in a revolt from his own formalism, be seduced into a display of showy, sensational tricks that are all very well in the studio but dangerous to their practitioner on the actual dueling ground.

Jean-Louis was guilty of no such excesses. He relied on basic parries rapidly and flawlessly executed. As one contemporary observed, Jean-Louis

> omitted everything that was superfluous; the affected salutations, the counter-coups, the capricious pauses, all shocked him and appeared to him unworthy of such a serious art. One admires both his simple, natural, and well-

becoming defense, and the development and rapidity of his attack, his sure judgment, his impassibility in the defensive, as also the regularity, even in the most unforeseen circumstances, of all his movements, which followed each other like the rings of a chain.

By the time Jean-Louis was 18, the French Republic had become an empire. Napoleon opposed the practice of dueling among his officers, but it was too deeply ingrained to be suppressed. Jean-Louis had a number of personal encounters, but his skill was such that he could afford to be merciful, disarming his opponents or inflicting only minor wounds.

After participating in a fencing display at the regimental fencing hall, Jean-Louis overheard an observer remark, "This is all very fine, but the fencing floor and the *terrain* are two different things, and as clever as this fellow may be with the foil, he might cut a different figure if the buttons [the protective buttons on the point of the foil] were off."

Glancing around, Jean-Louis recognized the speaker, a boastful but poor-quality swordsman, and shrugged off the insult.

After the next *assaut d'armes*, at which Jean-Louis beat several strong contenders, he overheard another conversation.

"You are very difficult to please," said one. "Jean-Louis has not been touched at all."

"Nonsense!" replied the other. "These fine foil-players would play a very different game if their points were sharp."

Noticing that it was the same man who had criticized him previously, Jean-Louis clapped him on the shoulder and asked, "Do you intend your words to apply to me?"

Assured that he did, Jean-Louis said, "Am I to understand, then, that you are attempting to force a duel upon me?"

To which the other replied, "The sword is not intended for the hand of a nigger; keep to your foil play."

Jean-Louis responded that he was not particularly anxious

to cross weapons with his critic, but since the latter was so keen to fight it would take place on one condition. Jean-Louis continued, "I cannot, for conscience sake, fight on equal terms with a tenth-rate performer like you. This is how it shall be: I will use a buttoned foil, and you shall have your sharp sword."

Though enraged by this insult, the man accepted. Jean-Louis' friends called him crazy for proposing such unequal terms. He responded, "Tomorrow you may judge if I am crazy, after I administer Monsieur the punishment to which he is entitled."

The following day Jean-Louis, armed with his practice foil, faced off against the military man with his sword. In the first rapid exchanges, Jean-Louis did nothing but parry the furious blows the other tried to land on him, breaking ground slightly to allow his enemy to expend his energy. After a particularly strong parry, Jean-Louis suddenly swung his foil back and slashed his foe across the face with its edge,

·KIRCHNER·

174

knocking him to the ground. Bleeding profusely, his beauty completely spoiled, the man left, a whipped dog.

Jean-Louis took part in 30 battles of the Napoleonic wars, fighting in Egypt, Italy, Prussia, and Russia. In 1814 his 32d Regiment went to Spain as part of the French army's 3d Division. Several regiments of other nationalities were part of this division, and conflict frequently broke out between those soldiers and the French troops. While stationed in Madrid, some troops of the 32d got into a drunken brawl with troops of the 1st Regiment, composed of Italians. Both sides were reinforced by their comrades, and the ensuing melee had to be broken up by two companies with fixed bayonets. Those who had incited the trouble were arrested, but men had been wounded on both sides and rancor ran high. A council was convened to determine how *fraternité* would be restored, and it unanimously decided that 15 fencing masters and their provosts (assistants) from each regiment would represent their units and fight duels.

The regiments were assembled in a hollow square on a plain outside Madrid. At its center was a natural elevation forming a platform where, two at a time, 30 champions would duel for the honor of 10,000 men. As the premier fencing master of the 32d Regiment, Jean-Louis was the first up. His opponent was Giacomo Ferrari, a celebrated Florentine swordsman and fencing master of the First Regiment.

Drums rolled. The troops were ordered to parade rest, and as they slammed down the butts of their muskets in unison, the earth shook. Jean-Louis and Giacomo Ferrari stepped onto the fencing strip, each stripped to the waist to show that they wore nothing that would turn a thrust. An expectant silence filled the air as every eye was fixed on the two masters. The traditional rivalry between Europe's two theories of fencing, the French and the Italian, added a piquance to the duel. The French school was formalistic—movements were made according to rules, as quietly as possible, and following in logical sequence; even when fighting a duel, Frenchmen seemed to work together like a piece of fine machinery. The Italian style was looser, freer, less formal, and more individualistic—a bout between Italians resembled a furious struggle involving shouts, stamping of the feet, whirling about, and leaps forward and back. The French said that the Italian technique was more *bruyant* (rowdy) than *brilliant*, and decried it as inartistic and crude. The French were considered the world's best fencers, but the Italians the deadliest duelists. The Frenchman was never free from the thought of the picture he presented, while the Italian was fixed on one thing—to kill. He would take a severe wound to deliver a fatal one.

The fencing masters crossed swords and the bout began. Ferrari took the offensive, but Jean-Louis followed all his flourishes with a calm but intense attention; every time Ferrari tried to strike, his sword met steel. With a loud cry Ferrari jumped to the side and attempted an attack from below, but Jean-Louis parried the thrust and with a lightning riposte wounded Ferrari in the shoulder. "It is nothing, start the fight again!" cried Ferrari, getting back to his feet.

Jean-Louis' next thrust struck home, and Ferrari fell dead. Jean-Louis wiped the blood from his blade, resumed his first position, and waited. His battle had only begun. The victor in each bout was to continue until he was injured or killed, and Jean-Louis still faced 14 swordsmen of the 1st Regiment, all of them eager to avenge their comrade.

Another adversary came at him. After a brief clash, Jean-Louis lunged and, while recovering, left his point in line. Rushing at him, his opponent was impaled. A second corpse lay at the French master's feet.

His third opponent, a taller man, attacked fiercely, with jumps and feints, but Jean-Louis' point disappeared into his chest, and he fell unconscious.

The next man approached.

The regiments watched in fascinated silence. They were accustomed to the wholesale music of slaughter: the booming of artillery, the bursting of shells, the rattle of musketry, the clash of sabers. All are impressive, but none so keenly painful as the thin *whisk* of steel against steel as men engage in single combat. As one contemporary observer wrote, "it goes clean through the mind and makes the blood of the brain run cold."

After 40 minutes only two Italian provosts were left awaiting their turn, pale but resolved. A truce was called, and the colonel of the 32d approached Jean-Louis.

"*Maître*," he said, "you have valiantly defended the regiment's honor, and in the name of your comrades, and my name, I thank you sincerely. However, 13 consecutive duels have taken too much of your body stamina. Retire now, and if the provosts decide to finish the combat with their opponents, they will be free to do so."

"No, no!" exploded Jean-Louis, "I shall not leave the post which has been assigned me by the confidence of the 32d Regiment. Here I shall remain, and here I shall fight as long as I can hold my weapon." As he finished his statement he made a flourish with his sword, which cut one of his friends on the leg. "Ah," cried Jean-Louis, distraught, "there has only been one man of the 32d wounded today, and it had to be by me."

Seizing upon the incident, the colonel said, "This is a warning; there has been enough blood. All have fought bravely and reparation has been made. Do you trust my judgment in the matter of honor?" After Jean-Louis said he did, the colonel said there was nothing more to do but extend a hand to the 1st Regiment. Pointing to the two provosts who still waited, he said to Jean-Louis, "They cannot come to *you!*"

Jean-Louis dropped his sword, approached the two Italians, and clasped them by the hands. His regiment cheered, "*Vive* Jean-Louis! *Vive* the 32d Regiment!"

Jean-Louis added, "*Vive* the First! We are but one family! *Vive l'armée!*"

Reconciliation was complete.

Jean-Louis had dealt 27 strokes, several of them fatal. In the chronicles of swordplay there are men who claimed to have had a dozen or more deadly encounters in their lifetimes, but to have defeated so many recognized masters one after the other is an unparalleled feat.

Jean-Louis was awarded the highest order of the Legion of Honor, and later, the Médaille de St. Hélène, which the imprisoned Napoleon bestowed only upon his most faithful troops. Jean-Louis' prestige had reached stellar heights, and he was frequently brought in as an arbiter in matters of honor. He always stressed reconciliation. "The blood of a soldier must not be wasted stupidly," he said.

He eventually married and fathered a daughter. He trained her to be the most celebrated swordswoman of her time, and she married into the nobility. Even after his retirement from the army at age 65, Jean-Louis' instruction in the art of fencing remained in great demand. He had that rare quality the French call *sentiment de fer*, a "sense of the iron," an almost supernatural affinity for swordplay. Through years of experience, after learning has become instinct, a fencer may develop such sensitivity in his grip that he can gauge the intentions of an adversary through the feel of his *pressions* (beats) and *froissements* (running of one blade over another with pressure), and thus anticipate his every move. In later years cataracts robbed Jean-Louis of his sight, but he continued to give lessons, his *sentiment de fer* enabling him to fence with students and identify their errors by touch alone.

He died at 80 in 1865. The fencing academy he established in Montpellier in 1830 still exists, and his techniques form the basis of French instruction to this day.

21 "Turkey Creek"
Jack Johnson

> *Whenever you get into a row*
> *be sure and not shoot too*
> *quick. Take time. I've known*
> *many a fellow slip up for*
> *shooting in a hurry.*
> —Wild Bill Hickok

G unfights in the Old West were not generally won by the man who got off the first shot but by the man who saw to it that his bullet struck home. Deliberation was essential. As Bat Masterson put it, "A man who essays to arbitrate a difference with a pistol . . . may possess both courage and experience and still fail if he lacks deliberation. . . . I have known men in the West whose courage could not be questioned and whose experience with the pistol was simply marvelous, who fell easy victims before men who added deliberation to the other two qualities."

Jack Johnson got into an argument with his two mining partners in the Montana Saloon in Deadwood, Dakota Territory, in the winter of 1876, and challenged them to settle the matter with six-shooters. Proper form was for them to fight him one at a time, but it was Johnson's choice that they face him together in the road alongside the fence surrounding the cemetery. A crowd of 20 or 30 gathered to watch, among them Wyatt Earp. Johnson said that he had chosen that particular spot because at least one man, and probably two, would soon need burying and he aimed to make things as convenient as possible for the undertaker.

The fence was about 50 yards long. Johnson positioned himself at one end of it, a Colt in his hand and another one holstered. His disgruntled partners stood at the other end, each with a Colt in each hand. At a signal they advanced toward each other. The partners started to shoot immediately, and by the time they had closed the distance to 40 yards, both had emptied one revolver and switched to the other. Johnson had two or three flesh wounds where bullets had grazed him but had not yet fired a single round. At 30 yards, as his ex-partners continued to spray lead, Johnson fired his first shot, hitting one of them in the midsection. The wounded man dropped to the ground and died in minutes. The remaining one kept walking and shooting. Suddenly Johnson stopped. For a moment observers thought he had been hit, but it was only so that he could fire more carefully. He put a slug through the heart of his remaining opponent, who fell face down.

Earp recalled that when the second miner's body was turned over his revolver was still cocked, his finger still on the trigger. This miner had fired nine times with the two revolvers and had one round left.[13] The first miner had fired seven times from his two pistols. Johnson had fired twice.

Deliberation: Johnson had it.

The crowd drifted back to the Montana Saloon. "Disillusioning as the truth may be," said Earp, "I can't recall

---

13. A Colt revolver could be loaded with six cartridges but was normally carried with the hammer resting on an empty chamber. Lacking a hammer safety, it could fire if dropped.

that Turkey Creek bought drinks for the camp." He did, however, graciously pay for his late partners' burial—even though the ground was frozen so hard their graves had to be blasted out with dynamite.

Johnson later relocated to Tombstone, Arizona Territory, where he allied himself with the Earp faction (of the storied shootout at the O.K. Corral), served as deputy marshal, and in March 1882 took part in the revenge killings following the murder of Wyatt Earp's brother, Morgan. He then drifted off to Utah, and Texas, and out of history's view. There is a character based on him in the 1993 movie *Tombstone*.

22 Charles E. "Commando" Kelly

The best soldiers are in the guardhouse. They are the best fighters.

—Charles E. Kelly

Almost as soon as The United States entered World War II, the search was on for the next Sergeant York (the U.S. Army hero of World War I), a soldier who could stand out as the most extraordinary combat infantryman of the war. We now know who came to hold that title—Audie Murphy—but for a time it appeared that it would be Cpl. Charles E. Kelly of Company L, 143d Infantry, 36th Division, the Fifth Army. Early in 1944, when Murphy wasn't yet known of, Kelly came home to a hero's welcome, with the Congressional Medal of Honor and 10 other decorations for valor. His hometown of Pittsburgh declared a "Charles Kelly Day," honored him with the biggest parade in its history, and gave him the key to the city. The *Saturday Evening Post* paid him

$15,000 for his life story, which it published in five parts, and a Hollywood producer gave him $25,000 for the movie rights. He used the money to buy a house for his family.

Kelly hadn't always been regarded as a model citizen. He and his eight brothers had grown up in a dilapidated shack without electricity or indoor plumbing. He dropped out of school after the sixth grade, then hung out with his gang, chewing tobacco and playing stickball on Middle Street. What he liked best about stickball was the crashing sound a storefront window made when a ball was hit through it. And until his father confiscated his BB gun, he also enjoyed shooting out streetlamps. Gangly, with jug ears and a long nose, Kelly could have doubled for Huntz Hall of the Bowery Boys.

His blacksmith father passed along a simple philosophy to his sons: "If you get into a fight, and he's bigger than you, and you can't beat him with your fists, beat him with a club." If young Kelly went home and admitted to his father that he'd been beaten up, he would get a "whaling" and be sent back to fight the winner again. Once, he recalled, he had to go back three times to beat his man. Even at home, disputes between the brothers were settled with boxing gloves. As a teenager, Kelly was arrested several times for brawling but was never convicted.

Kelly enlisted after Pearl Harbor—World War II was one rumble he didn't want to miss. "I'll go fight while you 4-Fs guard the vegetable wagons," he told the cops on the beat. (Evidently, he even *talked* like Huntz Hall.)

In basic training Kelly found he couldn't fire his '03 Springfield in the normal fashion. After putting it to his right shoulder, he had to crane his neck over and sight with his left eye. Doing so, he could punch three holes in the target at 100 yards you could cover with a dime. His instructor forced him to aim with his right eye, though, and then it would have taken a dollar bill to cover his group. Finally allowed to shoot as he pleased, Kelly qualified as a marksman.

Kelly volunteered for the paratroops, but his enthusiasm

National Archives

185

faded when he visited a hospital ward full of men injured in jumps, some of whom would never walk again. He asked for a transfer, and while he waited for it he went AWOL and visited home. When he reported back, he was fined a month's pay and given 28 days restriction.

In training Kelly had shown a lack of comportment and discipline, but on the battlefield he made up for it in pure fight. On September 13, 1943, while on patrol shortly after the landing at Salerno, he earned a Silver Star for killing 40 Germans in less than an hour. But it was on the following day that he put in the berserker performance that would earn him a seat on the dais in Valhalla's mead hall.

Altavilla was a town of some 200 to 300 houses, 20 miles inland from Salerno. The Germans still held most of it, as well as the surrounding hills. Kelly's Company L had taken over the three-story, solidly built mayor's house on the town square and prepared for a siege, stocking it with weapons and ammunition, barricading it with furniture and mattresses, and setting up machine gun nests in its windows and walled courtyard. Kelly was assigned guard duty on the front steps.

The next morning, just as Kelly stepped inside for breakfast, German machine guns opened up from a nearby hill that offered an excellent field of fire. The machine gun crew in the courtyard was cut to pieces, its weapon nicked and covered in blood. Bullets smacked into the house, and plaster dust began wafting from the ceiling. Within minutes, the air was filled with desperate cries of "Medic!"

Kelly picked up a Browning Automatic Rifle (BAR) and positioned himself by a second-floor window. A few feet away a machine gunner set up, sawing off the bars on his window with bursts of his Browning model 1919. He and Kelly decided to take turns, each firing only until the enemy brought fire against him, but no sooner had the machine gunner made his presence known than he was struck and wounded by an enemy bullet.

Through field glasses, Kelly spotted a group of Germans he

hadn't been able to see with his naked eye. Knowing where they were, he took careful aim with his BAR and gave them a burst. When he examined the scene again, three of the men were lying still. "A fourth, who had fallen into a foxhole, was still moving one foot, so I upped with the BAR and let it chatter once more. When I peered through the glasses, that foot slowly straightened out and lay flat on the ground," Kelly later told the *Saturday Evening Post.*

Kelly slurped sludgy cocoa from his canteen cup and ate biscuits while a sergeant next to him borrowed the field glasses and directed fire for a mortar in the courtyard. The NCO spotted a GI on a nearby hill who was unwittingly heading into a hidden pocket of the enemy, but he was unable to direct the mortars with enough precision to hit the Germans. Kelly emptied a magazine into them.

"I seemed to have been appointed official sniper for the room," recalled Kelly. Anytime anyone spotted the enemy, he called Kelly over to shoot them. Luck was with Kelly—whenever the machine guns he was shooting at returned fire he happened to be lying on the floor reloading, and it was the guys who were filling in for him who kept taking the slugs.

Kelly fired his BAR so steadily that it finally seized up. Tossing it on a bed, he went into the next room to get another. When he returned, the bed was on fire, ignited by the gun's red-hot barrel. He worked the next BAR until its barrel turned reddish-purple and warped. Unable to find another, Kelly picked up a Thompson submachine gun and emptied it at the Germans. There was a bazooka in the house, but to get rounds for it he had to climb to the third floor, over American corpses that littered the stairway. Kelly wouldn't have bet much on his own long-term survival. "We seemed a hell of a small island in a sea of Germans," he recalled.

Kelly brought down six bazooka rounds. He'd never been trained on the weapon but got it to fire after experimenting a little. The back blast knocked him off his feet and shook the house so badly that the other men thought they'd taken a direct hit from German artillery. Kelly fired the rest of his rounds nevertheless. Looking around, he found an incendiary grenade and threw it into a nearby building that was occupied by Germans, setting it ablaze. Kelly then uncovered a case of 60mm mortar shells and had the inspiration that he was convinced ultimately won him the Medal of Honor: after removing the primary safety lock, he tapped a shell on a window ledge until its secondary safety lock dropped out, making it a live bomb that would detonate if it landed with 12 pounds of pressure on its nose.

The Germans picked that inopportune moment to mount an assault. Kelly spotted them coming up a small ravine at the rear of the house, and threw one of the three-pound shells into their midst. With seven times the bursting charge of an ordinary Mark 2 grenade, the 60mm shell had a much larger lethal radius. He threw nine or 10 shells, and all but two exploded, turning about 20 of the enemy into steaming stew meat. (The foolhardy stunt was depicted in the street battle at the end of *Saving Private Ryan*.)

Weapons were at hand all over the house, and Kelly picked them up and fired them until they either ran out of ammunition or overheated and seized up; he had no time to see to their proper care and feeding. As he put it, "All we thought of was keeping on sticking hot lead out of the windows like the bristles of a porcupine, so that any Germans who tried to close in around us would give it up as a bad job." He did some work with an M1 carbine, but it had only two 15-round magazines, which he had to reload each time he emptied them. He picked up a Springfield '03, found some loose rounds on the floor, loaded it, and picked off a few Germans who were attempting to make their way toward the house. After a few minutes, a lieutenant watching over Kelly's shoulder said, "Let me borrow your shooting iron for a minute, Kelly." With his second shot the lieutenant picked off a sniper.

Spotting a 37mm antitank gun in the courtyard below, Kelly

ran out, grabbed a shell off a stack, and threw it into its breech. He aimed at a church bell tower that was providing a vantage point for German snipers, then fumbled with the gun's knobs and handles until it went off. The recoiling breech slammed him a glancing blow on the cheek, and the shell hit the court-yard wall only a few feet away. Sheer dumb luck had saved him again—had he happened to have loaded the gun with a high-explosive rather than an armor-piercing round, the explosion might have killed him. As it was, the shell took off the top of the wall and left him with a clear shot. Kelly fired the cannon again and again. As holes appeared in the bell tower and sections of it crashed to the ground, Kelly said he "began to feel like a real artilleryman." He fired a canister shell at a group of Germans heading down a hillside, which "hit one of them squarely and didn't do the others any good." Those who weren't injured turned and ran. Kelly himself became a target for enemy artillery, and as shells began to drop around him he headed back into the house. A shell blew a hole through a wall, burying two men under the rubble.

He picked up another BAR, loading its 20-round magazines with rounds he plucked from a machine-gun belt. A GI who was firing an M1 rifle out the same window as Kelly got excited and stood up—a tracer went through his shoulder and hit the wall behind him, where it burned. The GI slumped to the floor, and the inevitable cry of "Medic! Medic!" went up.

German snipers had picked off several men in the kitchen, and Kelly went down to try to help out. He was flabbergasted to find a couple of GIs in there cooking up a spaghetti dinner—they had even set a table with a tablecloth, knives and forks, and a basket of bread. He cursed them out, but they told him to "quit blowing his top," and went on fussing with the sauce. Not inclined to wait to be served, Kelly picked up a bottle of cham-pagne, smashed off its top, took a swig, then broke four eggs into a C-ration can and swallowed them raw.

Kelly shot a sniper who had been giving them trouble from

a treetop perch. The sniper's rifle fell to the ground, and moments later he followed. As Kelly looked around for more targets, two Germans ran out to pick up the body. Kelly shot them both. Shortly afterward three others ran out to pull those men in, and he shot them as well.

Someone showed up with about 50 loaded magazines for the BAR, handing a fresh one to Kelly every time he finished off the last. Among other targets, he took out the crew of a 20mm semiautomatic cannon on a distant hillside.

As night fell ammunition was running low. Of the 100 or so GIs who had started the day, there were only 28 left on their feet when the order came to pull out. They were to withdraw at intervals in groups of six. Kelly volunteered for the rear guard, and as he waited he fired off the rest of the 37mm gun rounds and bazooka shells at buildings he knew housed Germans. Then he went back to the upstairs room where the wounded lay. As they loaded weapons and slid them across the floor to him, he fired from the windows until it was his group's turn to leave. The wounded who were able to travel had already gone, and the ones too badly injured to move were left behind.

Kelly's group mustered in the basement. There was a dead GI there from whom Kelly requisitioned an M1 rifle, two bandoleers of ammunition, and a couple of grenades.

As his group drifted into the darkness, Kelly could hear Germans entering the house, then gunfire as they went upstairs—the wounded had saved a few rounds for a last firefight. The shooting gradually petered out.

As they left the house, a P-38 flew over, strafing the Germans in the streets but also wounding one of the GIs, who was stashed in an empty house and left behind. The rest worked their way toward the American lines as quietly as possible. Sometimes a sound betrayed them—a helmet clinked against a wall, or a metal gate creaked as they opened it—and then the German machine guns barked, forcing them to hit the ground and press their faces into the muck. Occasionally they heard

Germans moving around, "but we had no heroic ideas about dying there, as we had done an honest day's work and our idea was to get away alive to fight some other time." An enemy sentry popped up in front of them, but Kelly's lieutenant buttstroked him before he could let out a warning and then brought the rifle down on the back of his neck as he fell, killing him. The group rested in a pigpen, then moved on. They had traveled 10 miles or so when they came upon another sentry. The lieutenant had his knife out ready to silence him if he turned out to be in the wrong uniform, but he was a U.S. paratrooper. They had reached their own line.

The following day, an officer from division headquarters found the survivors of Company L and said, "I'm hunting for you guys. You're AWOL."

"That handed us a laugh," said Kelly. "We told him we had come from Altavilla, where a small portion of fighting had been served to a select few. Nothing greedy, we told him, nothing unladylike. Just a jigger full of hell." (The Bowery Boy influence again apparent.)

Kelly continued to see some of the heaviest fighting of the war, at the crossing of the Rapido River and the assault on Monte Cassino. On March 11, 1944, Kelly, dubbed "Commando" Kelly by the press, was awarded the Medal of Honor. He went back into battle, the medal stuffed in his pocket, until he was sent home a few weeks later.

Kelly died in 1985, at 64. The obituary writers found it ironic that he had spent his postwar years in poverty and obscurity, knocking about as a gas station owner and house painter, living for a period on welfare in public housing. Why this should be ironic is not clear—it was pretty much what he had expected of life as he grew up, and he was not a particularly intelligent or ambitious man. He was good at one thing—fighting—and got his chance to shine, but such a skill has little application in the civilian world, where the ability to surmount death is not nearly as useful as the ability to surmount difficulties.

23 José "Pepe" Llulla

José Llulla was 19th-century New Orleans' foremost master of arms, its most famous duelist, and a highly successful businessman, among whose many properties was a private cemetery said to be filled with his victims.

Llulla was born in 1815 near Port Mahón on Menorca, one of Spain's Balearic Islands. As a boy he went to sea, sailing on whaling ships to the Arctic and slavers to the West African coast, at last settling down in New Orleans in his 20s. Agile and sinewy, skilled with his fists and the knife, Llulla was hired as a bouncer at a combination ballroom-café. After a few encounters with Llulla, the rowdy element took its trade to more congenial establishments.

In those days a gentleman's honor was a fragile thing, easily injured by a jostle, a glance, or a word, and a night out often led to a morning at the dueling ground. In the 1830s and 1840s New Orleans saw an average of a duel a day, and some days as many as 10. To improve their odds, the sporting set supported a number of *salles d'armes*. Exchange Street, on which some 50 were located, was said to resound day and night with the beat and click of blade on blade.

Llulla took up the study of the sword, and his Alsatian fencing master, L'Alouette, was so impressed with him that he soon appointed him his assistant. Even though there were some who could score points against Llulla with the practice foil, he was considered unbeatable with the rapier, saber, or broadsword. He developed equal skill with firearms, and his friends thought nothing of letting him shoot silver dollars from between their fingers and pipes out of their mouths. He would sometimes balance an egg on his son's head and shoot it with a Colt at 30 paces. With a rifle he could usually hit a ball, a cork, or a coin tossed into the air.

The bowie knife was then a novel and popular weapon, and L'Alouette insisted that Llulla fight him in a public exhibition with wooden knives made to the bowie's pattern. Llulla had what one account called "the Spaniard's congenital cleverness with knives," and once the bout was under way, L'Alouette found himself repeatedly touched yet unable to score a point. Losing his temper, he made a violent thrust. Llulla parried it and countered so heavily that he broke two of his teacher's ribs and knocked him to the floor. Fortunately, their friendship survived, and Llulla succeeded L'Alouette as master of his school.

Llulla left the day-to-day operation of the fencing school to assistants and pursued his business interests, for which he seemed to have the Midas touch. He opened a bar and grocery, built slaughterhouses, speculated in cattle and real estate, invested in fleets of river flatboats, operated a sawmill, and in 1857 bought the St. Vincent de Paul Cemetery on Louisa Street. He amassed a fortune, and after the Civil War he purchased the island of Grand Terre.

Llulla aged into a vigorous, keen-eyed, distinguished-looking gentleman, with a low voice and grave demeanor. He was, according to John S. Kendall, "a man of fine instincts, generous to a fault, and charitable in endless simple, unostentatious ways.

Ordinarily, he was as gentle as a woman." A lifelong teetotaler, when asked to explain his legendary nerve, he explained, "It's just that I never drank." At the same time, he was the trainer and confidant of most New Orleans duelists and acted as second more than 100 times. His formidable reputation discouraged most challengers but he did fight some 20 or 30 affairs.

Before one duel, Llulla told his second that he would thrust his sword through a specific button on his opponent's vest—and did so seconds after the duel commenced.

On another occasion Llulla was acting as second when his opposite number, a German fencing master, announced that he would step in because his principal was in no condition to fight.

"We accept," said Llulla, "but in that case you shall deal not with my principal, but with me." Ten seconds later the German lay on the ground, his arm severely gashed and his lung perforated.

In the spring of 1840, the city's fencing masters held a grand tournament for the broadsword. Llulla was not allowed to participate, because he lacked the proper European certification. Llulla called out the Frenchman who had excluded him and after "opening the master's flank in two places" with his broadsword, apologized for having done so without the necessary qualifications.

Most of those who challenged Llulla were caught short on nerve at the moment of reckoning. A Cuban proposed to fight him with machetes, believing none could be found in New Orleans, but when Llulla produced a pair the Cuban made himself scarce. After a quarrel with the Grand Terre lighthouse keeper, a Mr. Douglas, Llulla told a friend, "You may see Mr. Douglas and tell him I am ready to settle our little difficulty. I will be on the beach tomorrow morning with my shotgun. Let him be there with his shotgun and we will settle everything to his entire satisfaction." The keeper did not appear, evidently having decided that living with dissatisfaction was, at least, still living.

Llulla dueled without rancor or vengefulness, but with a sort of impersonal professional pride. He liked to finish as quickly and efficiently as possible and always maintained an uncanny calm. He earned the gratitude of a good many prominent citizens, but the only rewards he would accept for his services were weapons. In the course of his lifetime he accumulated enough swords, cutlasses, poniards, pistols, revolvers, shotguns, and rifles to establish an arms museum.

A staunch defender of his motherland, Llulla was always at odds with the Cuban revolutionaries who had long found sanctuary in New Orleans. During anti-Spanish rioting in 1853, he personally escorted the Spanish consul out of the city, saving him from an angry mob. After this Llulla's life was frequently threatened, but no one dared to face him openly, and his instincts and reflexes were so well honed it was almost impossible to catch him off guard. When in his saloon, he would spin to face the front door whenever it opened, his hands flying to the brace of pistols he wore in shoulder holsters. Only when he recognized the entrant would he relax. A Mexican would-be assassin hid behind Llulla's door with a knife; Llulla wrestled it out of his grip and gave him a severe beating with his fists. Another time, seven drunken sailors attacked him in his saloon, but after Llulla laid five of them out with an iron bar, the last two fled. Two killers sent from Cuba in 1869 attempted to ambush him in his cemetery at dusk but ended up vaulting over gravestones and scrambling over tombs as Llulla chased them with a pistol in each hand. When he heard that a crowd of rowdies was collecting near his house after dark to launch an assault, Llulla went out and preemptively attacked, scattering them single-handedly.

During the Cuban revolt of 1873–1874, Llulla papered New Orleans with posters challenging any and all Cuban revolutionaries to mortal combat. He had a few takers: as was always the pattern, at the appointed time they contrived to be elsewhere. Llulla's skill with weapons was so renowned that even men who laid claim to honor felt it acceptable to refuse his challenge—honor required a man to risk his life, not throw it away, and to duel with Llulla was certain death. At last, a champion was found to represent the Cuban revolutionary cause, a retired Austrian army officer. He chose lead over steel, the distance being 30 paces. On command, the combatants were to advance toward each other and fire at will. When the command was given Llulla stood stock still, his face averted from his opponent. Reserving his fire, the Austrian stalked toward him, but Llulla still faced away. When, at last, the Austrian raised his gun to fire, Llulla suddenly turned and shot him through the lungs. The Austrian collapsed, but lingered a few months before dying. Contrary to the widespread belief that Llulla's victims could populate a necropolis, he claimed that this was only the second man who had died at his hands.

His willingness to champion the cause of his nation and defy an entire revolutionary movement made Llulla a hero to Spanish loyalists in New Orleans and Cuba. Thousands of photographic portraits of him were sold, and they were displayed in New Orleans homes for a generation afterward. He was showered with adulatory letters and telegrams, as well as commendations from military units and high-ranking officials. Writer Lafcadio Hearn, who visited Llulla a few years before his death, saw stacks of these tributes, as well as one especially romantic tribute—a portrait of the hero surrounded by a laurel wreath, atop a Spanish inscription that read: "To Don José Llulla, Determined Defender of the National Honor Against the Traitors of New Orleans." It appeared to have been done in lustrous black silk, but had actually been embroidered from hair that the ladies of Havana had cut off and donated.

Llulla died of natural causes on March 6, 1888. His grave can still be seen in the St. Vincent de Paul Cemetery.

24 Frank Luke

*"We had any number of
expert pilots and there was
no shortage of good shots,
but the perfect combination,
like the perfect specimen of
anything in the world, was
scarce. Frank Luke was the
perfect combination."*
—Major Harold Hartney

F rank Luke was born in Phoenix, Arizona, in 1897. With his pugnacious nature, good eye, quick reflexes, and steady nerve, he might have become a gunfighter had he been born a generation earlier, but in 1917 the gunfighters were dogfighting in the skies over Europe. Wanting to get in on the action, Luke enlisted in the U.S. Signal Corps and requested flying duty. Before he shipped out he told the owner of the *Arizona Gazette*, "I'm going over as a combat pilot, and you'll hear of me before I'm through. . . . One thing will not happen: I'll never be taken prisoner." The statement had some credibility coming from a man who, as starting tailback on his high school football team, once played the second half of a game with a broken collarbone.

In training at Issoudun, France, Luke proved himself an excellent pilot and marksman, but afterward found himself ferrying planes from Orly Airfield to the front. He made it clear that he considered the job beneath him, frequently taking the planes for joyrides. "I came here to fight, not ferry," he retorted when asked to explain himself.

Luke finally got an assignment to the U.S. 27th Pursuit Squadron, arriving with a group of replacement pilots on July 25, 1918. They were addressed by the commanding officer, a Captain Hartney, who told them that if they found that they weren't brave enough for aerial combat, they should at least be brave enough to admit it and get out. He concluded with, "You are in the 27th in name only. When you have shown your buddies out there that you have guts and can play the game honestly and courageously, they'll probably let you stay. You'll know without my telling you when you are actually members of this group."

Hartney later recalled being irritated that Luke grinned throughout the speech as if to say, "Don't kid me." It was true that Luke was fairly unimpressed with the 27th. Its landing field was a muddy mass of plowed-up turf, the buildings were shabby and decrepit, and, except for Hartney, none of the pilots had more than one kill. When Luke first met them he observed, "I can't imagine how some of you guys have stayed up here so long and still haven't knocked down your five planes to become aces." The response was a chilly silence that, within days, hardened into icy dislike as Luke continued to make tactless and boastful remarks.

Taking Luke and another newcomer, Joe Wehner, up in the air for a few mock dogfights, Hartney tried to quickly give them the benefit of his two years' experience—lessons such as *When you see one Boche, look for his partner. . . . Watch for the Hun in the sun. . . . Keep your head on a swivel. . . . Don't dive to shake a Hun on your tail—you're giving up precious altitude. . . . Take advantage of your opponent's weakness, however momentary.*

National Archives

On August 16, 1918, Luke took off in his Spad XIII an hour
after his formation. He claimed he'd had engine trouble, but he
hated formation flying, and it may be that he thought he'd have
better luck hunting alone. According to his after-action report,
while looking for his unit he found himself above a German formation. He dived on a straggler, opening fire at 100 feet and
breaking off at very close range, then went back for another
pass. The German flipped over, then sideslipped down. Luke
reported the kill, but because there were no witnesses few of the
pilots believed the man they had already dubbed the Arizona
Boaster. Hartney accepted Luke's claim. As he later wrote, "His
verbal account of the battle contained those little differences
that give such a report the touch of verisimilitude. But the
squadron didn't believe him, and that made Luke bitter."

One pilot who believed Luke was Joe Wehner. They became
friends and began flying as a team. As personalities, they had
little in common: Wehner was modest, reserved, and from a
respectable Boston family, while Luke was a born hell raiser.
However, they both had German backgrounds and their patri-
otism was therefore suspect—Wehner had actually been for-
mally investigated—so they shared a sense of having something to prove.

As Allied commanders planned the 1918 Argonne offensive, the 27th was charged with taking on the German balloon
corps. These balloons, called *drachen*, were the bane of the
infantry. They floated 500 to 2,000 feet above the battlefield,
providing a vantage point for observers who directed artillery
on Allied troop concentrations. Though large, immobile, and
filled with explosive hydrogen gas, the balloons were far from
sitting ducks. They were tethered to winches so that they could
be lowered quickly. A pilot who attacked from above would be
swallowed up in any ensuing fireball, but if he attacked from
the side he had to fly through a wall of lead thrown up by rings
of antiaircraft machine guns. Furthermore, the *drachen* were
often guarded by fighter planes circling high above, ready to

pounce. Most pilots felt that attacking balloons was close to suicidal, but Luke wasn't the cautious type. He decided he could take on the balloons as long as Wehner watched his six. He loaded the left-side Vickers machine gun on his Spad fighter with a belt of tracers only, and the right-side one with a standard mix of ball and tracer ammunition, which fed more reliably. He would use the ball ammo to tear open a hole in a balloon and release the gas, then the tracers to ignite it.

Luke filed this report on his first balloon kill:

> Combat report—Sept. 12th 1918
> "Lt. Frank Luke reports:—
> Saw three Fokkers and gave chase until they disappeared toward Metz. Saw enemy balloon at [Marieulles]. Destroyed it after three passes at it, each within a few yards of the balloon. The third pass was made when the balloon was very near the ground. Both guns jammed so pulled over to one side. Fixed left gun and turned about to make one final effort to burn it but saw that it had already started to burn. The next instant it burst into flames and fell on its truck, destroying it. There was a good field near our balloons so landed for confirmation. Attached is confirmation signed by Lt. Fox and Lt. Smith."

This time Luke was determined to get credit for his victory. The American infantrymen he landed next to were only too glad to sign his claim. As one said, "That thing was spotting us for three days, and our whole gang's waiting to give you a hand." Afterward Luke was unable to take off because his plane had been badly chewed up by ground fire. It was the first of five Spads he would destroy. (Wehner went through three.)

Two days later, on a midmorning flight over Boinville, Luke

and Wehner peeled off from their squadron to take on another balloon. Luke went straight for it while Wehner climbed high to provide cover. The German ground batteries opened up, but Luke flew through the fusillade until the balloon was in range. He had to dive on it six times, twice correcting stoppages in his left gun. The balloon didn't explode but hit the ground "in a very flabby condition." He used some of his remaining rounds in strafing an antiaircraft crew. Two other pilots who had made passes on the *drachen* after Luke disputed his right to the kill, provoking further friction in the 27th.

On the afternoon of the 14th, Luke and Wehner were assigned to take out a balloon near Buzy. Luke methodically prepared his plane and inspected each link and round of his machine-gun belts for the tiny irregularities that could cause stoppages.

As Luke approached his target, he saw between five and eight German Fokker fighters racing to intercept him from above, but he counted on the speed of his dive to give him one unmolested run. He started his first burst at long range, holding the nose of his Spad up to compensate for his bullets' drop. As he closed in he flew directly at the target, continuing to fire short bursts until his guns overheated and jammed. It didn't matter, since his work was done; he broke left as the balloon exploded. His plane was raked by bursts from the pursuing Fokkers, but Wehner dived on them from out of the sun, shooting down one and scattering the others.

The base was buzzing with news of Luke's double victory, but rather than return to group headquarters he landed and tried to have his badly shot-up plane refueled and rearmed so he could have a go at another balloon nearby. The ground crew stymied him by tearing a few yards of fabric off his badly shot-up wings.

The 27th was getting a reputation as a balloon-busting squadron, and as a result of its success the weight of the duty fell on Luke and Wehner. Not only had they proven able and willing to take it on, but they were also considered expendable, particularly Luke. He may have shown he could "play the game courageously and honestly," as Hartney had said, but his fellow pilots made it clear he was not a member of the group.

On September 15, on two daytime patrols, Luke took out two more balloons and that evening decided to try an experiment. He had noted that the German fighter cover lessened at dusk as Allied pilots returned to their bases before dark. It occurred to him that he would also be harder to spot at that time. Getting his ground crew to rig some lights to mark the landing field, he took off at sundown, heading for artillery flashes on the horizon, near which he knew there would be a spotting balloon. He dived on it and set it ablaze.

His six confirmed kills earned Luke the title of ace, and he was put in for the Distinguished Flying Cross. He continued to butt heads with his commanding officer, one Captain Grant (Hartney having been promoted to major), but his sudden celebrity status made it difficult for Grant to discipline him.

Chagrined by their recent losses, the Germans increased their precautions. They quickly winched down their balloons the following day as Luke and Wehner approached. Luke suggested another evening patrol.

Before he took off, he was summoned to Hartney's headquarters. There he was surprised to meet Gen. Billy Mitchell, chief of the Air Service, as well as a couple of colonels. Though Luke was initially ill at ease, his cockiness kicked in and he made a surprisingly confident assertion: that evening he and Wehner would flame two gasbags near Boinville, one at 7:15 and the other at 7:19.

The brass didn't know quite what to make of this, but as the time approached they walked to the crest of a hill and looked toward the eastern horizon. Eddie Rickenbacker, America's top ace, was with them. At exactly 7:15, there was a bright flash of light over the German lines as a balloon exploded. At 7:19, everyone strained their eyes, and within a moment the other one blew up. "By God, there she goes!" shouted Mitchell, who, with uncharacteristic exuberance, danced up and down. There was yet another explosion as Wehner took down a third *drachen* by himself.

On September 18, at 5 P.M., Luke and Wehner decided to try for two balloons over Labeuville. As Wehner circled above for cover, Luke dove on his target. The antiaircraft batteries opened up, but he flew through the torrent of lead and aimed a stream of tracers into the balloon until it exploded and collapsed. As he banked sharply and headed for the second balloon, nine Fokkers dropped out of the clouds above. The balloons were bait, and the trap was now sprung. Wehner fired a red flare, signaling danger. Either out of recklessness or because he didn't see the flare, Luke left Wehner to engage the Germans and headed for the second balloon. He was only 90 feet above the ground when he flamed it. As he pulled out of his dive, Luke saw Wehner under attack by three Fokkers. Wehner's Spad rolled over and hurtled down in flames. In a blind fury, Luke lit into the Fokkers without even maneuvering for advantage. He locked on to one and pumped bullets into it until it went down. By this time the other two were on his tail, but with a quick *renversement* he got the second in his sights and took him out. The third turned tail.

Low on fuel, Luke headed back for the American lines. Ahead of him he saw a German Halberstadt two-seat observation plane, its tail gunner holding off four French fighters. Luke dived through the French, came up under the Halberstadt, and killed the pilot and gunner with one quick burst.

Luke had downed two balloons, two Fokkers, and one Halberstadt in less than 10 minutes. With 14 confirmed kills he was now the top U.S. pilot, but there was little satisfaction in it for him. The death of his best friend plunged him into depression. It was at this time that he was photographed for the newspapers, and the bleakness of his mood is evident. He was given two weeks' leave in Paris but returned early, claiming there was "nothing to do there."

On September 26, at the beginning of the Marne offensive, Luke teamed up with Lt. Ivan Roberts, who had joined the 27th at the same time he had and was perhaps the only man left he considered a friend. Attacking a formation of five Fokkers, Luke downed one and would have gotten another had his guns not jammed. Unfortunately, Roberts was shot down and presumed dead.[14] If Luke was depressed before, he was now nearly suicidal.

Two days later, he flew off without authority and shot down a balloon near Bethenville. When he landed he was ordered to report to Captain Grant's office. Rather than comply immediately, Luke went to his quarters, packed some of his things, and filled out a combat report. When he finally turned up at his CO's office, he received a scorching reprimand and was told he was grounded. Luke did not answer, so Grant asked him if he had understood. "Yeah," responded Luke, flipping his combat report onto Grant's desk. "By the way, I got you another balloon."

Luke walked from Grant's office to the line, tossed his overnight bag in his Spad, ordered his mechanics to spin the prop, and took off. He spent the night with a French unit. Grant ordered him arrested, but Hartney countermanded the order, knowing there was no way they could court-martial a hero who had been featured on the front page of the *New York Times*.

The next day, September 29, Luke took off at about 6 P.M. Swooping low over the U.S. Army Balloon Headquarters at Souilly, he dropped a message reading: "Watch out for those three nearest balloons at D-1 and D-4 positions." Luke slipped across the lines in the fading light. A fighter cap of eight to 10 Fokker D-7s spotted the flashes of antiaircraft fire directed at his Spad and went after him. So confident were the German aviators that a lone pilot posed no serious threat that they didn't bother to winch down the three balloons. French civilians reported that there was a dogfight in which Luke shot down two

---

14. Roberts was taken prisoner and killed in an escape attempt the day before the war ended.

of his opponents, but this has never been confirmed. Finally, Luke plunged thousands of feet toward the ground in a spin, apparently out of control. The pursuit broke off, but Luke pulled out just above the treeline and headed for the first balloon. With precisely aimed bursts of his tracers, he set it ablaze. Buffeted by the wave of heat and concussion, he banked and headed for the second. He toasted it too, then stood his Spad on its wingtip and headed for the third. The ground fire intensified. Thousands of rounds had been fired at Luke in the past few weeks, and it was inevitable that some must eventually connect. A series of hits rocked his plane—his engine sputtered, badly damaged, and Luke took a bullet in the shoulder. Nevertheless, he continued toward the third balloon, and as the ground crews frantically winched it down he put a red-hot burst into the bag. It convulsed and belched out a fireball that left a towering column of black smoke.

Luke lost altitude. He flew unsteadily over the small farming village of Murvaux, barely clearing the church steeple. He spotted a German patrol outside town and strafed it, killing six and wounding six more. Crash-landing his plane in a muddy field, he walked to a nearby stream for a drink of water. A German patrol found him and ordered him to surrender. Customarily, pilots only fought in the air, not on the ground, but Luke wasn't much for honoring custom. He drew his .45 and fired at the Germans. Some say he killed three before they dropped him with a volley.

The average life span of a fighter pilot at the front was six weeks, so Luke lasted about as long as expected. Captain Grant, who had wanted him arrested, put him in for the Medal of Honor, which Luke was the first pilot to receive. Luke Air Force Base, west of Phoenix, is named in his honor.

25 Bat Masterson & Luke Short

> *He was a chunk of steel and anything that struck him in those days always drew fire.*
> —Billy Dixon

He was christened William Bartholomew in Quebec in 1853. For most of his life was called "Bat," from a shortened version of his middle name, not, as the story goes, for using a walking stick as a weapon. His family moved to Kansas while he was still an infant. At 19 Bat and two of his brothers, Ed and Jim, joined up with a group of hunters following the buffalo herds into Oklahoma and the Texas panhandle. In 1874, Bat was one of 14 buffalo hunters who used their long-range Sharps rifles to successfully defend the Adobe Walls outpost against several hundred Comanche, Arapaho, Kiowa, and Cheyenne warriors. He served as an army scout for three months before falling out of sight for a few years. He popped up again in Sweetwater, Texas, where on January 24, 1876, he killed his first man.

Masterson was visiting a girlfriend, Mollie Brennan, after

hours at the Lady Gay Saloon. U.S. Army Corporal Melvin King was also interested in Brennan, and in cowboy parlance had "thrown a brand on her." King showed up at the saloon late one night, drunk and angry, and banged on the door. Masterson, who didn't know him, opened it. King burst in brandishing his six-gun and shouting threats. Brennan jumped in front of Masterson just as King opened fire. A slug tore through her abdomen and struck Masterson in the hip. Staggering under the blow, Masterson drew his own gun and shot King in the heart.

Masterson set off for the mining fields of the Black Hills of the Dakota Territory but found there was more money to be made running the faro game at a Cheyenne saloon than panning for gold. In 1876 he met Wyatt Earp, who became a lifelong friend, and whom Masterson considered "absolutely destitute of physical fear." Earp advised him to run for sheriff of Ford County, Kansas, which encompassed Dodge City. "But I'm not even 23," Masterson protested.

"You're as much of a man as you'll ever be," Earp assured him.

Dodge was a rough town, where cowboys finishing cattle drives let off steam. They got drunk, got laid, and left whatever remained of their wages at the gaming tables. As one cowboy described Dodge, "It was a plumb hair-triggered country, filled to the nozzle with hair-triggered gents, totin' hair-triggered side guns. A man walked soft and light in Dodge City, or he quit walking."

Bat's brothers had preceded him to Dodge and established themselves, Ed as assistant marshal and Jim as proprietor of a combination saloon-dance hall.

Almost as soon as he arrived, Bat got into trouble. He was in the crowd on a street listening to Bobby Gill, a small, innocuous drunk, deliver a derisive dissertation on 300-pound city marshal Larry Deger when Deger happened by. Deger, who did not find the roast amusing, collared Gill and marched him toward the hoosegow, hastening him along with swift kicks to

Kansas State Historical Society

211

the backside. His sense of fair play offended, Masterson looped an arm around Deger's neck from behind, allowing Gill to escape. Deger called for help, and a half-dozen men piled on Masterson. Deger pistol-whipped him until he was bloody, but Masterson continued to put up a fight as he was dragged to jail. As the *Dodge City Times* put it, "Bat Masterson seemed possessed of extraordinary strength, and every inch of the way was closely contested, but the city dungeon was reached at last, and in he went. If he had got hold of his gun before going in there would have been a general killing."

Six months later, Bat Masterson ran against Deger for Sheriff of Ford County and had the satisfaction of defeating him, albeit by three votes.

The day before the election, Bat's brother Ed got into a shootout. Under the headline "FRONTIER FUN," the *Dodge City Times* described it in the lighthearted manner in which it invariably described incidents of gunplay. It opened with,

"Last Monday afternoon one of those little episodes which serve to vary the monotony of frontier existence occurred at the Lone Star dance hall," and went on to explain that Ed Masterson had intervened in an armed altercation between Bob Shaw and Texas Dick Moore. Shaw refused to surrender his weapon to Masterson, and

> again proceeded to try to kill Texas Dick. Officer Masterson then gently tapped the belligerent Shaw upon the back of the head with the butt of his shooting iron, merely to convince him of the vanities of this frail world. . . . The aforesaid reminder . . . failed to have the desired effect, and instead of dropping, as any man of fine sensibilities would have done, Shaw turned his battery upon the officer and let him have it.

Ed Masterson, wounded but not seriously, fired two bullets

into Shaw, "rendering him *hors de combat*." Ed returned to the Wichita homestead for two weeks to recover.

Bat was sworn in on January 14, 1878, and within two weeks had a chance to prove himself. A gang of six bandits had twice tried to rob the Santa Fe Railroad near Dodge, and the railroad wished to entertain no further attempts. Three separate posses took off in pursuit of the desperados but failed to find them. Masterson was asked to try. He formed a posse of three former buffalo hunters who knew the country and could be counted on if any shooting was required. But after they set out, a blinding snowstorm blew in, and after three days they had to take refuge at an isolated ranch. Realizing that there was a good chance the men they wanted would also be forced to seek shelter, the posse was ready when two of the bandits showed up. One of the bandits was Dave Rudabaugh, who later rode with Billy the Kid. He started to go for his gun but changed his mind when he heard the hammer being cocked on a Colt revolver pointed at his back by Masterson.

A few weeks later, another posse led by Masterson arrested two more members of the gang outside Dodge City. The outlaws tried to put up a fight, but they were swarmed before they could get off a shot.

Five months after Bat's election, brother Ed got into a shootout with two drunken cowboys he had tried to disarm. He killed one and wounded the other but was badly wounded and subsequently died. Bat's worst fears about Ed had been realized—his trusting, easygoing manner had enabled the badmen to "outmanage" him. Bat also had an affable, live-and-let-live approach, but troublemakers never thought they could push him. He had an unmistakable resolve—*sand*, as they called it. To reinforce his image, Bat regularly put on demonstrations of his shooting skill. He could kill rabbits shooting from the hip and, for a bet, would put a hole through a tin cup tossed into the air. Masterson ordered his Colts direct from the factory, made to his specifications with hard rubber stocks, nickel plating, and front sights higher and thicker than normal. Then, Masterson wrote, he would "file the notch of the hammer till the trigger would pull sweet, which is another way of saying that the blamed gun would go off if you looked at it." Because reloading took time, he often carried two revolvers, one in reserve.

Bat's reputation as a gunfighter was based on the widespread belief that he had killed between 26 and 38 men. The *Kansas City Journal* wrote that

> the gentleman who has killed his man is . . . a ubiquitous individual in this city and may be met at every corner . . . but when you see a man who has entered upon his third dozen, it is about time to be civil, for he may begin to fear that material is about to run out and may have an uncontrollable desire to hurry up and finish that third dozen. Such a gentleman . . . is . . . known, by those whom he has not shot, as "Bat" Masterson. In answer to a very leading question, Masterson said he had not killed as many men as was popularly supposed, though he had "had a great many difficulties."

The *Atchison Champion* challenged the figure of three dozen under the headline "TOO MUCH BLOOD":

> The *Champion* is the last paper to discourage any citizen in a worthy pursuit, or to deprive any Kansan of the fruits of his honest toil, or of honors earned; but really the newspaper correspondents East and West credit some of our people with more bloodshed than rightfully or reasonably belongs to them. We do not stickle about a few tubs full of gore, more or less, nor have we any disposition to haggle about a corpse or two,

but when it comes to a miscount or overlap of a dozen, no conscientious journalist, who values truth as well as the honor of our state, should keep silent. To credit unjustly a man with having killed thirty or forty people when this accomplished bookkeeper, with the undertaker to check off, can only find two dozen has a tendency to bring Kansas statistics into disrepute, and also to discourage some humble beginner in the field of slaughter who has sent only four or five to act as foundations for the daisies.

Masterson's reputation was useful to him, which may be why he chose to be vague about his tally. In fact, he is not known for certain to have killed more than one of his fellow citizens (Mexicans and Indians not usually being included in such tallies). He was "not one of those human tigers who delighted in shedding blood just for the fun of the thing," as he described Earp (a gunfighter with not a single confirmed kill on his record), but handled most of his opponents with his fists or by "buffaloing" them—knocking them cold by smacking them across the forehead with the heavy barrel of his Colt.

Masterson was relaxing in Dodge City's Alhambra Saloon one evening when a young rowdy named Bell came looking for him, revolver in hand. In an instant Masterson was on his feet, his Colt cocked and pointed directly between Bell's eyes. Bell stood frozen as Masterson advanced on him, till the two stood at arms' length, eyes locked, each holding a weapon on the other. Suddenly, Masterson lowered his Colt's hammer and buffaloed Bell. "I didn't think I had to shoot," Masterson mused, years later. "I once saw Bell jump over a bar-counter to get at a man, when he might just as well have gone round, and it struck me all at once that he was much too *dramatic*."

Masterson assisted Earp in this same fashion one May evening in 1879. Three Missouri roughnecks traveling through

Dodge were raising hell when Assistant Marshal Earp interrupted their festivities, grabbed the biggest and rowdiest by the ear, and began marching him off to jail. The man's friends followed and confronted Earp at gunpoint on a dark corner. They demanded that he let go of their friend, but Earp was not one to give in to threats. The two then urged their friend to break free so they could get a clear shot at the marshal. Struggle as he might, the man was unable to break Earp's vise-like hold on his ear, though he was able to keep Earp from aiming his revolver. Masterson saw the situation from across the street and rushed to Earp's assistance. He administered a sleeping tonic to the prisoner's forehead, then swung his gun up beside Earp's to cover the two men. The Missourians meekly submitted to arrest.

Masterson also had guile in his arsenal. On one occasion he received a telegram saying that an escaped criminal named Davis was on an eastbound train that would make a stop in Dodge City. With no physical description, only the warning that Davis was armed and extremely dangerous, Masterson was requested to take him into custody. As the train pulled in, Masterson entered the end car and walked through the carriages casually studying the passengers, his sheriff's badge hidden under his coat. After his suspicions pointed him toward one particular man, he strode purposefully toward him, flashed a warm smile and stuck out his hand for a shake, calling out, "Why, hello, Davis! How are you?" Davis, no doubt searching his mind desperately for the identity of this old friend, obligingly stuck out his right hand—his gun hand. Masterson trapped it in a grip of iron, yanked Davis out of his seat, and handcuffed him.

Masterson lost his reelection bid for another two-year term as sheriff, due largely to his refusal to respond to the scurrilous charges of his opponents. He headed west, working as a faro dealer in frontier saloons. For a time he was employed at Wyatt Earp's Oriental in Tombstone, Arizona Territory. Earp backed himself up with well-known gunfighters to put fear into the gamblers, as well as the hostile "Cowboy" faction. Among Earp's dealers was

Kansas State Historical Society

Luke Short, whom Masterson described as "a small package, but one of great dynamic force." Short had been a buffalo hunter and a cowboy and later sold liquor to the Indians. He had reportedly killed nine Indians and two white men in Nebraska, earning the nickname of the Undertaker's Friend because "he shot 'em where it didn't show." Always nattily attired in a dark suit, he carried a snub-nosed Colt .45 in a leather-lined pants pocket he kept dusted with talcum powder. Like all successful gunfighters, he had a hair-trigger homicidal reflex.

On February 25, 1881, an altercation arose between Luke Short and gambler Charlie Storms, another friend of Masterson. Fearing that Storms might make the mistake of underestimating Short, Masterson separated the men. Storms left the scene. In *Famous Gun Fighters of the Western Frontier,* Masterson described what followed:

> I was just explaining to Luke that Storms was a very decent sort of man when, lo and behold, there he stood before us. Without saying a word, he took hold of Luke's arm and pulled him off the sidewalk, where he had been standing, at the same time pulling his pistol, a Colt's cut-off .45-caliber single-action, but . . . he was too slow, although he succeeded in getting his pistol out. Luke stuck the muzzle of his own pistol against Storm's heart and pulled the trigger. The bullet tore the heart asunder, and as he was falling, Luke shot him again.

Storms reflexively fired as he fell but was dead when he hit the ground, his wool shirt aflame from the muzzle flash of Short's gun. Short turned to Masterson and said, "You sure as hell pick some of the damnedest people for friends, Bat."

Masterson testified in favor of Short, and the case was dismissed.

The shooting had the effect of intimidating local gamblers,

but eight months later Earp's difficulties with the "Cowboys" erupted in the shootout at the O. K. Corral. Masterson might have been a participant had his stay in Tombstone not been cut short by a telegram entreating him to return to Dodge City because his brother Jim's life had been threatened by two business associates, Updegraff and Peacock. Bat took the first train available.

Thirty hours later, not knowing whether Jim was dead or alive or what kind of reception to expect, he swung down off the train as it pulled into Dodge and walked toward the depot. He spotted Updegraff and Peacock walking ahead of him and called out, "I have come over a thousand miles to settle this. I know you are heeled—now fight!" Recognizing Masterson's voice, the men ducked behind a building, and within seconds the Colt fandango was on, with supporters of each faction joining in. A bullet hit the ground close enough to Masterson to kick dirt into his mouth and then ricocheted into a bystander, wounding him slightly. Updegraff took a bullet in the lung but eventually recovered. The brief shootout produced no fatalities. Bat declined to be arrested but condescended to a fine of $8 for shooting inside the city limits. The authorities were no doubt relieved when he and Jim left Dodge that evening.

In the spring of 1883 Masterson was again out of town when he received a call for help, this time from Luke Short, who had returned to Dodge to operate the Long Branch Saloon.

Short's license had been revoked and all his girls arrested by Masterson's old nemesis Larry Deger, now Dodge's mayor. When Short found that Ab Webster, a rival saloon keeper and Deger crony, was still in business, he "smelled a mouse." On the evening of February 28, Short strapped on his guns and headed for the jailhouse. City Clerk Lou Hartman, who was in front of the jail, saw Short coming and threw a few shots his way. Short pulled his gun and responded in kind. Knowing Short's deadly reputation, Hartman turned to run and, in his panic, tripped over his own feet and fell to the ground. Assuming he'd killed him, Short returned to his saloon, loaded his shotgun, and barricaded his door. The following morning, after the sheriff told him he had not injured Hartman and would only have to pay a small fine, Short left his premises. Going back on his word, the sheriff arrested him and ran him out of town. Short then contacted Masterson.

Masterson put out the call, and from all over the West itinerant dealers in lead began drifting into Dodge City. Modern readers would recognize the names of Wyatt Earp and Doc Holliday, but equally notorious in their day were Shotgun Collins, Rowdy Joe Lowe, Dynamite Sam, Three-Fingered Dave, and Black Jack Bill, all rumored to be lining up behind Short. In a meeting with the mayor, Earp suggested that his friends "signified a willingness to participate in whatever festivities might arise." Newspapers across the nation called it the Dodge City Saloon War, so Masterson dubbed his contingent the Dodge City Peace Commission. Dodge's sheriff requested two companies of state militia to handle the situation but was turned down by the governor. At this point members of the Deger faction acknowledged that they had perhaps been a bit unfair, and Short got his saloon back.

In 1885 Dodge went "dry," and Short relocated to Fort Worth, Texas, where he set up shop in the White Elephant Saloon. "Longhaired" Jim Courtright, a gunfighter with four kills, made the mistake of thinking he could intimidate the "Undertaker's Friend" into paying protection money. Masterson happened to be visiting Short when the situation came to a head. As Short discussed the matter with Courtright on the street, the latter went for his revolver. Before he could get off a shot, Short drew and fired. His first shot mangled the thumb on Courtright's gun hand and damaged the cylinder of his pistol. As Courtright tried to shift the gun to his left hand, Short shot him in the chest and then fired three times more, hitting him in the shoulder. Courtright died on the spot. Short was held in jail overnight, and word got out that Courtwright's cronies were planning to bust in and lynch him. Masterson announced he would spend the night outside Short's cell, armed with his brace of Colts and bringing an extra pair to hand his friend should the need arise. At that, "the would-be lynchers . . . virtuously resolved that the law should take its course, and went heedfully home to bed," as one account put it. Short was never indicted.

One night in 1890, a crooked gambler Short had exposed fired a shotgun at him from a dark alley. Short was wounded in the leg and left hand, but before he fell he got off a shot that smashed his assailant's wrist, ending his days as a cardsharp. It was Short's fifth and last gunfight. He died in bed three years later of kidney and liver failure.

Masterson continued to roam the boomtowns of the West, settling wherever opportunity presented itself. He worked as a gambler in Leadville, Colorado, and as the town marshal in Trinidad in the same state. In 1892 he covered both bases in the mining town of Creede, Colorado. A reporter for the *St. Louis Globe Democrat,* who met him there, wrote:

> Bat Masterson is generally recognized in the camp as the nerviest man of all the fighters here. He has a record for cool bravery unsurpassed by any man in the West. . . . There is no blow or swagger about him. He is of unusually pleasant address, and his language is that of a man of uncommon education. His deportment and bearing are such that, despite the fact you know his record, you could never summon hardihood enough to ask him about some of his escapades. But all the toughs and thugs fear him as they do no other dozen men in camp. Let an incipient riot start and all that is necessary to quell it is the whisper, "There comes Masterson."

Masterson lived in Denver for a while, where he managed prize fighters and wrote for a local paper. One of his acerbic columns angered a gambler named O'Neal, who slipped a pair of six-shooters into his overcoat pockets and, accompanied by a hired tough, lay in wait for Masterson on a dark street. The goon was supposed to grab Masterson so O'Neal could shoot him. The plan went awry when Masterson decked the tough with his left hand and drew his shooting iron with his right, leveling it at O'Neal before the gambler could get out his own revolvers. "Don't kill me!" O'Neal begged. In an accommodating mood, Masterson merely dosed him with a Dodge City tranquilizer. Later, his forehead swathed in bandages, O'Neal requested that Masterson visit him at his sickbed to give him a chance to explain. Masterson agreed, but warned him to keep his hands above the covers while he did his "explaining."

At age 50, Bat Masterson left the "zone of fire," as he called it, and moved to New York City. Shortly after his arrival he was charged with carrying a concealed weapon and had to surrender his .45 Colt and pay a $10 fine. Despite the rude welcome, he soon made himself at home. He found a spot as a columnist on the *New York Morning Telegraph*, writing about boxing and the city's nightlife. Among his circle were Damon Runyon, Theodore Roosevelt, and Irwin S. Cobb. The latter was disappointed by the mild appearance of the famous gunfighter, but then noticed "the flecks of mica" that glistened in his pale blue eyes when he was aroused. A reporter for the *New York Sun* accompanied Masterson to an off-Broadway saloon frequented by a tough crowd and was struck by the way the hooligans instinctively quieted down in his presence.

During this period, a collector pestered Masterson for one of the six-shooters with which he had supposedly filled a subdivision on Boot Hill. Unwilling to part with any of his personal weapons, Masterson purchased a worn Colt at a pawnshop and carved 22 notches on its butt with his penknife. After paying a hefty price for the treasure, the awestruck collector asked him if he had really killed 22 men with it. Masterson didn't lie. Rather than answer yes or no, he shrugged and allowed as how he hadn't counted Indians or Mexicans.

Bat Masterson died at his typewriter in 1921.

26 La Maupin

> *Beautiful, valiant, generous*
> *and superbly unchaste . . .*
> —Cameron Rogers

Honor has always been defined in a contrary manner for gentlemen and ladies. The gentleman might debauch himself as he pleased, as long as he displayed courage and a constant readiness to fight. For the lady, however, honor rested on her chastity, and fighting was frowned upon.

Even as a young girl, La Maupin aspired to the honor of a gentleman.

She was born in 1670, in the gay and vicious France of the *ancien régime*, and her given name is not known. Her father, Monsieur d'Aubigny, secretary to the Comte d'Armagnac, was a dashing fellow, known to be "as brave as steel"—it was said he feared neither God, man, nor the devil, and was equally adept with cards, women, and the sword. He gave his daughter a gentleman's education in writing, dancing, grammar, and drawing, and saw to it that she learned to ride and fence as well. Fencing with the smallsword favors[15] skill and finesse over brute strength, and by the time she was a teenager Maupin had mastered the art of "striking without being struck." She was described as tall and athletic, with blue eyes, dark auburn hair, very white skin, and "perfect" breasts, and had a beautiful singing voice. At 14 or 15 she seduced her father's employer, the count, and through him was introduced to Paris society and the royal court. To disguise their relationship, the Comte d'Armagnac had her married off to a dull but respectable older gentleman named Maupin, who maintained an indulgent myopia. After a year or so, she began to find the count tedious, so "La Maupin," as she now called herself, ran off with a fencing master, Sérranes, whose swordplay was more to her liking.

Together they frequented the Parisian *salles d'armes*, honing their skills, and picked fights in the street. After Sérranes killed a man in a duel they had to leave town. La Maupin traveled in male guise, a fashion statement that she maintained off and on for the rest of her life.

They took a room in Marseille, supporting themselves with La Maupin's singing and by giving nightly fencing demonstrations in the inn's taproom. Fencing in a doublet and hose, her assaults, parries, and ripostes were so strong and flawlessly executed that many in the audience expressed disbelief that she was a woman. One evening the debate on the subject grew so loud that La Maupin was distracted and got herself pinked a few times. To put an end to the argument she tore open her shirt. Although that evening produced a gratifying return, on a day-to-day basis she found the enterprise insufficiently lucrative. She auditioned for the music academy of Pierre Gaultier and entranced him with her fine contralto. Contralto roles were until then exclusively filled by castrated males, "the maimed ones" as they were called, but Gaultier signed her up immediately and she made her professional debut at 18.

---

15. The smallsword was a further development of the rapier, shorter and lighter, designed primarily for thrusting.

La Maupin was not one to limit her amorous pursuits to one sex, much less one man, and her eye was soon caught by a young blonde who regularly attended the opera with her parents. When La Maupin seduced her, the girl's mortified parents quickly packed her off to the Visitandines' convent at Avignon. Not to be denied, La Maupin entered the convent herself. There the affair continued, till La Maupin decided they needed a less confining environment. After an older nun died, La Maupin took the body, put it in the bed of her inamorata, and set the room on fire so that the two could cover their escape. Three months later, she grew bored, and sent the girl home to her parents. In the wake of the scandal the tribunal of the Parliament of Aix published an edict condemning La Maupin to death by burning at the stake. She took some comfort from the fact that it mistakenly identified her as "Monsieur" Maupin, but to be on the safe side she decided to return to Paris, singing for her supper at inns along the way. She was performing in male attire at the Ecu-Neuf Inn in Villeperdue,

· KIRCHNER ·

where a group of young squires was dining and drinking. One of them, Louis Joseph d'Albert, the son of the Duc de Luynes, saw through her disguise and called out, "Tell me, oh pretty bird, I've listened to your chirping, but now tell me of your plumage?"

"My chirping and my plumage are all of a piece, you insolent coxcomb," she answered, and reached for her sword.

They stepped outside. D'Albert was confident in his skill, but La Maupin parried two of his thrusts and then pierced his shoulder, sending six inches of steel out his back. She returned to her room, leaving his friends to carry him from the courtyard.

That night she slept poorly due to an unfamiliar sensation—a troubled conscience. The next morning, she asked the town's barber (who doubled as a surgeon) about her victim and was told he would recover. D'Albert's friends passed along his apologies for having insulted her, and she agreed to meet with him. Apparently, her *épée* had had the effect of Cupid's arrow. He insisted she nurse him back to health and she agreed, beginning a love affair that was interrupted only when he was recalled to his regiment.

Hitting the road, La Maupin fell in with Gabriel-Vincent Thévenard, a singer who, like her, hoped to make a career in Paris. She first had to attend to the untidy matter of her death sentence, though, and dropped by the country estate of the Comte d'Armagnac. The count must have retained a soft spot for her because he interceded for her with the king, who personally remanded her death sentence, saying he could not see consigning someone so talented, lovely, and wanton to the ash heap.

Both Thévenard and La Maupin took Paris by storm. In about 1691, she debuted at the Paris Opera as Pallas Athena in *Cadmus et Hermione* and was lauded as the most beautiful woman in the company. It was the fashion for gentlemen to choose their mistresses from among the Opera's dancers and singers, but while La Maupin dallied with them, she continued to pursue "amours in keeping with her dress," as Cameron Rogers put it.

According to Cameron Rogers' 1928 book *Gallant Ladies*, there was a leading tenor at the Opera named Duméni, a drunkard known for making crude advances to his female costars. After he dispensed one such remark to La Maupin, she quietly responded, "We shall speak of this again." He laughed but did not find it so amusing when, on his walk home, a figure stepped out of the shadows and cuffed his head. Disguised as a man, in a wide hat that hid her face, La Maupin challenged him. He pleaded that he did not know how to use his sword.

"Then, as you insult women and lack the courage to defend yourself against men, I shall give myself the pleasure of punishing an insolent rogue and humiliating a coward," she replied. She spun him around, bent him over, and administered 50 strokes to his backside with a cane. She left him quivering; then, in an afterthought, returned and took his watch and snuffbox.

The following evening, Duméni told the assembled theatrical company about the assault, although in his version he had been jumped by three robbers. "Realizing that I was in a tight corner, I determined to make a fight for it and went for them like a lion—the beggars won't have forgotten yet the weight of my arm—and despite the odds against me, I made them take to their heels," he said.

La Maupin let him milk the story for all it was worth before interrupting him:

> Ladies, what Duméni has just told you is a flagrant untruth. He was attacked but by me alone. This abject animal who so glibly insults women trembles like an aspen at the point of a sword. After giving him a buffet I asked for satisfaction; he shook like a chicken. On his refusal to cross swords I gave him a sound thrashing, and to prove his cowardice I took his snuffbox and watch.

She displayed them to the hooting company. What was left of Duméni trickled through the floorboards.

In 1695, d'Albert had a respite from war in the Low Countries (present-day Belgium and Holland) and returned to Paris. He fought a few duels, broke a few hearts, and had a brief, passionate reunion with La Maupin before returning to the Siege of Namur. Looking for stimulation after his departure, she put on her best cavalier costume and crashed a ball at the Palais Royal given by the king's brother, who was himself a notorious cross-dresser. There her eye lit upon an attractive marquise. La Maupin showered her with unwanted attention, at last kissing her passionately on the mouth. The marquise's three gentleman suitors sprang to her defense, demanding that La Maupin leave. She agreed on the condition that they all face her on the street outside, cold steel in hand. Not realizing she was a woman, they accepted.

The street lamps had not been lit because there was a full moon that night, but it was obscured by clouds. As the duelists waited for the clouds to pass, the first gentleman twice tried to surprise La Maupin with sudden thrusts. She easily batted them away and chided him, "Be patient. Why do you want to end the evening so quickly?"

The clouds parted.

"Now I'm going to strike you properly," she said, and she did so. He slumped bleeding to the street.

The second gentleman attacked, shouting, "This steel is wielded by a sure hand!"

La Maupin parried his blows, while maneuvering him until the moon was to her back and shone full upon him. "Now that I have gotten a good look at you—*farewell!*" she said, pinning his shoulder against a wall.

The third did not even wait until she had returned to en garde before he began his assault. He fought with a mixture of fury and desperation, but La Maupin maintained her sangfroid, mocking him as she turned aside his every thrust. As the shafts of steel flickered in the moonlight, she teased, "Slowly, slowly, your turn will come! Getting angry never helped anyone. Be calm, my kind gentleman. Look, you almost scratched me!"

She indulged herself for a few minutes of blade crossing and badinage, then feinted and launched a thrust *par la ligne basse* (on the low line), piercing his thigh.

"*Touché!*" he gasped.

"The contrary would have surprised me," she responded. Sheathing her sword, she saluted her fallen opponents, then returned to the ball and sought out the king's brother.

"Monseigneur," she told him, "in the Rue Saint-Thomas du Louvre three gentlemen lie stretched on the pavement, who have need of prompt assistance. Less than an hour ago they were excessively hot in the head, but the night air might perhaps cool them a little over-much. Kindly give orders that they may be taken to their homes."

Seeing in La Maupin his own mirror image, the king's brother was amused, but not so the king himself. Once again discretion seemed the better part of valor, and La Maupin relocated to Brussels where she became the pampered mistress of Maximilian Emanuel, the Elector of Bavaria. After a year, he switched his affections to a countess and tried to pay Maupin off with 40,000 francs, which he sent to her via his new mistress's own husband. La Maupin threw the money in the count's face, saying it was a present fit only for a cuckold such as the count himself. After a sojourn in Spain, where she was reduced to working as a chambermaid, she returned to the Paris Opera in 1698. Three years had passed, all was forgiven, and she was welcomed back exuberantly by her public, as well as by d'Albert.

La Maupin had a falling out with Thévenard, her former lover and costar at the Opera, whom she felt had insulted her publicly. Remembering very well what had happened to Duméni, Thévenard was terrified. He didn't even dare venture from the theater, but ate and slept in his dressing room. Finally he could stand it no longer and wrote her the following letter, which appears in *Gallant Ladies*:

My Dear Julie [this is the only evidence we have that her first name was Julie]: Everyone in the world has his good points and bad. I freely admit that you handle a sword far better than I do; you will admit that I sing better than you. With this settled, you will understand that were you to embed only three fingers of steel in my chest, my voice, providing that I were not killed, would be seriously injured, and I rely absolutely on the livelihood it wins me apart from the pleasure it affords me by allowing me to mirror myself in your eyes when we act together and you do not glare at me, a procedure which much alters the sweetness of your expression.

Let us, then, make peace, my dear Julie; I come to place myself bound hand and foot before you (in writing of course, considering the danger of an interview); pardon a blunder which I sincerely repent and be merciful to me.

She responded,

Since M. Thévenard so frankly admits the distaste he entertains for a meeting sword in hand, even with woman, which leaves me no course but to congratulate him upon his prudence, I consent to forgive him, but I desire that since I have promised him my pardon, he should ask me for it in the presence of those who were witnesses of the insult to which it refers. Let him assemble those witnesses together and I will keep my word.

Thévenard duly apologized to Maupin in the foyer of the Opera. She also dealt with the ungentlemanly Baron de Servan, a fop and braggart who liked to boast of real and imagined conquests of the ladies of the theater, as well as his triumphs at dueling. Finally he went too far, impugning the reputation of a young dancer who had resisted his advances. Disguised in her male garb, La Maupin presented herself as the Chevalier de Raincy, called the baron out as an infamous liar, and let the wind out of him with a thrust through the arm. When he learned that he had been defeated by a woman, he closed his townhouse and retired to his country estate.

On September 6, 1700, La Maupin was the subject of a police report. Arriving late at her Rue Saint-Honoré lodging, she had demanded supper, and when her landlord wasn't quick enough about it she grabbed a spit from beside the fireplace and gave him a beating. The servants tried to subdue her, but she soon laid them all out. Once again the good offices of the Comte d'Armagnac were required to get the charges dismissed.

She maintained her on-again, off-again romance with d'Albert, who, like herself, spread his affections rather widely. She generally took his dalliances in stride, but grew jealous of his budding relationship with the Duchesse of Luxembourg. La Maupin sat beside the noblewoman at Sunday mass, and as they knelt in prayer whispered to her that she would cut her throat if she ever again invited d'Albert to her boudoir.

There are different versions of the rest of La Maupin's brief life. One has it that she and d'Albert settled down and lived happily until her death. According to the other, d'Albert was arrested for killing a man in a duel, and after serving two years in prison he left Paris and married one Mademoiselle de Montigny, who came with an income of 40,000 crowns. A disconsolate La Maupin swore off men and struck up with Madame Marquise de Florensac, but their two-year affair ended with the marquise's sudden death. La Maupin then retired from the Opera and entered a convent. A biographer suggested that the struggle to devote her unruly passions exclusively to the incorporeal body of Christ was too much for her, and she died at the age of 37.

27 Donald McBane

I t is rare to find a war memoir written by the common foot
soldier before the 19th century. One of the few is by
Scotland's Donald McBane, a fencing master, duelist, pimp,
and gambler who fought in the War of the Spanish Succession
(1701–1714) and set down his experiences in *The Expert Sword-
Man's Companion: Or the True Art of Self-Defence. With an
Account of the Authors Life, and his Transactions during the Wars
with France.*

In 1687, at age 23, McBane left his apprenticeship to a
tobacco spinner and joined the army in search of adventure. In
his first battle, a struggle between clans, his side was outnumbered two to one. As the enemy charged, waving swords and
Lochaber axes, wistful thoughts of his prior occupation flitted

through McBane's mind. His wooden-handled plug bayonet was cut from the muzzle of his musket, and when he attempted to use his musket as a club, his stock broke in two. He participated enthusiastically in the general rout.

Over the next few years glory continued to elude him. He was routed in another battle, and in 1692 an older soldier was assigned to handle his pay because McBane had proven unable to manage it himself. Unfortunately, the old soldier treated it as his own, and when McBane asked for money he got a blow instead. It did no good to complain: military men were expected to settle such difficulties themselves. McBane had no dueling weapon but took two weeks of fencing lessons, borrowed a smallsword, had a few drinks, and challenged his foe.

The two went to a lonely spot at dusk, and McBane learned that a few lessons do not a swordsman make. After two passes the old soldier knocked McBane's weapon from his hand with his broadsword, then chased him, beating him with the flat of its blade. In a further indignity, he retrieved the sword McBane had dropped and pawned it for two gallons of ale.

McBane returned to the fencing master and took a lesson on how to employ the smallsword against the broadsword. On the following payday McBane again demanded his money, was again rebuffed with a blow, and again arranged a rendezvous. Having lost one sword already, he couldn't find anyone to lend him another and had to borrow one without permission.

The old soldier warned McBane that he didn't intend to let him off so lightly this time and would lop off an arm or leg, but after a few passes McBane put his lesson into action. He kept a low guard, and when the old soldier slashed at his leg he slipped the blow and, before the other could recover, McBane thrust him through the body. As he fell forward, McBane skewered him through the leg "lest he should run after me as before."

McBane took the old soldier's sword and went to the alehouse, where he traded it for the sword he had lost, and then returned the sword he had purloined. True to the code, the old soldier refused to tell his superiors how he had been wounded, so McBane suffered no repercussions. From that day on he was master of his own pay as well as that of his former exploiter. "I then began to think something of myself, and purchased a sword," he wrote. He continued studying fencing until he was his master's top student.

In 1695, McBane helped guard a party of men being marched to Leith for shipment to Flanders. After completing his duty, he went aboard ship for a few drinks, passed out, and woke up at sea. Having thus volunteered, he participated in the Siege of Namur, taking part in six assaults and receiving three wounds from bullets and six from bayonets. He convalesced in Brussels.

A few years later McBane was stationed at Perth. After his corporal discovered him absent from his guard post, he gave him a beating. McBane waited until the corporal was off duty, then challenged him. The corporal accepted, asking, "Are you for life or death?"

"I am for anything that happens," responded McBane.

McBane dropped his man with a thrust to the chest.

"Run, you rogue, for I am killed," the corporal cried, as blood coursed from his wound. A man of honor, he not only forgave McBane but gave him three shillings, all the money he had, to help him make his escape. (To his amazement, McBane later encountered the corporal in Holland, fully recovered—"I took him by the Hand and we went and took a Bottle.") As McBane fled, he encountered his commanding officer and told him of his plight. His officer gave him an additional half-crown (two and a half shillings) and provided an introduction to a captain in Glasgow with whom McBane could enlist.

While McBane was passing through Stirling, a press gang of two soldiers and a drummer attempted to make him their prisoner. McBane jumped to the far side of a ditch and drew his sword. As the soldiers came at him, he stabbed one through the shoulder and the other through the hand. Begging his pardon, they retreated to have their wounds dressed.

Fearing pursuit, McBane kept a low profile for the rest of his journey. He hooked up with the captain in Glasgow and shipped out for Ireland the following morning. He was stationed in Dublin, where he studied fencing with a French master. After 18 months of training McBane was qualified to call himself a master and set up his own school.

Late in life McBane compiled his lessons in his combination fencing manual-autobiography *The Expert Swordsman's Companion*. They included nothing he had not tried out in combat and were uninhibited by punctilious concerns. He recommended the smallsword over the broadsword because a man wielding the latter tires sooner. He also favored the thrust over the cut, for "you may Receive Forty Cuts and not be Disabled," while a single thrust can kill. If you are able to spring to the side of your opponent and thrust him in the back, do so, "for all is fair play, whil'st Swords are presented and you are Disputing the Victory." He also favored attacking an opponent's sword arm, hand, and wrist, because it allows disabling him without leaving oneself open. He taught that it is less dangerous to retire than advance, "and not at all Scandalous," because an opponent often throws himself open when he attempts a thrust. One should be prepared for the possibility that an opponent may have a hidden pistol or a pocketful of sand to throw in one's face. For such knaves, McBane reserved his "Boar's Thrust," dropping his sword hand to knee level and thrusting upward under the opponent's guard: "This is what is called a Poke," he wrote, "which many find fault with. I would never make use of this Thrust but when engaged with a *Ruffin* or some Person that I had a mind to Kill. Before and after a fight, you should never turn your back on an opponent, let him get near you without having your weapon in hand, nor accept his admission of defeat until he is disarmed." He also advised that one keep one's temper, saying that

> if you do Command it, and are Engaged with a Person who can not, you will have very much the Advantage of him, for his Passion will make him Play wild and wide, and consequently exposes himself to be Hit very often, whereas your thoughts not being in Hurry or Confusion, you may Defend your self with ease and Judgement, and take an Advantage readily when ever you have a mind.

At the end of the 17th century McBane's regiment was shipped to Brabant (present-day southern Belgium), where there were eight English battalions, eight battalions of Dutch and Scots, and eight regiments of horse and dragoons. Perceiving an opportunity, McBane began giving fencing lessons. As was often the case, the established masters resented the competition, forcing McBane to fight and win 24 bouts before he was allowed to teach in peace.

McBane discovered that four of the local swordsmen had a lucrative sideline in prostitution and gambling, and he

> resolved to have a share of that Gain, or at least to have a fair Tryall for it. I Fought all the four, one by one: the last of them was Left-hand-ed; he and I went to the Rampart where we searched one another for Fire Arms. Finding none, we drew and had two or three clean Turns: at last he put up his Hand and took a

Pistol from the Cock of his Hat; he cocked it against his shoulder and presented it to me, upon which I asked Quarters, but he refused, calling me an *"English* Bouger," and Fired at me and run for it. One of the balls went through my Cravat. I thinking I was shot did not Run as I was wont to do, but run as I could after him, crying for the Guard . . . at last I overtook him...and gave him a thrust in the buttocks . . . . [I] call'd for his Commerads that same Night, who agreed to give me a *Brace* of Whoors, and Two *Petty Couns* a Week. With this and my School I lived very well for that *Winter.*

McBane noted that he risked his life four or five times a day on account of his operations.

The year 1701 saw the outbreak of the War of Spanish Succession, in which France, then the dominant power in Europe, fought Great Britain, Austria, Holland, Denmark, some of the German states, and Portugal. McBane served in the Royal Scots Regiment in the force commanded by the Duke of Marlborough. Between battles he continued to run an alehouse, a gambling tent, and a string of prostitutes.

While on his way to purchase a barrel of beer, McBane lost his purse to a roadside bunco artist. Not one to accept defeat graciously, McBane took back his money and the swindler's as well. The swindler called for help, and seven of his cronies fell on McBane with their swords. McBane held a stick in his left hand to parry blows and wielded his double-edged spadroon with his right. Fighting his way back to his camp, he put five of them out of the fight, but was severely pressed by the remaining two until he reached safety. Badly cut up, he called to his mistress to get him a surgeon, but she screamed at him for coming home without the beer, "calling me Rogue and a Hundred worse Names," and only calmed down when he gave her half the money he had stolen.

The Battle of Blenheim, on August 13, 1704, was the first major defeat a French army had suffered in 50 years. Casualties were unusually heavy, the French losing 18,000 men, the British and their allies 12,000. McBane was shot four times and received five bayonet wounds and was left for dead on the battlefield. At night, plundering Dutch troops (allies, yet!) stripped him of his clothes, clubbing him when he was reluctant to give up his shirt. He lay "expecting Death every minute, not only by reason of Wounds, but by reason of the Cold and great Thirst that I had, I drank several handfulls of the Dead Mens Blood I lay beside, the more I Drank the worse I was."

McBane was found the following day and sent to the rear to recover. A month later he was on the street in Marelykin, walking with crutches, when he came upon a gambling operation run by an Italian soldier serving in a German regiment. Seeking a share of the profits, McBane sent for a sword and challenged him. As he described the scene, "The Italian and I went to it, he was Lame of his Left Arm, and I of my Legs, you may judge how the Spectators did Laugh to see two Lame Men Fight." McBane earned a partnership.

Even war was a bit of a racket for our hero. He regularly led parties of men "partisaning" behind French lines, collecting a bounty of enemy troops, horses, and weapons.

In 1707, according to his memoirs, McBane quarreled over a woman with a French swordsman attached to a Dutch regiment:

> He challenged me immediately to Answer him, so we went out to the back of an old Trench where he shewed me Five Graves which he had filled, and told me I should be the Sixth, (we had a great many Spectators both *Dutch* and *English*) if I would not yield him the *Lady*, for shame I could not but Fight him, he drew his Sword, and with it drew a Line, saying, that should be my Grave; I told him it was too short

for me, likewise I did not love to ly wet at Night, but said it would fit him better; we fell to it, he advanced upon me so I was obliged to give Way a little, I bound his Sword and made a half Thrust at his Breast, he Timed[16] me and wounded me in the Mouth; we took another turn, I took a little better care, and gave him a Thrust in the body, which made him very angry; he came upon me very boldly, some of the Spectators cryed stand your Ground, I wished them in my Place, then I gave him a Thrust in the Belly, he then darted [threw] his Sword at me, I Parried it, he went and lay down on his Coat and spake none. . . . His Commerads were glad he was off the Stage, for he was very troublesome.

McBane had less luck with a quartermaster who took the sum of 10 crowns and the earrings from one of his ladies. The quartermaster accepted his challenge, and the two went to an out-of-the-way place where the quartermaster laid out his booty, to be returned if McBane could beat him. Wrote McBane:

> Then we took a Turn . . . but I could make nothing of him, so we took Breath a little, and fell to it again and Closed one another, and secured one another's Swords, but none of us could get Advantage of another; we had Five such Turns, but could make nothing of it, we were Four or Five Times through [each] others Shirts, but could not draw Blood.

The quartermaster, as it happened, was an Irish fencing master. They called it quits, with the Irishman returning the

---

16. A time thrust is made against an opponent as he attacks.

whore's earrings, and, as McBane summed it up, "As for the Money we agreed to Drink it and let the Whore work for more."

The results were far worse when McBane tried to muscle in on a gambling concession when he was stationed in Soignies, and, according to his own account, "The Master answered, he had a Point on his Sword, I told him mine had another, then we went to try it in a little Wood in the Rear of the Camp; we no sooner drew but he cryed for help." A mob of the man's cronies chased McBane, beat him, and threw him in a watering hole where he lay all night. He spent a month recovering.

In 1709 McBane was put in charge of six cannon, with 16 men under his command. During the siege of a citadel near Tournai, he was among the men sheltering in a trench when the French raked it with enfilading cannon fire. As he told it in his memoirs,

> With one Shot they Killed Forty-eight Men, I Escaped the Shot, but one of the Heads of the Men that was Shot, knocked me down, and all his Brains came round my Head, I being half Senseless put up my Hand to my Head, and finding the Brains, cryed to my Neighbour that all my Brains were knock'd out; he said were your Brains out you could not speak.

Yet another personal difficulty arose when two Dutch dragoons tried to take a captured horse from him. Drawing his sword, McBane recalls, "I Defended as I could, but some of them was so Foolish as to run upon the Point of it . . ." The incident nearly got McBane hanged, but the Earl of Orkney's aide-de-camp interceded and helped him slip the noose.

By the time the war ground to a halt, McBane had fought in Holland, Germany, Flanders, and France, taken part in 16 battles and 52 sieges, and been in too many scraps to count. He had been wounded 27 times, was "Carv'd with Cuts and Scars," and carried two musket balls in his thigh and a plate of silver in his skull. Surprisingly hale, he returned to England, took a new wife, and set up a school and an alehouse in London. Making his debut at 50, he fought 37 times at the Bear Garden, where gladiatorial bouts with the backsword attracted large crowds.

During the Jacobite rebellion of the 1740s he enlisted as a sergeant of dragoons and had the honor of guarding the regimental colors at the Battle of Preston. During a hard winter his leg wounds began suppurating, and he was recommended for Chelsea Hospital, but preferred a transfer to Fort William in the Western Highlands of Scotland, where he served as a gunner.

In 1726, McBane was living in Edinburgh when an Irish swordsman, Andrew O'Bryan, arrived in town and stationed himself along one of the main thoroughfares, beating a drum and derisively challenging all Scots. O'Bryan was touring Britain after a winning season at the Bear Garden. The Duke of Hamilton and the Duke of Argyle sent for McBane and requested that he take up the challenge if he thought himself up to it. As evidence that he was, McBane picked up a claymore and swept it around over his head, making it whistle in the air. By way of letting O'Bryan know that his challenge had been accepted, McBane put his foot through one side of his drum and his fist through the other. As the bout approached, some passersby in the street asked McBane if he was confident his arm still had sufficient strength. He leapt up, grabbed a crossbar on a lamppost with one hand, and swung for a moment before dropping down. "She'll do yet," he assured them.

The bout took place on a stage erected in St. Anne's Yards at the back of the cavalry grounds attached to the palace, and it lasted several hours. McBane was the victor; as he wrote, "I gave him Seven Wounds, and broke his Arm with the *Fauchion* [a short curved sword], this I did at the Request of several *Noblemen* and *Gentlemen*. But now being Sixty-three Years of Age, resolves never to Fight any more, but to Repent for my former Wickedness."

Repentance: indeed a worthy project for McBane's golden years.

28 Mgobozi

I have lived by the spear,
and today I die by the spear.
That is how it should be.
— Mgobozi,
in his last battle

No man was more devoted to Shaka, king of the Zulu, than his friend from childhood Mgobozi-ovela-entabeni (Mgobozi-of-the-Hill). When both were common warriors in the army of Chief Dingiswayo, there were many times that the huge, powerful Mgobozi covered Shaka's back. Even though Mgobozi belonged to a tribe the Zulu considered inferior, when Shaka rose to power he appointed him drillmaster of his army. In fact, Shaka offered him the position of commander in chief, but Mgobozi declined, saying, "Nay, my father, that would be a mistake, for when I am in a battle I see only my own *assegai* [spear] and the man before me, and I forget all else. A small command at most I could manage in battle. To drill your army in peace, and to advise you in council, that I could do, but when it

243

comes to fighting, just let me be your leading warrior who starts the killing."

Mgobozi typified the ideal of the Zulu warrior: strong, proud, fierce, fearless, and loyal to his chief and comrades. Every young recruit in the Zulu army strove to emulate him. He relentlessly drilled them to execute orders instantly and flawlessly. Warriors marching at double time had to keep a straight line even over rough ground, and those who fell out without good reason were killed on the spot with their own spears. Close-quarter combat was practiced in war games, where warriors were trained to fight in silence so that they could hear the orders of their officers. Complex maneuvers had to be mastered, in which the "horns of the bull" (flanking elements) would encircle the foe and "shut the back gate" (cut off retreat).

Mgobozi was a strict taskmaster, but his men knew he had their best interests at heart. "Do I want to see you eaten by buzzards and hyenas after the next battle, merely because you were too stupid or lazy to understand that what I am trying to teach you today will save you tomorrow?" he would ask. In battle, Mgobozi led the attack, wading into the enemy and issuing few orders to his regiment beyond an enthusiastic, "Stab, lads, stab!"

In 1818, Shaka's army fought the mighty army of the Ndwandwe chief Zwide at Qokli Hill. Mgobozi and his men were kept in reserve early on, duty under which he chafed. When Shaka at last ordered him into battle, Mgobozi plunged his small phalanx into the midst of the enemy. Shrugging off stab wounds as if they were pinpricks, he slew Ndwandwe by the bushel, but suddenly, in the midst of the fighting, he collapsed. His men shouted, "They have killed Mgobozi-of-the-Hill!" and the cry was picked up by hundreds of voices. The Zulu went mad with rage, slaying 1,500 Ndwandwe within such a small area that there was a mound of corpses over Mgobozi's body. In all, the battle cost the lives of about 7,500 Ndwandwe and 1,500 Zulu.

Despite their great victory, there was gloom that night in the

Zulu camp. Shaka visited the mound of corpses beneath which Mgobozi lay, and beside which one of the bodyguards devotedly stood. After a moment of respectful silence, Shaka observed, "Someone is dragging dry hides [snoring] in there." Recognizing the sound, he called out, "Mgobozi!"

After he called three times he heard a deep response, as if out of a tomb: "*Yebo, Baba* [Yes, father]."

"What are you doing in there?" asked Shaka.

"I don't know, but the hill has collapsed on top of me," came the answer.

The men quickly freed Mgobozi, who had received no serious wounds but had passed out from blood loss. He sat up, still clutching his spear in his hand, looked around, and said, "*Hau,* it looks as if there has been some fighting here."

A joyous cheer went up that Mgobozi had returned from the dead. His fierce, leonine visage broke into a smile. "Yes, men, I have returned!" he announced. "Who otherwise would have continued to plague you?"

With belief in witchcraft strong throughout Africa, those who claimed to be able to "smell out" witches wielded great power. They traveled with a retinue of club-wielding "slayers," who would seize and execute those they fingered, usually those who had offended the witch doctors or were otherwise unpopular. The Zulu chief was safe from denunciation, but he could not interfere in the witch doctors' judgments. However, a condemned man could appeal for sanctuary if he escaped from the slayers and reached the foot of the chief.

After a series of bad omens, five witch doctors came to Bulawayo, Shaka's kraal, to hold a smelling-out ritual. Among them was Nobela, a notoriously vicious woman. They whipped themselves into a frenzy and then prowled past the assemblage. Nobela stopped before Mgobozi. While "driving goats" (a Zulu euphemism for being drunk), he had once spat at the mention of her name and likened her to a hyena's anus. This was her chance to settle the score, and Shaka was powerless to intervene.

Four slayers grabbed Mgobozi, but he was more than their match. He kneed one in the groin, drove his head into the solar plexus of another, tore free of the two still standing, and, grabbing a club that one of the slayers had dropped, finished them off. Then he ran to Shaka's feet and received sanctuary. Shaka, who himself did not believe in witchcraft, accused Nobela of wrongfully accusing Mgobozi, and advised her to reconsider her verdict carefully; after all, he pointed out, Mgobozi still wielded a club, and there was no one present who could prevent him from using it to spill her brains. With this in mind, Nobela quickly concluded that Mgobozi had been the unwitting—and therefore entirely *innocent*—tool of a sorcerer.

In 1826, the northern branch of the Ndwandwe tribe again went to war against Shaka. As the massive armies neared each other, Shaka decided that the only way to defeat the Ndwandwe force was to divide it. According to E.A. Riter's *Shaka Zulu*, Mgobozi immediately volunteered to spearhead the thrust. In a tribal custom called *giya*, he gave a wild performance in front of the Zulu army, leaping, spinning, and spearing the air. When he was finished, he announced: "Thus shall I go, spearing my way through the serried ranks of the foe, until I emerge in their rear or die—and so must we all do for our Father."

Inspired by Mgobozi, other champions pledged to join him, but Shaka was disheartened, fearing that his best friend would be killed. When he raised his concerns, Mgobozi answered,

> My Father, we must all die sooner or later, and if my time has come nothing will hold it back. It is far, far better to die with the joy of battle in the heart than to pine away with age, or like a sick ox in a kraal. I have lived by the spear and I shall die by it. That is a man's death. You would not deprive me of that, who are my friend as well as my Father?

Unable to dissuade him, Shaka ordered beer that they might celebrate together.

The following day, Mgobozi led his champions against the Ndwandwe front. They stabbed their way completely through the ranks, including regiments of veterans, and when they broke through, found themselves facing a boulder the size of a house. Mgobozi and his men put their backs to it and made their stand, completely cut off from the rest of their army. The Ndwandwe recognized Mgobozi as the warrior who had single-handedly inflicted such heavy losses on them at Qokli Hill and attacked him in a fury. Their first wave broke against his men's spears, and Mgobozi expressed satisfaction with his champions' fine work. As the Ndwandwe pulled back to regroup, Mgobozi called out to the main Zulu force, "We have got the bull by the testicles here. Do you now stab him in the chest!"

At the order from their drillmaster, the Zulu tore into the Ndwandwe. Forty thousand warriors fought a desperate battle. The air was filled with their grunting and screaming, the bumping and scraping of their shields, and the sound of spears thudding into flesh. The Zulu victory cry—"*Ngadla! Ngadla!*"—rose above the din.

Once again there came a lull as both sides stepped back for a moment's respite. Mgobozi still stood against the rock, bleeding from numerous flesh wounds but strong, his eyes gleaming with battle lust. "What a fight," said Mgobozi. "This is what I have always wished for." He then bade farewell to his men, saying,

> In the next clash we will all eat earth. For us the sun will rise no more, but I for one do not regret it. I have lived by the spear and today I die by the spear. That is how it should be. Look at the "mat" of corpses we have made for ourselves. It is a fit resting place for a king—and you are kings—all of you. Our enemies are men,

too, and have fought well, but they no longer relish closing with us, even though we are but few
now, and sorely stricken.

He then led his champions in a salute to Shaka: "The Zulu!
Their very essence! Hail, King of Kings! Thy will be done!"

Mgobozi's voice, and the realization that he still lived,
brought the main Zulu army to a fever pitch. It renewed its
attack in the desperate hope of rescuing him. Meanwhile,
Mgobozi was fighting like a berserker, leaping in among his enemies and scattering them. One by one his comrades fell until
only Mgobozi and one champion, Mashaya (Striker), were left.
In fending off yet another rush, Mashaya was stabbed in the
lungs and sank to the ground. Mgobozi stood alone, his blood—
mingled with that of his enemies—dripping off him, his red eyes
staring madly, and his chest heaving for breath. Over the heads
of his enemies he could see the Zulu army drawing nearer. The
Ndwandwe flung themselves at him, sticking him again and
again, but like a lion shaking off a pack of dogs he knocked them
away. For 30 seconds more, he piled up enemy corpses even as
the blood flowed from his gaping wounds, the battle madness
seeming to infuse him with inexhaustible power. At last, even
that was no longer enough and he sank beneath the onslaught.

Mgobozi's death availed the Ndwandwe little. The army he
had trained soon overwhelmed them, and only a few escaped.
The Zulu's victory celebration was muted, though. They realized
that the unimaginable had happened. Mgobozi was no more.

29 Usamah ibn-Munqidh

An Ismaili Muslim attacking Shayzar Castle charged Usamah ibn-Munqidh with an upraised dagger. With one sweep of his sword, Usamah cut the offending weapon in two and severed his assailant's arm at the elbow. The dagger left an imprint in his blade, easily recognizable as the trace of a knife. When an artisan offered to remove the dent, Usamah replied, "Leave it as it is! This is the best thing in my sword."

Usamah wore his battle scars proudly. Born in 1095, at the outset of the turbulent period of the First Crusade, he grew up a prince in Shayzar Castle, where his uncle was sultan. The castle was built atop a rocky ridge along the Orontes River, strategically placed to block one of the main approaches to Syria from the north. Usamah fought numerous battles there, not only against the Franks (the local term for European crusaders), but also Ismailis, Byzantines, Batinites, and assorted bandits. Shortly before his death, he dictated his memoirs, recounting events that struck him as noteworthy. They provide a rare and vivid depiction of life and war in 12th-century Syria.

Usamah's father, Majd-al-Din abu-Salamah Murshid, was a scholar and devout Muslim who spent his evenings transcribing the Koran, until by the end of his life he had made 46 complete copies, one in gold with lengthy annotations. He was also a man of action, "greatly addicted to warfare," who told his son, "It is in my horoscope that I should feel no fear." Although his father lived a long time and died in bed, "his body bore scars of terrible wounds," and Usamah gave the stories behind some of them. In one battle, his father received a chest wound in a small spot exposed because his attendant had failed to close a hook on his mail coat. In the same battle, a lance pierced his forearm, severing a nerve and causing him to drop his weapon. (Fortunately, Usamah noted, it didn't affect his calligraphy.) An arrow once hit him in the lower leg but was stopped by a dagger he had in his boot. Another time, he was in full armor when a javelin struck the nose guard of his helmet, bending it inward and causing his nose to bleed, but otherwise bringing him no harm. As Usamah notes, "If Allah (praise be to his name!) had decreed that the javelin should deviate from the helmet's nasal, then it would have killed him."

As a young man, Usamah received 10 years of private tutoring in grammar, calligraphy, poetry, and the Koran, but his real training was as a warrior. From an early age he hunted with his father, learning to spot game, handle weapons, and use terrain. He thought so little of bloodshed that as a child of 10 he stabbed to death one of his father's attendants who had shoved him, and the only thing that struck him as noteworthy about the incident was that another servant fainted at the sight of the blood. There was no parental rebuke; indeed, he wrote, "I never saw my father (may Allah's mercy rest upon his soul!) forbid my taking

KIRCHNER

part in a combat or facing a danger, in spite of all the sympathy and preference he cherished towards me." He could think of only one exception—a time when, while hunting, he approached a crouching lion, alone, armed with his spear. His father yelled, "Face it not, thou crazy one! It will get thee!" But Usamah continued to advance and killed it with a single thrust.

In his first combat, Usamah led a small cavalry detachment accompanying a group of peasants who were to pillage the crops of the city of Afamiyah, from which the Franks had just been driven. No resistance was expected, but as the peasants spread over the field a large army of Frankish horsemen appeared and began pushing the Muslim horsemen back. As Usamah wrote in his autobiographical *An Arab-Syrian Gentleman and Warrior in the Period of the Crusades,*

> Death seemed an easy thing to me in comparison with the loss of that crowd in my charge. So I turned against a horseman in their vanguard, who had taken off his coat of mail in order to be light enough to pass before us, and thrust my lance into his chest. He instantly flew off his saddle, dead. I then faced their horsemen as they followed, and they all took to flight. Though a tyro in warfare, and never before that day taken part in a battle, I, with a mare under me as swift as a bird, went on, now pursuing them and plying them with my lance, now taking cover from them.

Hearing of his son's performance, his father proudly quoted the Koran:

> The coward among men flees precipitately before danger facing his own mother,
> But the brave one protects even him whom it is not his duty to protect.

His uncle the sultan often entrusted Usamah with important missions and personally oversaw his military education, stressing presence of mind in combat. In a battle against the army of Hamah, one of the enemy's best knights, Alwan al-Iraqi, charged Usamah's company of 15 cavaliers. When they refused to give ground, Alwan al-Iraqi turned and headed back toward his army. Usamah rode after him, caught him as he reentered his line, and killed him with a lance thrust, breaking the lance in the process. Weaponless, beneath the very battle flags of the enemy, Usamah wheeled his horse and headed back toward his men, who were charging forward in support. Afterward, his uncle, who had observed the action, asked him, "Where didst thou thrust Alwan al-Iraqi?"

"I meant to thrust him in the back," Usamah replied, "but the effect of the wind on my streamer made the weapon swerve and fall on his side."

"Thou art right," responded the sultan. "Thou certainly hadst presence of mind on that occasion." While presence of mind was key to the warrior's success, victory could never be guaranteed. Once, when the sultan sent him into battle, Usamah asked, "O my lord, instruct me as to how I should conduct myself when I meet the enemy." He never forgot his uncle's reply: "O my boy, war conducts itself."

Usamah spent time in all the capitals of the Muslim world—Damascus, Jerusalem, Cairo, Mosul, Mecca—and fought in Palestine, Egypt, and the Sinai. His rambling narrative mentions incidents haphazardly, usually to illustrate a larger point (its original title means "teaching by example"). For example, he mentions that in one battle his horse was killed and he received 50 sword blows because his groom failed to properly attach his reins to the bit—this to teach the lesson that seeming "trifles may lead to serious results." He tells us that he once chased a band of brigands through a ravine, without waiting for the rest of his troops to back him up, trusting that the narrowness of the pass would prevent more than one of his enemies being able to fight him at a time. He drove them back and they jettisoned some of their stolen goods, but he admitted that had he waited for the troops he might have killed all the brigands and recovered all their loot, pointing out "the disadvantages of excessive audacity." He tells of the time he and an uncle, Jum'ah, were reconnoitering a crusader castle and spotted eight mounted Franks in the road ahead. His uncle wished to press the advantage of surprise, but Usamah chivalrously replied, "This is not fair. We should rather make an open assault on them, both thou and I." They attacked them head on and routed them. For a few moments Usamah swelled with pride, until a foot soldier began shooting arrows at them from the hill on which the castle stood. With no bows and arrows of their own, Usamah and his uncle were forced to flee—two knights routed by an infantryman, he ruefully reported. "One should not put too much trust in his own courage, nor take too much pride in his own intrepidity" was the moral he drew from that experience.

Usamah was related by marriage to Amir Iftikhar-al-Dawlah, the lord of the castle of abu-Qubays. Four brothers had resolved to assassinate the lord at a time when he was alone in the castle with his son. They stealthily entered his bedroom and stabbed him as he slept, and then, leaving him for dead, went in search of his son. But al-Dawlah, Usamah tells us, "was endowed by Allah with unusual strength." He arose from his bed, naked, picked up his sword, and went after them. Encountering their leader, al-Dawlah swung at him and then jumped aside, afraid the assassin might reach him with his knife. But when he looked back the man lay face down on the floor, slain by that single blow. He then killed the second man, again with one blow. The other assassins fled, jumping from the castle wall. One died from the fall, but the other escaped. When the news reached Usamah and his family at Shayzar, they sent congratulations and, a few days later, paid him a visit. As they talked, al-Dawlah said, "The back of my shoulder is itching in a place where I cannot reach it," and summoned an attendant to find out if he had an insect bite. The attendant found the tip of one of his assailant's daggers, which had broken off under his skin and caused an infection.

Usamah noted that al-Dawlah was so powerful that he could grab a mule by the hoof and give it a beating without its being able to free its foot from his hand. He could also hold a horseshoe nail between his fingers and drive it into an oak board.

Another of Usamah's tangential tales, too good to omit, concerns the Atabek Tughdakin.

Ilghazi, prince of Maridin, had captured Robert, a wealthy Frankish lord who claimed that he would fetch a ransom of 10,000 dinars. Ilghazi sent him under guard to his lord, Tughdakin, hoping that he could intimidate Robert into offering an even higher sum for his release. Tughdakin was in his tent drinking when Robert arrived. He walked out of his tent, drew his sword, and lopped off Robert's head.

Ilghazi was aghast. "We are in need of even one dinar to pay our Turkoman soldiers," he railed. Here was a man who had fixed his own ransom at 10,000 dinars and whom I dispatched to thee so that thou mightest scare him and he might increase for us the sum, and thou hast killed him!"

Tughdakin replied, "I have no other way of scaring but this."

Usamah got to know the Franks in peace as well as in war, and though there were some he counted as friends, for the most part he found them crude, "animals possessing the virtues of courage and fighting, but nothing else." Nevertheless, he does not fail to provide examples of their valor. In one pitched battle, a Frankish knight charged into the midst of the Muslims. His horse was killed and he was pitched to the ground, where his enemies rained blows on him. He was wounded several times, but he kept fighting until he had broken through the Muslim crusader ranks and made it back to his own side. Some months later a crusader appeared at Shayzar

Castle with a letter of safe conduct, wishing to meet the knights there before he returned to Europe, having completed his pilgrimage. Usamah noted that his body was covered with scars and the mark of a sword cut ran diagonally across his face. When Usamah asked about the Frankish warrior, he was told that "this is the one who made a charge against the army of Isbaslar Mawdud, [and] whose horse was killed and who fought until he rejoined his comrades." Usamah observed, "Exalted is Allah who can do what he pleases as he pleases! Holding aloof no more retards fate than adventure hastens it."

It was fundamental to Usamah's belief that the duration of life is predetermined. As he declared in his memoirs:

> Let no one therefore assume for a minute that the hour of death is advanced by exposing one's self to danger, or retarded by overcautiousness. In the fact that I have myself survived is an object lesson, for how many terrors have I braved, and how many horrors and dangers have I risked! How many horsemen have I faced, and how many lions have I killed! How many sword cuts and lance thrusts have I received! How many wounds with darts and arbalest stones have been inflicted on me! All this while I was with regard to death in an impregnable fortress until I have now attained the completion of my ninetieth year!

A respected scholar and poet in his old age, Usamah was installed in a palace in Damascus by the great Saladin himself, who looked to him for counsel. By now Usamah had attained venerable status, but he chafed at a life of forced inaction. His hand, he noted, was "too feeble to carry a pen, after it had been strong enough to break a lance in a lion's breast." Several of his poems expressed his view that a long life was a mixed blessing:

I have always been the firebrand of battle:
every time it abated
I lit it again with the spark struck by apply-
ing the sword to the heads of the enemy.
My whole ambition was to engage in combat
with my rivals, whom I always took
For prey. They therefore were in constant
trembling on account of me.
More terrible in warfare than nighttime,
more impetuous in assault
Than a torrent, and more adventurous on
the battlefield than destiny!
But now I have become like an idle maid
who lies
On stuffed cushions behind screens and cur-
tains.
I have almost become rotten from lying still
so long, just as
The sword of Indian steel becomes rusty
when kept long in its sheath.
After being dressed with coats of mail, I now
dress in robes
Of Dabiqi fabric. Woe unto me and unto the
fabrics!
Luxury has never been my idea nor my
desired goal;
Comfort is not my affair nor my business.
I would never consent to attain glory
through ease,
Nor supreme rank, without breaking swords
and lances.

Usamah ibn-Munqidh died on November 16, 1188, at age
93. The historian Ibn-al-Athir attributed to him "a degree of
valor to which there is no limit," and Al-Dhahabi called him "a
veritable hero of Islam."

30 Audie Murphy

An officer who knew him once remarked that "had it not been for World War II, Murphy would have been a zero, a cipher." As it was, Audie Leon Murphy, of Company B, 15th Infantry Regiment, 3d Division, emerged as the best-known and most highly decorated American enlisted man of the millions who served. In two years of combat he took on snipers and machine gunners, captured prisoners and knocked out tanks, and went through the Wehrmacht like an angel of death, killing 241 by one count.[17]

Murphy was born to a poor Texas tenant-farming family, the seventh of 12 children. As a youngster he went to school in

---

17. This calculation was made by Murphy's friend David "Spec" McClure, coauthor of his memoirs. It includes German troops killed by artillery Murphy directed.

overalls that had shrunk up to his knees, earning him the nickname of Short-Breeches. Anyone who called him that had to fight him, though, and when Murphy fought he usually won.

To put meat on the table, he hunted with an old .22. He had a rare ability to spot squirrels in thick foliage at the tops of trees—in fact, he said he could actually *hear* the scrabbling of their claws against the bark. Once he spotted his target, a quick shot inevitably tumbled it from its perch. He could also hit rabbits on the run, even from the window of a moving car.

Murphy impressed his friends with his daring as much as his marksmanship. He would do anything on a bet, hopping on and off freight trains, climbing to the top of a water tower and sliding down a guy wire, and once diving almost 20 feet into a storage elevator filled with cottonseed. He and his friends often shot snuff cans off each other's heads and books out of each other's hands and even staged ".22 shootouts," shielding themselves behind trees. Stupid and dangerous games, but ones that may have helped instill Murphy's coolness under fire.

While Murphy was in his early teens his father deserted the family. Murphy, who hadn't gotten past the fifth grade, left school and picked up whatever work he could find, from farm labor to bagging groceries. His mother—"brokenhearted and broken in body"—died when he was 16. The three youngest Murphy children were put in an orphanage, and the older ones fended for themselves.

When World War II broke out Murphy was desperate to get into the service; combat seemed to be the one form of escape and adventure open to him. He tried to sign up with the marines and the paratroops, but, at a mere 5 feet 5 inches and 112 pounds, he was turned down. On June 20, 1942, his 18th birthday, the army took him in.[18] At first it didn't look like he would amount to much. He fainted during his first close-order drill, got bloody noses when he fired his .30-06 Springfield, and

---

18. Murphy may have lied about his age to join. Because he did not have a legally recorded birth certificate, he may have actually been 17, and some say 16.

couldn't carry the regulation 60-pound pack. His commanding officer felt he was better suited for cooks-and-bakers' school, and his sergeant, taking one look at his chubby, beardless face, gave him the unenviable nom-de-guerre of Baby. Murphy felt at home in the army, though, and soon proved himself a good soldier. He demonstrated leadership and received regular promotions. It was the first time in his life that he'd had decent clothing and good food, and during the next few years he grew four inches and put on nearly 40 pounds.

On July 4, 1943, before Murphy's 3d Division entered combat, it was addressed by Gen. Lucian Truscott, who told them, "You are going to meet the Boche! Carve your name in his face!" Murphy took the message to heart. Shortly after the invasion of Sicily, his patrol spotted two Italian officers on horseback. As they galloped away, he dropped to one knee and fired twice, tumbling both from their saddles. A shocked lieutenant asked him why he'd killed them. "That's our job, isn't it?" Murphy replied. In his postwar memoir *To Hell and Back*, Murphy described his reaction: "Now I have shed my first blood. I feel no qualms; no pride; no remorse. There is only a weary indifference that will follow me throughout the war." He had just been initiated into what a buddy sardonically called the Brotherhood of International Killers.

On March 2, 1944, Murphy, now a sergeant, earned his first medal, a Bronze Star. From an observation post he spotted a column of 20 Mark VI Tiger tanks heading toward American lines. Murphy called in an artillery strike. The lead tank was disabled, effectively blocking the route because the others didn't dare attempt the rain-soaked ground on either side of the hard-surfaced road. It was clear that there would be an attempt to repair or remove the tank, so after dark Murphy led a small patrol to finish it off, bringing along Molotov cocktails and grenades. The tank was easy to find in the darkness because an interior light showed from an open hatch. At 200 yards Murphy told his men to wait, and crept closer alone. He threw two Molotov cocktails against the tank, which failed to ignite, then tossed a grenade into the hatch, which didn't even put out its interior light. Murphy then blasted off its treads with six rifle-fired grenades. Nearby Germans began firing at him—as he recalled, the tracers were "a few inches from the ground and not nearly far enough away." He ran back to his patrol and led it to safety. This was the pattern that he would follow throughout the war: undertaking a dangerous mission alone rather than risking the lives of his men.

On August 15, after approaching Ramatuelle, France, Murphy's squad came under machine gun fire from a boulder-covered hillside. Leaving his men under cover, Murphy worked his way up the slope by following a gully. Rounding a bend, he ran into two Germans, who recoiled in surprise. He didn't, and killed them both with a burst from his M1 carbine. After dueling with a group of Germans in foxholes, he ran out of ammunition. Going back down the gully, he made his way to a U.S. light machine gun squad, but no amount of coaxing or cursing could induce the GIs to follow him. He commandeered their weapon and dragged it to the base of the hill, dousing a German machine gun crew with jacketed lead as they exposed their heads, killing two and wounding a third. He picked up the Browning and began climbing the hill, and again came under fire. Firing back, he killed two more. The ammunition belt now empty, he raced for the safety of the gully. While pondering his next move, empty carbine in hand, he was joined by his best friend, Lattie Tipton, who had brought along some loaded magazines. Tipton jokingly accused him of trying to hog all the glory, and added his favorite joke: "Come on—they can kill us, but they can't eat us."

As Murphy and Tipton moved forward, two Germans popped out of the brush and fired. Tipton whirled and killed them both. One of their bullets had clipped off part of his ear, but he insisted on continuing. He and Murphy came across two Germans huddled in a foxhole and shot them. Another machine gun opened up, and the two GIs responded with grenades and a burst of carbine fire. The machine gunners shouted "*Kamerad!*" and waved a white handkerchief. Against Murphy's better judgment, Tipton stood up to receive the Germans' surrender. He was promptly shot through the heart and collapsed, his last word, "Murph."

Murphy went berserk. He took out the crew of a nearby machine gun with a grenade, then picked up their belt-fed MG 42 and headed up the hill. He flanked the gun crew that had killed Tipton and closed in on them as they concentrated on targets downhill. He aimed deliberately and raked them with fire, watching their bodies flop and squirm, holding down the trigger until the rage left him, long after they were dead. Later he said, "That was a personal score to settle. I only went off the rail that once." For his action Murphy won the Distinguished Service Cross.

A month later, Murphy suffered his first wound. He was standing conversing with five men when a mortar shell landed between his feet. The explosion tore the heel from his shoe, gashed his foot, and cracked the stock on his carbine but otherwise left him uninjured, while two of the men beside him were killed and three badly wounded. After less than two weeks in the hospital, Murphy returned to his unit. He made a point of getting his old carbine back and fixed its stock with wire. He'd had good luck with it and prized it for its light, crisp trigger.

On October 2, after his unit had been halted for days at Cleurie Quarry by heavily entrenched German forces, the battalion commander and executive officer decided to get a first-hand look at the situation, picking four infantrymen to escort them up the hill. Describing himself as "bored with the lack of activity, which breeds the thinking I try to avoid," Murphy picked up his carbine, put a few grenades on his belt, and followed at a distance.

Ahead of him he heard the explosions of two German "potato masher" grenades and the tearing-silk sound of a burst from an MG-42. Three of the enlisted men were hit. The officers dived into a shallow hole, but it was only a matter of time before they would be finished off. Murphy made his way behind a large boulder flanking the German machine gun nest, then stepped out with his carbine in one hand and a grenade in the other. The Germans frantically swiveled their machine gun toward him, but its muzzle got caught on a branch and they missed. With two bursts of his carbine and a couple of grenades, Murphy killed four of them and wounded three. An eighth tried to run away. He was a fat man, and as he ran he struck Murphy as clown-like, but clown-like or not he had a gun, wore a German uniform, and had not surrendered, so Murphy cut him down.

The Silver Star was the next award.

Murphy was lucky, a fugitive from the law of averages if there ever was one, but it's hard to say where luck left off and his extraordinary skills took over. He moved quietly, used the terrain for cover, and was able to detect the enemy's presence from a misplaced bit of camouflage, the scent of tobacco, or the crack of a twig. He was a crack shot and had a cool nerve, cat-like reflexes, and the intelligence to analyze a combat problem quickly. He also understood the value of audacity, which, he said, "is a tactical weapon. Nine times out of ten it will throw the enemy off balance and confuse him. However much one sees of audacious deeds, no one really expects them."

Murphy claimed to have experienced gut-wrenching fear frequently, but it's hard to find evidence of it. After each of the three times he was seriously wounded he returned to combat and took the same chances he always had. As he told a nurse during one of his hospital stays, "As long as there's a man in the lines, maybe I feel that my place is up there beside him." Murphy claimed that he hated the war and fought as hard as he did only to hasten its end and to protect his comrades, but at the same time combat clearly filled a void in him. As an exasperated officer once told him, "You couldn't stay out of a scrap at a Peace Convention!"

Murphy said he looked at the Germans "as an enemy to be hated only impersonally," but he had a "vendetta feeling" for snipers, and on several occasions he hunted them down. On October 3 or 4 of 1944, after a sniper had killed two men in his company at the Cleurie Quarry, Murphy got permission to go after him. The mortar barrage was suspended for an hour to allow him to do his work. He shed every piece of equipment that might rattle or make a noise and pulled socks over his boots to muffle his footsteps. He described the challenge: "This is the most lonely game on earth, two men stalking each other with powerful guns; two men trained to kill in split seconds; two men without an atom of mercy toward each other." Figuring out that the sniper was covering the same line of approach that the American officers had tried two days before, Murphy circled around, reaching the same boulder he had used for cover then. He leaned against it with his left arm as he carefully surveyed the terrain. He heard a slight sound and saw the sniper's head rise above a clump of brush 10 yards away. He slowly raised his carbine with his right hand while continuing to lean against the boulder; he wanted no sudden movement to give him away. Just as he had his carbine in position the sniper looked toward him. Their eyes locked, but Murphy put two bullets in his head before he could react. In the dead man's pockets he found documents indicating that the sniper had earned extra furloughs for his proficiency. Murphy kept his scope-sighted rifle as a trophy.

On October 5 Murphy won another duel, when a patrol he was leading came under fire from a concealed machine gun nest and sniper emplacement. Again alone, he crawled to cover within 200 yards of the German position. The Germans knew where he was but, despite firing furiously, were unable to hit him. He shot two of their snipers and used his radio to direct mortar fire on the rest, killing 13 and wounding 35.

Murphy was made a 2d lieutenant on October 14, 1944, along with two other battle-weary dogfaces, by a colonel who declared: "You are now *gentlemen* by act of Congress. Shave, take a bath, and get the hell back into the lines."

Prime targets and always at the pointy end of things, 2d lieutenants had an average life expectancy of about six weeks. In less than two weeks Murphy and his radio operator came under sniper fire. The first shot killed the radio operator and the second tore through Murphy's right buttock as he dived for cover. Feeling like he'd been struck by a baseball bat, Murphy fought to remain conscious. His helmet had fallen off and lay a few feet away. Thinking Murphy was still under the helmet, the sniper, some 30 yards away, made the mistake of raising his camouflage net to fire at it. Raising his carbine pistol-style, one-handed, Murphy snapped off a shot that hit the German between the eyes. "It was his brain or nothing," Murphy explained. "He would not have missed the second time."

As Murphy waited to be evacuated, a sergeant asked for the "lucky carbine" that Murphy had carried since Italy. Murphy was so attached to the weapon that he knew its serial number by heart, but he agreed to the loan.[19] Unfortunately, the dispensation Murphy enjoyed from fate was nontransferrable: the sergeant was killed in a firefight the following day along with most of the platoon.

The hip wound was Murphy's most serious yet, growing gangrenous and costing him two months in the hospital. He returned to the front in January 1945, where his carbine was returned to him. The 3d Division was trying to take the Colmar Pocket, Germany's last foothold west of the Rhine. The Germans were dug in and well supported by armor, while most of the U.S. armor had been halted by a collapsed bridge.

Snow lay a foot deep, and it was so cold that it was impossible to dig in, so the GIs sheltered in shell craters. On January 25 Murphy awoke with his hair frozen to the ground. Later that

---

19. Murphy's carbine, serial number 1108783, one of the greatest artifacts of World War II, was turned in and "reconditioned" at the war's end, its broken stock tossed out and worn parts replaced.

National Archives

day, as his company crossed an open field, it came under machine gun fire. One of his men, Bill Weinberg, recalled Murphy saying, "Cover me," and then "he trotted up to the bunker where the machine gun was, shooting as he went, and killed all the Germans there. I don't know how he did it." That day, both men promoted alongside Murphy the previous October were killed in a mortar barrage. He suffered minor wounds, his legs peppered with steel fragments.

Murphy's Company B was at the edge of the woods near the town of Holtzwihr, supported by two M10 tank destroyers. Because the 1st lieutenant had been badly injured a day or two before, at 3 A.M. on January 26, 1945, Murphy assumed command.

At about 2 P.M., following an artillery barrage, two German-reinforced rifle companies approached—250 men in winter camouflage supported by six Mark VI Tiger tanks, 60-ton behemoths mounting 88mm guns. The 75mm shells of the M10s bounced right off the German armor. Faltering on the icy terrain, one M10 slid into a ditch and got stuck, its gun pointing uselessly at the ground. With their opening salvo the Tigers took out Company B's machine gun squad and its remaining tank destroyer and moved in spraying automatic-weapons fire.

Soon only 40 men were left of Company B's original 128. As the sole surviving officer, Murphy ordered his men to withdraw while he stayed to try to hold back the Germans the only way possible—by directing artillery with his field telephone. It was a "one-man job," he said. He fired on the approaching Germans with his carbine until he ran out of ammunition, then looked over at the burning M10 and spotted a machine gun and several cases of ammunition on top of it. Despite the fact that the vehicle's fuel and ammunition could have blown at any moment, he climbed onto it, noting that it was the first time in weeks that his feet had been warm. The M10's commander lay sprawled half out of its turret, dead, and Murphy had to roll him out so that the swivel-mounted .50-caliber machine gun could traverse freely.

He fed an ammo belt into the gun and racked the bolt handle. Its grips felt hot to his touch, but when he pressed the trigger the gun let out a hammering burst. "I bore into any object that stirs," he wrote, adding that his "numbed brain" was "intent only on destroying." In actions such as these, he entered a state he described as "coolness and calm fury." He showered lead upon every German that moved, only pausing to reload and direct artillery over his field telephone. Asked how close the Krauts were, he joked, "Just hold the phone and I'll let you talk to one of the bastards"; in fact, their infantrymen got within 10 yards of him. Murphy's body was completely exposed above the tank destroyer, but it took the Germans a while to spot him because they couldn't believe he would be standing amid the smoke and flames. They fired at him with rifles, submachine guns, machine guns, and tank guns to no avail. Twice the tank destroyer took direct 88mm hits. Murphy was tossed around, but not dislodged from his perch. Twelve Germans tried to approach him by following a gully under cover of smoke, but when the smoke momentarily lifted he turned the .50-caliber on them and "stacked them up like cordwood." His contact on the other end of the field telephone asked him how he was doing. Murphy cracked, "I'm all right, Sergeant. What are *your* postwar plans?"

If the Germans had gotten past Murphy they might have punched through the 15th Infantry Regiment's defense line, possibly endangering the entire 3d Division's position, but his hour-long one-man stand, combined with the artillery barrage he directed, brought them to a halt. He killed between 50 and 100 enemy troops, and, deprived of their infantry support, the Tiger tanks couldn't advance.

After his field telephone went dead Murphy stumbled away from the M10 tank destroyer, which exploded moments later. Murphy's leg wounds of the day before had opened up and were bleeding, but he was otherwise unhurt. He immediately reorganized his men and pursued the enemy. The battle continued for seven weeks until the Germans were pushed across the Rhine.

For his extraordinary action, Murphy was awarded the Medal of Honor. The army didn't want to lose such a hero just as the war was coming to a close, so he was taken out of the front, much to his chagrin. While at headquarters, Murphy received a dispatch that Company B was pinned down at the Siegfried Line, its captain and senior lieutenant killed. He immediately drove to rejoin his men. Finding them huddled in a trench, bewildered and demoralized, he got them onto their feet and led them past the line. Not a shot was fired. The fortresses were empty, abandoned as the Wehrmacht had retreated.

According to his biography *No Name on the Bullet,* Murphy was in Lyon, France, when he heard the war was over. "I could feel the blood drain out," he said. "My blood pressure went way down and stayed there, and I've been tired ever since."

Of the 235 men in his original company, Murphy was one of two noncasualties by the war's end. He had fought in nine major campaigns. With an eventual total of 37 medals—at least one of every kind the U.S. military handed out—as well as decorations from France and Belgium, he was probably the most decorated soldier of the war. That, his boyish good looks, and his shy, unpretentious manner made him America's most popular hero. His portrait on the cover of *Life* brought him to the attention of Hollywood.

In his first film test, Murphy was asked to play the part of a juvenile delinquent. His performance was wooden and unimpressive until the scene called for him to pick up a gun. As soon as he did the eyes in that baby face turned suddenly cold, and his body seemed charged, powerful, like a coiled spring. The transformation astonished the director. Later, directors found that they had to be careful not to close in on Murphy's eyes when he was portraying anger—they were too frightening. Lawrence Tierney, a burly character actor with a reputation for drinking and brawling, once felt their force. Murphy was with a date at a party where a drunken Tierney was making a scene. Murphy approached him and quietly asked him to stop swearing, but Tierney contemptuously brushed him off. Ten minutes later Murphy again asked Tierney to clean up his language, and was once again told to get lost. The third time, Murphy said, still quietly, "Mr. Tierney, I've told you twice and I'm not going to tell you again. Get your hat and coat and leave right now." This time Tierney was looking directly into Murphy's eyes. Without a word he got his hat and coat and left.

One man who didn't get the message in time was a 6-foot, 2-inch-tall, 190-pound hitchhiker Murphy picked up after the war. He was wearing an army uniform, and Murphy wanted to help out a fellow veteran. Once in the car the man shoved what he said was a .45 into Murphy's ribs and announced a robbery. Murphy warned him that he was making a mistake. The man backhanded him across the face and ordered him to stop the car and get out. As Murphy did so he made a grab for the gun and realized the man was merely simulating one with his knuckles. Murphy punched the man, knocking him out of the car, and then fought with him for 10 minutes. By the time the police arrived Murphy had beaten the man unconscious and declined to press charges. He dealt similarly with two men who tried to manhandle him in a traffic altercation, beating both of them to the ground with his fists and a riding crop.

As late as 1970 Murphy was accused of taking a shot at a hulking dog trainer with whom he he'd had an altercation. Murphy pleaded innocent and professed to be miffed that anyone would think he could have missed such a large target. He was acquitted.

Murphy made more than 40 films, mostly B-Westerns, and, in a unique twist, played himself in the 1955 movie adaptation of *To Hell and Back*. (The movie minimized his actual record of slaughter for reasons of taste, it being decades before *Rambo*.) Even so, Murphy never felt a part of the Hollywood community, which he described as "full of phonies." As he put it, "I have seen too many good men die to humble myself before people whom I do not respect."

For a generation after World War II, the standard line drill instructors used on overeager recruits was, "Who do you think you are, Audie Murphy?" He had come to be the apotheosis of the invincible hero, but he was uncomfortable with adulation. He turned down an invitation from President Kennedy to appear at a White House gathering of Medal of Honor winners; in fact he attended no functions that would require him to wear his medals, many of which he lost or gave away to friends, relatives, and neighborhood kids. He often said that the real heroes were the guys who didn't come back.

Combat had left him with what would later be termed "post-traumatic stress." For seven years he suffered from insomnia, and when he slept he had a recurring nightmare in which he was on top of a hill, fighting off a faceless horde; a piece fell off of his rifle with every shot until he was left holding only the trigger guard. He was put on tranquilizers and became addicted. He felt detached from everyday life, finding release in reckless gambling and womanizing. In 1962 he said, "War robs you mentally and physically. It drains you. Things don't thrill you anymore." In 1967 he observed, "With me, it's been a fight for a long time to keep from being bored to death."

It seemed that his two years in combat had been the most meaningful of his life. As he told an interviewer from *Esquire*,

> There's this to say about combat: it brings out the best in men. It's gory and it's unfortunate, but most people in combat stand a little taller. . . . You have a comradeship, a rapport that you'll never have again, not in our society anyway. I suppose it comes from having nothing to gain except the end of the war. There's no competitiveness, no money values. You trust the man on your left and on your right with your life, while, as a civilian, you might not trust either of them with ten cents.

On Memorial Day in 1971, Murphy's burned and dismembered body was recovered from the crash site of a small plane and identified by the nine-inch scar on his hip. He was laid to rest with full military honors in Arlington National Cemetery, where his grave remains the most visited after that of John F. Kennedy. His funeral drew few Hollywood "names," but a number of the veterans who had served beside him were there. Said Perry Pitt, a paraplegic who had shared a hospital ward with Murphy, "He gave everything, took nothing, and never forgot who his friends were."

31 Miyamoto Musashi

> *The way of the warrior is*
> *the resolute acceptance of*
> *death.*
> —Miyamoto Musashi

apan's feudal fiefdoms were united under Shogun Tokugawa Ieyasu in the early 1600s, and after 150 years of internecine warfare the nation was largely at peace. To quote from Eiji Yoshikawa's *Musashi*:

> As the chance to use swords in actual combat diminished, martial skills were gradually becoming martial arts, and these increasingly came to emphasize the importance of inner self-control and the character-building qualities of swordsmanship rather than its untested military efficacy. A whole mystique of the sword grew up which was more akin to philosophy than to warfare.

Schools of swordsmanship were established all over Japan, each propounding the particular approach of its founder. In the absence of war, dueling was the only way that a samurai could achieve acclaim, and disciples of different schools put their techniques to the test, sometimes with wooden swords and sometimes with steel. Warrior society was strongly influenced by Zen Buddhism, with its emphasis on action and intuition, and swordsmanship was believed to hone the Zen ideals of focus, discipline, and detachment. Foremost among those whose martial skills brought them spiritual insight was Miyamoto Musashi, the so-called *kensei* (sword saint).

Musashi was born into Japan's samurai class in 1584 and lived with his mother after his parents separated. As a boy, Musashi visited his father frequently to study fencing and proved himself a prodigy. Their relationship was cold, however, and when Musashi was 12 his father threw a sword at him after a violent argument. Musashi didn't flinch but moved his head just enough that the blade flew past it. He left the house and never came back, having decided that his father had nothing more to teach him.

At age 13, while walking home from school, Musashi saw a posted placard that read: "Whoever wants to challenge me will be accepted. Arima Kibei." Musashi took a brush out of his school bag and wrote on the placard, "I will challenge you tomorrow," adding his name and address. That evening a messenger came to his home to inform him that his challenge had been accepted. His mother was horrified, for Arima Kibei was a famous swordsman of the Shinto Ryu school and had won numerous duels. She sent a priest to the field the following day to explain that Musashi was a mischievous boy, not to be taken seriously. But before the priest could make his case, Musashi appeared and shouted "Stand up and fight!" to his waiting opponent. Wielding a long wooden staff against Arima's sword, Musashi knocked him to the ground, creating a local sensation.

Musashi continued to develop his technique and killed

·KIRCHNER·

Tadashima Akiyama in a duel when he was 16. A few years later he left home and embarked on his *musha-shugyo* (warrior pilgrimage), wandering the country seeking duels.

Even as Musashi's swordsmanship became more polished, his appearance grew increasing disheveled. Eschewing the meticulously styled topknot of the samurai, he wore his hair long and unkempt. He refused to bathe, a marked eccentricity in a nation noted for its fastidiousness. He never changed his clothing no matter how tattered and filthy it became.

Musashi fought in the Battle of Sekigahara in 1603 against the forces of Tokugawa Ieyasu. Although Musashi was on the losing side, he managed to survive the three-day battle in which 70,000 were killed.

At 21, he went to Kyoto and challenged Genzaemon, head of the Yoshioka clan, famous for its swordsmanship. Genzaemon could have easily dismissed a challenge from an unknown upstart like Musashi but chose to accept. The weapons would be wooden practice swords. A location was picked and the time for the meeting set at five the following morning.

At the appointed time, Genzaemon was at the spot, accompanied by several disciples. Musashi was nowhere to be seen. Two hours passed. Suspecting that his unknown challenger had scurried away in the night, Genzaemon sent his disciples to Musashi's inn. When they returned they told him, "Musashi was still sleeping. He was so impertinent that he said, 'I have overslept but I will come soon. Please give my regards to your master.'"

Enraged, Genzaemon loudly promised to destroy him when he finally made his overdue appearance.

For another two hours Genzaemon waited, seething, until at last, near noon, Musashi appeared, with insolent equanimity.

His patience having been pushed beyond its limit, Genzaemon attacked in a fury. Musashi coolly parried the blows. They separated and then clashed several times. Both bled from cuts to their foreheads, but Genzaemon's white headband was stained red with blood, while the deep red headband Musashi wore concealed the evidence of his wounds.

Suddenly Musashi launched an attack that Genzaemon failed to stop, and he beat him to the ground with a flurry of blows. Genzaemon lost consciousness and had to be carried off the field on a shutter, his right arm broken in several places. He was so unnerved that he hung up his sword and entered a monastery.

Genzaemon's younger brother, Denshichiro, actually considered the more skillful of the two, then challenged Musashi to retrieve the family's honor. Having seen Musashi's technique, Denshichiro was convinced he could defeat him. A duel was arranged, this time with steel blades. When the hour came Musashi was late again, despite his solemn vow to be punctual. A furious Denshichiro cursed and fretted while he waited. He might have made better use of these hours, for Musashi killed him seconds after he arrived.

Another fencer of the Yoshioka school, Matashichiro, then challenged Musashi. With no intention of fighting him fairly, he planned to have a number of the school's swordsmen set upon Musashi as soon as he showed up. His deviousness was no match for Musashi's. This time, Musashi arrived hours before the duel and waited in hiding. Matashichiro and his backup showed up on time and, expecting Musashi to be late, lay down on the grass. Musashi ran out from his hiding place, shouting, "I've been waiting long enough! Draw your sword!"

He struck Matashichiro across the forehead and killed him and then killed and wounded the other swordsmen as they tried to scramble to their feet.

Musashi's practice of arriving for a duel when he chose was considered dishonorable by many, but there was a philosophy behind it. He believed that the tactics of personal combat should be applicable to clashes of armies—as he put it, "The spirit of defeating a man is the same for 10 million men." Since even a surprise attack is permissible in war, he did not consider it unfair that he control the time and circumstances of his individual bouts.

In his lifetime Musashi fought about 60 duels against masters of a wide variety of weapons and fighting styles. His most famous was against Sasaki Kojiro in 1613. Kojiro was the founder of the Ganryu school of fencing in Kyushu and a retainer of the lord of the province. Kojiro used a long, straight sword he called the Drying Pole and a fencing technique called *tsub-ame-gaeshi* (swallow counter) for its resemblance to the movement of a swallow's tail in flight. Funashima, a small island just east of Hikojima in the Kanmon Straits, was chosen as the site. The duel was set for early morning.

Musashi spent part of the morning painting and as usual set out late. He hired a fisherman to row him the two miles to the island. It was clear that they wouldn't arrive until after midmorning, which seemed to suit Musashi fine. He asked the fisherman if he could have a broken oar that lay on the bottom of the boat, and he proceeded to carve it into the semblance of a sword. That done, he braided a string from small squares of paper and used it to tie up the sleeves of his kimono. Then he folded a hand towel lengthwise four times and tied it around his head.

As the boat got within 200 feet of the island, the water became shallow. Musashi leapt out, taking the carved oar and leaving his long sword in the boat. Kojiro ran into the water, berating Musashi for his tardiness. He drew the Drying Pole and tossed its scabbard into the water. Musashi studied him and quietly observed, "You've lost, Kojiro."

Kojiro demanded to know what he meant.

"The fight's already been fought. I say you've been defeated," Musashi replied.

"What are you talking about?" asked Kojiro.

"If you were going to win, you wouldn't throw your scabbard away. You've cast away your future, your life," explained Musashi.

Kojiro lunged at him. Musashi evaded the thrust and ran onto the shore. The antagonists faced each other, poised for the attack, each searching out the other's stance for an opening.

Kojiro brought his sword down, but Musashi blocked it. The duelists bounded away from each other, Kojiro finding advantage in a position where the sunlight was no longer reflected off the water into his eyes. Musashi then startled Kojiro by striding straight at him. Kojiro sliced at him, cutting off Musashi's headband. A second later, Musashi's wooden sword crushed Kojiro's skull.

The sight of his headband lying on the ground gave Musashi a momentary shiver. He had never fought a swordsman as strong and skillful as Kojiro, but it was his belief that a battle's outcome was determined in the hearts of the warriors before their swords even crossed. As Yoshikawa put it: "Kojiro had put his confidence in the sword of strength and skill. Musashi trusted in the sword of the spirit. That was the only difference between them."

After his duel with Kojiro, Musashi's reputation rose even higher. At the same time it changed him, marking the beginning of the more spiritual phase of his life. He devoted himself increasingly to brush painting, calligraphy, and the tea ceremony. He continued to regard fencing as a path to spiritual awareness, as suggested in this passage from his *The Thirty-Five Articles on the Art of Swordsmanship*:

> The majority of people have supported staring at an opponent's face. When doing so, the eyes should be narrower than usual but the mind should be broad.
>
> The eyeballs should not move and when the opponent is near they should be focused as though they were looking into the distance. In this way, a man can look not only at an opponent's face but his whole body, thus being able to anticipate any thrusts he might make. In my

opinion there are two kinds of eyes: one kind simply looks at things and the other sees through things to perceive their inner nature. . . . Sometimes a man can read another's mind with his eyes. In fencing, it is all right to allow your eyes to express your [resolute] will, but never let them reveal your mind.

Musashi turned down opportunities to duel the most eminent swordsman of his time, Munenori Yagyu, the shogun's chief of fencers. Musashi's defenders say that having analyzed Munenori's style, Musashi was satisfied he could defeat him and did not want to make an enemy of the shogun unnecessarily.

He continued to demonstrate his mastery against lesser lights. While serving as a retainer to the lord of Akashi, he was challenged by an ambitious young swordsman named Aoki. With amused contempt, Musashi looked over the foppish upstart, whose sword hilt was decorated with crimson ribbons. Musashi called for a bowl of boiled rice and placed a single grain on the head of a pageboy. With a lightning sweep of his sword he bore down on the pageboy's head and then suddenly stopped motionless, slicing the grain of rice neatly in two but cutting not a hair. He performed the difficult technique two more times, causing his challenger to flee. Musashi thundered after him, "You and your empty ostentatious sword. That crimson ribbon is just empty display! How ignoble. How can you hope to excel in swordsmanship with that kind of mental attitude?"

Musashi also accepted a challenge from four fencers of the Himeji daimyo. The first to face him was Miyake Gunbei, in a bout with wooden swords. For the first time, Musashi publicly demonstrated the technique he had developed using the short and long sword at the same time. He parried Gunbei's attacks as effortlessly as if he were toying with a child. Finally Gunbei lost his temper and ran at him, swinging his sword. Musashi called, "Look out!" but Gunbei ran into his short sword, gashing his face. Gunbei's defeat was so humiliating that instead of taking their turns, the other fencers apologized for their effrontery in presuming to match their skill against Musashi's.

In one demonstration of prowess, Musashi defeated a sword-wielding opponent using only an iron-ribbed "war fan," with which he parried every attack.

Musashi never married, though he adopted two sons. He was rumored to have had a romance with a girl who sold her time, which might explain this poem attributed to him:

> When in love
> Avoid love epistles and
> amorous letters
> Avoid poems expressing love
> to your beloved
> In their place, devote all your strength
> To accumulating and saving
> money.

Musashi spent his last years as a recluse living in a cave, where he wrote *A Book of Five Rings*, an exposition of his principles of strategy. He died at age 61 on May 19, 1645. His calligraphy, sculptures, and brush paintings are considered among the greatest masterpieces of Japanese art.

32 Charles Nungesser

In 1909, 16-year-old Charles Nungesser left France for Rio de Janeiro to stay with his uncle and seek his fortune. Unfortunately, when he arrived, he found out that his relative had departed for Argentina some months before. Nungesser traveled on to Buenos Aires in search of him. Shortly after his arrival, he stopped at an airfield to watch the landing of a Blériot biplane. Approaching the pilot, a fellow Frenchman, he asked if he could take flying lessons. The pilot took one glance at him, ascertained that he was not awash in funds, and airily brushed him aside. Infuriated, Nungesser climbed into the plane and opened the throttle before anyone could stop him. The Blériot rolled erratically down the field, picked up speed, and took off. Nungesser realized that he had only moments to figure out what he was doing before his impulsive act would result in his death. After experimenting with the controls, he somehow managed to bring the plane back to earth intact. The airport personnel were severely shaken by the near disaster, but Nungesser was not; more than ever he was determined to become a pilot.

He found a job as an assembler at an automobile plant and spent a good portion of his pay on flying lessons. Having demonstrated driving skills, within a year he was the lead driver for the plant's racing team.

He eventually met up with his uncle and went to work with him on a ranch, where he began building his own airplane in his spare time.

One night Nungesser attended a 12-round bout between a touring French boxer and a popular Argentine light heavyweight known as the Giant. The Frenchman was knocked out in the first round. The Giant raised his fists in victory and apologized for the brevity of the contest, telling the laughing crowd, "As the world knows, Frenchmen like to talk a lot but can't back it up."

Nungesser tossed his cigar away, jumped out of his seat and pushed his way to the ring. Stripping off his suit jacket and rolling up his shirtsleeves, he said, "Let's see you try *this* Frenchman." The crowd roared.

Nungesser was powerfully built and a trained boxer, but at 5 feet, 9 inches and 150 pounds, he was several inches shorter and 30 pounds lighter than his opponent was. Nevertheless, he took the gloves off his fallen compatriot and put them on.

The fight began to cries of, "Kill the Frenchman!" The Giant hit Nungesser with a pile-driving right that knocked him to the canvas, and the crowd cheered. He got back to his feet and slammed the hometown favorite in the midsection, spinning him around. The two men pounded at each other, trading blow for blow. The Giant's cheek was torn open, and Nungesser's shirt drenched in blood. Nungesser couldn't match

his opponent's reach and power and was knocked to the canvas 15 times, but he kept getting back up. Awed by his courage, the crowd gradually quieted, and behind his guard The Giant began to wear a look of bewilderment. Nungesser faked left, then, empowered by "the fury of desperation," slipped past the Giant's guard and landed a solid blow to his solar plexus, then another to his kidney. The Argentine dropped to his knees and knelt swaying like a poleaxed cow. Nungesser was thoroughly spent, every muscle in pain, his knees shaking, but he had a message to deliver. "A Frenchman is the equal of any man!" he shouted to the crowd. He put his jacket back on, stuck a cigar in his mouth, and returned to his seat.

"Even when I have not one iota of strength left in my body I will always continue to fight," he later observed.

Bigger battles and bigger threats to French honor were on the horizon. With war about to break out in 1914, Nungesser returned home. He tried to join the air service but was rejected and instead enlisted in the 2d Hussar Regiment. When he parted from his mother, he promised her he would make her proud. Less than two weeks later, on September 3, 1914, he delivered on that vow.

During the French retreat to the Marne, Nungesser had lost his horse and become separated from his unit. He was wandering the war-torn countryside with two infantry stragglers, surrounded by elements of the German army, when they heard the sound of an approaching German staff car. They leaped into a ditch beside the road, near an open gate. While the car was still in the distance, Nungesser sprinted to the gate, closed it, and returned to his comrades. The Mors sedan was forced to a stop, and the Frenchmen opened fire, immediately killing two of the German officers. The others returned fire with their pistols, but Nungesser charged the car and shot them both.

Nungesser and the infantrymen gathered all dispatch cases, dumped the bodies, and drove off, with Nungesser at the wheel. As they passed a cluster of French troops, he shouted to them that he was making his way back to headquarters with valuable intelligence. They weren't convinced, and on the chance that he might be a spy fired a volley in his direction. For the next two hours, he drove through French and German troops and took fire from both, the French shooting because of the German car and the Germans shooting because of his French uniform. Somehow he made it.

The papers he had captured were so valuable and his deed so intrepid that he was not only awarded the Médaille Militaire but allowed to keep the Mors as a trophy. But Nungesser used his hero status to leverage something he wanted far more than medals or motorcars—a transfer to the air service.

On April 8, 1915, after flight training, he was posted to the 106th Bomber Group and flew 53 missions in an antiquated, slow-moving Voisin, bombing supply depots, railheads, coastal guns, and submarine pens. But it was aerial combat he craved. On April 26 he spotted a German Albatros two-seater and dived at it, despite the fact that his gunner was equipped with a bolt-action carbine while the Albatros carried a belt-fed Parabellum machine gun. The Albatros flew away, leading Nungesser over German antiaircraft positions. His plane was so badly shot up that its engine nearly sputtered out, but he managed to crash-land behind French lines. For months afterward, Nungesser tried to pick a fight with the Germans but only managed to get his own Voisin chewed up by rifle and antiaircraft fire. His mechanic, Pochon, worked late most nights repairing the damage.

On the night of July 31 Nungesser was posted as standby pilot, a duty he found onerous. When he couldn't be hunting Germans, he liked to hunt women in the bistros of nearby Nancy; they were far too patriotic to reject a charming and handsome hero of France. He was wandering through the hangars, bored, when he came across a brand-new Voisin equipped with a swivel-mounted Hotchkiss machine gun. Itching to try it out, he persuaded a gunner to join him and took off at dawn. Half an hour later, the alert sounded—five German Albatroses had been spotted approaching the airdrome.

Nungesser, of course, was nowhere to be found. His comman-der was still wondering what to do when, to his astonishment, he was notified that one of his planes had shot down an Albatros—something that had never happened before. Moments later, the triumphant Nungesser landed. For leaving his post he received eight days' confinement to base, and for his valor the Croix de Guerre.

At his request, Nungesser was transferred to a fighter wing, the 65th Escadrille, which he joined in November 1915, bring-ing Pochon with him. Nungesser was issued an agile single-seat Nieuport 17 armed with a drum-fed Lewis machine gun. He decorated his fuselage with a macabre emblem—a skull and crossbones under a coffin flanked by two burning candles, sur-rounded by large black heart—then put on an impromptu air show over Nancy, performing hair-raising stunts barely 100 feet above the town. When he returned to base, his commanding officer was in a fury, telling him that he ought to use his aero-batic antics to terrify the Germans rather than his fellow Frenchmen. Seeing his point, Nungesser climbed back into his plane, flew to the nearest German airdrome, buzzed the field at treetop level and repeated his performance of barrel rolls, loops, chandelles, and vertical turns. There were a number of German planes in the air at the time, but he adroitly maneuvered between them so they couldn't fire at him for fear of hitting one of their own. He returned to his base, saluted the CO, and announced, "It is done, *mon capitaine!*"

Again he received eight days' arrest.

Nungesser's punishment forbade him from leaving the base, but not from flying. After two days, he took his plane up and came upon a pair of Albatroses. One peeled away for home but the other stayed to fight. Nungesser traded bursts with the German gunner until three of his 47-round Lewis drums were empty, and still he had not scored a knockout. There was noth-ing to do but get in closer. He wrestled his last drum into place and flew at the Germans through streams of tracers. At 30 feet, he clamped down on the trigger. As his slugs tore up the Albatros, the pilot was killed and the plane nosed over. Thrown from his seat, the gunner clung desperately to the machine-gun mount, his body working convulsively like a man on a trapeze, his mouth wide open in a scream Nungesser couldn't hear over the roar of his engine. The plane plunged into the earth and exploded. Later, as Nungesser inspected the crash site, he found bits of the pilot and gunner stuck against the wire of a nearby fence.

For his victory, Nungesser was excused from the remaining six days of his punishment and awarded the Scarlet Ribbon of the Knight of the Légion d'Honneur.

On January 29, 1916, Nungesser agreed to test a new biplane, the Ponnier. It proved unstable, and in the middle of a climbing turn it fell into a spin and crashed. Nungesser was carefully extricated from the wreckage and rushed to the hospital. His jaw and both his legs were broken. The control column had smashed through his palate and knocked out most of his teeth. Blood flowed from his mouth and nostrils. The doctors wrote him off and parked his gurney with the dead. An hour later a nurse noticed he was still breathing. He was rushed into surgery.

Three days later, Nungesser was hobbling around his room on crutches. In two weeks, he was driving his car to the airfield daily. In a month, pale and sweating, his head swathed in bandages and his jaws wired, he appeared at the airfield and rasped out a demand that he be allowed to take up a Nieuport. He climbed to 5,000 feet and performed every aerobatic stunt he knew, and after 15 minutes touched down smoothly.

Eight weeks after his broken body had been pulled from the wreckage of the Ponnier, Nungesser returned to duty. He walked with a cane, shakily, but his nerve was as steady as ever. Within days he shot down two planes and a balloon.

On April 27, over the Spincourt Forest, he flew into a formation of six enemy planes—three Fokkers and three LVGs—

adroitly maneuvering between them so that they couldn't get a clear shot, just as he had over the German aerodrome. He shot down one LVG and made it back to his base with 28 bullet holes in his plane, including seven in his engine. There was a hole through his helmet, one through his boot, and five tears in his flying suit where bullets had grazed him.

On June 20, in a battle against two Germans, his plane was struck in the first pass and a bullet nearly tore off his upper lip. As Nungesser recalled, "After the first pass they knew I was wounded, so they were very confident. I toyed with them to let them know it would not be so easy." He stuffed his silk scarf into his mouth and bit down on it to stanch the bleeding. Like a bullfighter, he skillfully evaded their firing passes and began to employ maneuvers that they had difficulty following. "They realized their initial success was sheer luck. Through a series of passes I wore them out, planted the seeds of self-doubt, and let them know they were dominated. As they grew tired they began making mistakes." Though he was increasingly weak from loss of blood, Nungesser's concentration was absolute—he knew that any mistake he might make would be his last.

The *danse macabre* went on for nearly an hour. Whenever possible, he made his firing passes when the two planes were lined up so that he could rake them both. At last, with an Immelman turn, he got into position to take out one of the Germans and, moments later, dispatched the other. Feeling faint, he landed his own badly damaged plane in a field behind French lines. He was taken to the hospital in a farmer's cart. As always, he refused anesthesia, choosing to remain conscious throughout the operation and even assisting the surgeon by holding clamps and compresses to stop his bleeding.

It was after this battle that Nungesser was dubbed the Matador of the Sky.

His last kill of 1916 was earned under particularly unusual circumstances. He was test-flying a newly overhauled Nieuport when he spotted an LVG. As its observer opened up on him, Nungesser dived, then zoomed up under its tail in his favorite maneuver, the whipstall. It was only then that he realized that his machine gun had not been reinstalled. It was a serious predicament, for if he tried to pull out of the fight he would be at the mercy of the LVG's gunner. So Nungesser continued his attack, closing in as if he intended to ram the LVG and kill them all. Taken in, the Germans landed inside French lines, climbed out of their plane, and torched it.

It was Nungesser's 21st victory, and he had suffered an injury for nearly every one of them. He had survived crash landings and bullet wounds, and his legs were often so badly injured he had to be lifted in and out of his plane. He picked up another nom de guerre, the Human Jigsaw Puzzle.

Nungesser moved from his quarters at the air base to a room that was set aside for him at the hospital at Dunkirk, so that between missions he could have his latest injuries treated while continuing to recuperate from old ones. His recovery was speeded by his great physical strength, which he would demonstrate by lifting 70 kilograms (154 pounds) with one arm, or tearing a deck of cards in half lengthwise.

He still took jaunts to Paris to enjoy the sparkling nightlife. One evening he was at a club with his father, who looked at the dancers, then down at his son's bad leg and observed, "This time you have no advantage." Always pricked by a challenge, Charles took his date onto the dance floor. With sheer willpower he overcame his tendency to limp, and danced so impressively that the other couples stopped to watch.

On May 8, 1917, in a strange case of mistaken identity, Nungesser was attacked by a British biplane. Frantically trying to wave the pilot off, he took evasive action, but his adversary kept coming. After the Britisher put a 14-round burst into his plane, Nungesser could no longer afford to remain passive and shot him down, suspecting he might be a Hun in a captured aircraft. Sadly, that was not the case. Evidently, the novice pilot had taken Nungesser's skull-and-crossbones insignia for a Teutonic device. The incident put Nungesser in a sullen mood.

When he returned to his base, he learned that a German plane had dropped a message, addressed "To my worthy opponent, Monsieur Skull and Bones," inviting him to an aerial duel at four that afternoon above Douai. His fellow pilots warned him it was a trap, but Nungesser didn't care. Only Boche blood could cleanse his conscience.

At half past two he took off. Impulsively, he strafed a nearby German airfield, wasting precious fuel and ammunition. He reached the rendezvous point 15 minutes early and was immediately ambushed by six Albatroses hiding in the clouds. Nungesser dived to pick up speed, looped, then pulled an Immelman turn, which put him behind the German formation. Blazing though an entire drum of ammunition, he shot down two. His fuel and ammunition low, he disengaged and headed for home. The Germans did not pursue.

Throughout his meteoric career, Nungesser had shared his triumphs and travails with his friend and mechanic Pochon. Their relationship ended on a cold October night in 1917 as Pochon was driving Nungesser into Paris. He suffered a heart attack and was killed when the Mors ran into a tree. Nungesser broke his jaw again, among other injuries. He was hospitalized but by New Year's Eve was back in action.

By war's end, Nungesser was credited with 45 victories and 11 probables, making him France's third-ranking ace. Among many honors, he received the U.S. Distinguished Service Cross, the British Military Cross, the Serbian Cross of Karageorgevitch, the Croix de Guerre from France and Belgium, and the War Cross from Portugal. At the same time he had accumulated enough injuries to hospitalize a regiment: a skull fracture; a brain concussion; five upper and two lower jaw fractures; the loss of all his teeth; the dislocation of both knees; a shell fragment in his arm; bullet wounds in his ear and mouth; a dislocated wrist, ankle, and clavicle; multiple internal injuries; and lacerations and contusions too numerous to mention. His doctors marveled at his tolerance for pain, and one wonders how he endured his strenuous nightlife, not to mention aerial combat.

When Gen. Robert Nivelle decorated Nungesser with the Rosette of the class of Officer of the Légion d'Honneur, he asked him, "Lieutenant, can you tell me by what miracle of tactics you have managed to bring down so many of the Boche?"

Nungesser answered, "*Mon général*, when I am behind the adversary and believe that I have his airplane well and truly centered in front of my machine guns, I close my eyes and open fire. When I open them again, sometimes I see my opponent hurtling through space . . . and at other times I find myself in a hospital bed."

In wartime Paris, Nungesser was fond of saying that he had to return to the front in order to relax, and indeed, once peace returned he found it hard to settle down. He taught flying for a while, raced airplanes, and made a barnstorming tour of America. He starred in a movie, *The Sky Raider*. In 1927, at age 35, he decided to try for the $25,000 Orteig prize, offered to the first pilot to fly nonstop from New York to Paris in either direction. On the 10th anniversary of his duel against the German pilots, he set out from France in a plane he named the *Oiseau Blanc* (White Bird). He was never seen again. Had he succeeded, he would have beaten Lindbergh by more than a week.

33 Francisco Pizarro

> *Pizarro is the archetypal conquistador: crafty, cruel, treacherous, greedy, and very brave.*
>
> —Desmond Wilcox

Francisco Pizarro, the illegitimate son of an army officer and a whore, was born penniless and without prospects in Estremadura, a remote, hardscrabble part of Spain. Abandoned by his mother when he was old enough to walk, he began working as a swineherd and then joined the army as an adolescent. Tempered by hardship, the men of Estremadura were Spain's toughest soldiers, eager to go anywhere that they could make their fortune with "a cloak and a sword."

After military service in Italy, Pizarro shipped out to the New World and was in Balboa's 1513 expedition that first sighted the Pacific Ocean. Pizarro spent 20 years in Central America and the Caribbean, and by 50 had become comfortably well off. "Comfortable" was not Pizarro's goal, however. In 1524, fired by the success of Hernando Cortés and rumors of more gold to the south, he formed a partnership with another conquistador, Diego de Almagro, and a wealthy priest, Father Luque.

After years of grueling and fruitless exploration, Pizarro at last found evidence of the wealth he sought. He assembled an army of 180 men, 67 of them mounted.

As William H. Prescott wrote, Pizarro

> possessed something higher than mere animal courage, in that constancy of purpose which was rooted too deeply in his nature to be shaken by the wildest storms of fortune. . . . Had he faltered for a moment, had he stopped to calculate chances, he must inevitably have failed; for the odds were too great to be combated by sober reason.

But against all reason, Pizarro's band defeated the mighty Inca Empire by holding its ruler Atahualpa hostage, much as Cortés had Montezuma. At no other time in history has such a small number of men conquered such a vast territory, seized such riches, and subjugated so many people.

Success brought dissension to the conquistadors' ranks. Having been deprived of his fair share of honors and wealth, Diego de Almagro turned against Pizarro, who then had him executed. A dozen Almagro loyalists, led by Juan de Rada, gathered in Lima to plot revenge. They decided to kill Pizarro on Sunday, June 26, 1541, as he walked home from church. He got wind of the plan and skipped mass that day, although he was too accustomed to such threats to take serious precautions. The Almagrists, fearing that their intentions had been revealed, set out for his palace, swords in hand, shouting, "Death to the tyrant!" On the way, one of them turned to avoid a puddle in the road. Rada shoved the man out of the group, snapping, "We go to bathe in human blood, and you refuse to put your foot in a puddle of water!"

The assassins entered Pizarro's courtyard and immediately cut down one of his servants. Another servant ran and gave the alarm. Pizarro was in the dining room with his half brother Martín de Alcántara; an officer, Francisco de Chavez; his lieutenant, Juan Velásquez; the bishop of Quito; and several servants. As the Almagrists headed up the hallway, Pizarro ordered Chavez to bolt the door. Had Chavez done so the others would have had time to put on their steel cuirasses, but instead he stood in the doorway and tried to reason with the assassins and for his efforts was stabbed in the heart. The bishop, Velásquez, and a few others jumped from the windows. As Pizarro struggled with his armor, Alcántara and two servants rushed forward to meet the Almagrists. In a furious battle, two of the assassins and the servants were killed. Then Alcántara fell with multiple wounds to the chest. Unable to fasten his cuirass alone, Pizarro tossed it aside and wrapped his cloak twice around his left forearm.[20]

He faced the remaining eight Almagrists. His wealth and power meant nothing now; back to the sword and cloak with which he had started, he remained a true conquistador, outnumbered but undaunted. At 70 he was the equal in strength of any man half his age and in ferocity the lord of them all. "What ho, traitors!" he roared. "Have you come to kill me in my own house?"

He parried his assailants' blows and killed two of them. As they fell back, Rada angrily shouted, "Why are we so long about it? Down with the tyrant!" He grabbed one of his men and threw him onto Pizarro's sword. The body went halfway to the hilt, and before Pizarro could free his blade Rada stabbed him in the throat. The assassins then ran him through.

As the old man slumped to the floor, he dipped a finger in the pool of his blood, traced a cross on the floor, leaned over, and kissed it. His last words were, reportedly, "God have mercy."

---

20. The cloak was often used in combination with the rapier. The cloak would be wrapped twice around the forearm to protect it as it parried blows, and the remainder was allowed to drape in order to snag an opponent's point.

34 Robert the Bruce and the Black Douglas

> *In the art of fighting and in vigor of body, Robert had not his match in any time in any clime.*
>
> —John Fordun

R obert the Bruce, Lord of Annandale and Earl of Carrick, was born July 11, 1274, and from childhood was trained for war. He mastered the weapons of his day—the bow, the sword, the ax, and the lance—and learned to manage a horse in battle. Tall and strong, he was ranked among the three greatest knights in all Christendom as a young man in tournament competition.

When Scotland's King Alexander III died in 1286 without a successor, Robert had one of the strongest claims to the throne, along with John "the Red" Comyn, Lord of Badenoch, but England's Edward I invaded and brought Scotland under his own dominion. William Wallace raised an army in rebellion, and Robert joined him and fought for Scottish independence for five years until Wallace was defeated at the Battle of Falkirk. In 1302, with a letter of contrition and a reaffirmation of fealty, Robert returned to the English fold.

Three years later Wallace was captured and taken to London, where he was convicted of treason and subjected to the horrific punishment meted out for that crime. He was first stripped naked and dragged by horses through the streets; hanged, but cut down while he was still alive; castrated, disemboweled, and forced to watch as his genitals and entrails were fed into a charcoal brazier; and finally, beheaded, his heart cut out, and his body quartered. Edward I assumed that the example he had made of Wallace would crush the spirit of Scottish independence. Instead, it provided a martyr to inspire the struggle.

Robert secretly negotiated for the Red Comyn's support in his quest for the Scottish throne, but in January 1306 Comyn sent evidence of Robert's machinations to Edward. Learning of Comyn's betrayal, Robert requested a meeting at the Grayfriars Church at Dumfries. They withdrew to the altar, and the discussion soon turned angry. Comyn went for his dagger, but Robert used his first. Robert's men finished Comyn off as he lay bleeding on the altar steps.

Robert was given absolution by the Scottish church, which supported independence, and on March 25, in a makeshift ceremony, he was crowned King of Scots. He raised an army, including 100 landed knights, and rode to Perth, where he challenged the English Earl of Pembroke to battle. Pleading that it was too late in the day, Pembroke requested that their armies clash in the morning. Robert accepted and made camp a short distance away, so trusting in his foe's honor that he did not even post guards. That night, Pembroke attacked and slaughtered most of Robert's men. Robert and a few hundred followers managed to break free and take refuge in the mountains.

Some time later, while Robert's band traveled along a narrow hillside track above Loch Dochart, it was attacked by an army led by Alistair MacDougall, Lord of Lorne, a relative of the

Red Comyn who sought vengeance. Robert stationed himself at the rear of his men, repeatedly wheeling around to fend off the Highlanders. MacDougall ordered three stout members of the MacIndrosser clan to run ahead and ambush Robert at a point

New York Public Library Picture Collection

where the track was too narrow for him to turn his horse. As they jumped him, Robert swung his sword at one who grabbed his bridle and lopped off his arm at the shoulder. When another grabbed his leg, Robert stood, trapping the man's hand between horse and stirrup, and spurred his horse forward, causing the man to lose his footing and be dragged. The third jumped onto the horse behind Robert, wrapping his arms around Robert's cloak to prevent him from swinging his sword; Robert crushed his skull with his sword's heavy pommel. He then slew the man whose hand was trapped beneath his stirrup. After that, the Highlanders hung back. The Baron of Cowal, riding with the pursuit, was so obviously impressed that MacDougall angrily turned on him and said, "You seem to enjoy our discomfiture."

The baron replied, "No, but never did I hear tell of such a feat, and one should honor chivalry whether in friend or foe."

Robert was relentlessly pursued by the English army, as well as by the majority of the Scottish lords, who were still loyal to Edward. He adopted the life of a guerrilla, attacking small bodies of English troops and then quickly disappearing into the wild hill country. Beside him fought a small army of heroes, among them his impetuous brother Edward, of whom it was said that "had he one foot in Paradise, he would withdraw it to go and fight." Another was James "the Black" Douglas, Robert's champion, who planned and led a number of daring commando-style raids. The English so hated Douglas that they used his name to frighten their children.

Robert was accustomed to wander away from camp early each day "for his private purposes" (as the chronicle discreetly puts it), alone or accompanied by a page. One of his kinsmen, who had been bribed to assassinate him, decided that this would be the best time to make his attempt, and he brought as backup his two sons, one of whom carried a sword and an ax, and the other a sword and a spear. Robert, who had been warned of his treachery, saw them coming. Armed only with his sword, he said to his page, "Those men will slay us if they can. What weapon do you have?"

"I have but a bow and arrow," responded the page.

"Then give them to me quickly and stand far back," said Robert, "for if I win you shall have weapons aplenty, but if I die make haste away."

Robert called out to the men, "Traitors, you have sold me. Come no further, but stay where you are."

The traitor told him he had nothing to fear, that he brought information about the English. "Say what you will at a distance," said Robert. As they kept coming he drew back his bow and said, "You shall die if you come one foot nearer to me."

Still they advanced. Robert's arrow hit his kinsman in the eye, piercing through to his brain.

The older son ran at Robert with his ax, but Robert cut him down with his sword. When the younger son thrust at him with his spear, Robert lopped off the spearhead and, before the young man could draw his sword, killed him.

While Robert wiped the blood from his blade, his page congratulated him. Robert responded somberly, "As our Lord sees me, these were good fighting men until they were ruined by treachery."

Robert's popular support grew, but his situation remained desperate. Kildrummy Castle, where he had sent his family to be guarded by his brother Nigel, fell to English forces. His wife, sisters, and daughter were taken prisoner and confined under harsh conditions; his sister Mary was kept in a cage mounted outside a castle wall. Nigel asked for the special treatment normally accorded nobility, which Edward mordantly honored by having him hanged on a gallows 30 feet higher than normal. Two of Robert's other brothers were also hanged, drawn, and quartered.

Robert and his force of some 60 men were encamped in Carrick, his own earldom, when he learned that the Macdowalls of Galloway were approaching, 200 strong and led by bloodhounds. Robert moved his men across a steep-banked river and set up camp a half-mile beyond it. It was dark when Robert returned to the ford alone to assess the situation. He heard the clinking of armor and the movement of mounted men on the far bank but couldn't be sure whether the enemy was closing in or it was just a casual patrol. He didn't want to disturb his exhausted men without good reason, but as the moon came out from behind the clouds, he saw the enemy massed on the opposite shore, preparing to cross. At this point if he returned to his camp to rouse his men they would only be forced to flee, pursued by a superior force. However, if he remained atop the steep and narrow path cutting through the riverbank, sword and spear in hand and protected by his armor, he might be able to stop the enemy as did the legendary Horatius at Rome's narrow Sublician Bridge.

The Macdowalls, seeing only one man presuming to block their way, plunged into the river. As the first knight climbed out of the ford Robert killed him with a thrust of his spear, and then stabbed his horse. It fell back into the river, kicking and thrashing. As the others tried to clamber over the carcass of the horse, Robert hewed them down with his sword. The dead and wounded piled up, making it even more difficult for the men behind them to pass. After five men died the others drew back, but unwilling to be driven off by a single foe, they again threw themselves against Robert, and again were cut down. By this time Robert's followers had heard the clamor and rushed to join him, causing the Macdowalls to call off the attack. According to Robert's 14th-century biographer John Barbour, Robert's men found him "sitting alone, with his basinet [helmet] off to take the air, for he was hot. . . . They found lying in that place fourteen slain by his hand."

Here Barbour pauses in his narrative to comment on the nature of courage:

> No man can have honor who has not wit to
> . . . sense what to undertake or to leave alone.

> Valor has two extremes, foolhardiness and cow-
> ardice, and they are both to be avoided.
> Foolhardiness will venture all, things to leave
> alone as well as things to take up, while cow-
> ardice ventures nothing and utterly forsakes all.
> . . . For this reason valor is of such renown, that
> it is the mean betwixt these two.

Barbour argued that Robert's stand at the ford should not be considered foolhardy; it stood a reasonable chance of success.

Shortly afterward, the Black Douglas struck another blow for Robert's cause. With a small group wearing disguises, he attended mass near Castle Douglas on Palm Sunday. When the English garrison of his former castle entered the church, Douglas and his men pulled swords from beneath their cloaks and killed them. They then went to the castle and feasted on the slain men's dinner. Afterward, they carried off the castle's arms, armor, and treasure; poisoned its well; and set it ablaze. Outraged at this assault, Edward I sent messages to his lords demanding that Robert's insurrection be crushed.

The armies of the Earl of Pembroke and John of Lorne surrounded Robert's band in the forest where it was hiding. As the trap closed, Robert ordered his men to scatter and retreat in different directions. His main purpose defeated, John of Lorne sprung a backup plan, releasing a bloodhound that had once belonged to the Scottish king. As the dog took off after Robert's scent, John of Lorne ordered five fast men to follow it. Accompanied only by his foster brother, Robert ran, but as his pursuers gained ground he stopped to await them so that he might have a moment to recover his breath. Three of the pursuers attacked Robert, and two took on his foster brother. In Barbour's words,

> The king met the three that made at him, and
> dealt such a blow at the first that he shore through

ear and cheek and neck to the shoulder. The man
sank down dizzily, and the two, seeing their fellow's sudden fall, were affrighted, and started
back a little. With that the king glanced aside and
saw the other two making full sturdy battle
against his man. He left his own two, and leapt
lightly at them that fought with his man, and
smote off the head of one of them. Then he went
to meet his own assailants, who were coming at
him right boldly. He met the first so eagerly that
with the sharp edge of his sword he hewed the
arm from the body. . . . The strokes that were
given I cannot tell, but so fairly it fell out that the
king, though he had a struggle and a difficulty,
slew four of his foemen. Soon afterwards his foster brother ended the days of the fifth.

They took off running again. When they came to a stream,
they waded along it for a distance, throwing the hounds off
their scent and forcing John of Lorne and the Earl of Pembroke
to call off the pursuit.

Later that day, as Robert and his foster brother were crossing an upland moor, they encountered three rough-looking
men, one of whom carried a freshly killed sheep across his
shoulders. Needing food and shelter, the fugitives accepted an
invitation to join the men, though Robert suspected they might
have recognized him and be hoping to collect the price on his
head. After a dinner of roast mutton, Robert felt an overwhelming weariness. Taking a place at the opposite side of the
farmhouse from the three men, he asked his foster brother to
stand guard while he slept. Robert dozed restlessly, wearing his
mail coat, his drawn sword by his side. At last his foster brother fell asleep and the three men moved in. His eyes flickering
open, Robert saw them and got to his feet, sword in hand, kicking his foster brother awake. The latter was too slow to shake

off his drowsiness and was killed. It was now one against three, but Robert slew them all.[21]

Edward was furious at his minions' failure to deal with Robert, and in the summer of 1307 he decided to lead an expedition himself, despite his poor health. The strain was too much, and the "Hammer of the Scots" died—oddly enough—on July 11, Robert's birthday.

His son, Edward II, proved to be a less formidable opponent of Scottish independence. He was described as "strong, handsome, and brave," but also "weak-willed, indolent, and frivolous." Chief among his frivolities was his affair with Piers Gaveston, a knight on whom he bestowed considerable authority, provoking so much antagonism among the English lords that they withdrew their military support. Gaveston was eventually seized and beheaded on the orders of the Earl of Lancaster, precipitating a civil war.

The dissension among the English enabled Robert to further consolidate his power. In January 1313, he led a successful surprise attack on the heavily fortified town of Perth. His men had secretly taken soundings of its moat and found a place where a man could cross. Robert was the first to do so, wading into the icy, neck-deep water in full armor. Once across, he used his great strength to raise a heavy rope ladder over the castle wall with a long spear. A French knight who accompanied his forces observed, "What shall we say of our nobles in France who think only to stuff their bellies when so renowned a knight will risk his life for a miserable hamlet?"

The rebels took other castles through a similar combination of stealth and daring. William Bunnock, a farmer who sold produce to the castle at Linlithgow, concealed eight armed men beneath the hay in his wagon. When he was halfway beneath the castle's portcullis he stopped and cut his wagon's traces, pre-

---

21. The number of occasions on which Robert bests three or more opponents strains credulity. It is possible that some of these accounts may be garbled retellings of one original incident, or else effusive expressions of the storyteller's art.

venting that barrier from dropping completely. The men swarmed out from under the hay and quickly overcame the guard as others hidden nearby rushed to join them. Shortly afterward, the Black Douglas and 60 men approached Roxburgh Castle at night on their hands and knees, their armor covered with black cloaks, causing the sentries to mistake them for a herd of cattle. Scaling the walls with rope ladders, Douglas' men took the garrison by surprise, quickly overwhelming it. Even the great castle at Edinburgh, called the Maiden's Castle for its reputed impregnability, fell to Scottish cunning.

The conquests that had cost his father so much in blood and treasure were falling from Edward II's hands. Once he finally solidified his support among the nobles, he put together the greatest army yet to attempt to crush the Scottish insurgency. It was four times the size of Robert's, with 10,000 men, including 3,000 archers, 2,500 knights, and masses of peasant levies. So confident were the English that many of the knights brought along wagonloads of silverware, tapestries, and furniture to furnish the homes they had been promised. The king even brought a poet to immortalize his coming victory in verse.

Robert chose the advantageous terrain beside a stream, Bannockburn, on which to fight. The river and nearby forest prevented flanking maneuvers, and the Scots dug pits and erected spiked barricades to confine the enemy to a narrow battlefield.

On June 23, 1314, Sir Henry de Bohun, riding a bow's shot ahead of the English army as it approached, saw an armored figure inspecting the Scottish troops, riding a small horse and carrying an ax. Around his helmet was a golden crown—it could only be Robert. Seeing an opportunity not only to attain glory but to end the uprising with one blow, de Bohun couched his lance and spurred his great charger forward.

Prudence would have dictated that Robert withdraw—his life was too precious to risk, and he was not even equipped with a lance. But it was his heroic spirit that had transformed Scottish peasants into an army willing to confront one of the world's great powers, and he could not refuse a challenge in front of them. There was a personal motive as well: it was to the de Bohuns that Edward II had given the confiscated Bruce domains in Essex. Finally, perhaps most important, Robert *liked* to joust. He wheeled his horse and cantered toward Sir Henry. As they closed, Robert sideslipped his mount to avoid Sir Henry's lance, stood in his stirrups, and brought his ax crashing down through the knight's helmet, skull, and brain. The force of the blow splintered the handle of his ax.

For a moment the two armies were silent. Then the Scots let out a great cheer and rushed upon the English cavalry, stabbing them with their pikes and flinging them from their horses. It required all of Robert's authority to make them return to their lines and adhere to the battle plan. Robert's brothers and commanders reproached him for risking their cause on the impulse of a moment, but his only regret was that he had ruined his ax handle.

The English cavalry charged the Scottish infantry, which was organized into phalanxes, or schiltrons. A mounted knight carried around 70 pounds of armor and moved at 20 miles per hour, bringing all that force to bear at the sharp metal tip of a 10-foot lance. The most disciplined infantry would usually break up under such an attack, but the Scottish schiltrons refused to yield and the charge faltered against their 12-foot pikes. Knights were impaled before they could bring their own weapons into play, or killed on the ground after being thrown from their horses.

Thomas Randolph, Earl of Moray, was in charge of a schiltron that was surrounded by English knights. The Black Douglas was about to ride to his rescue when he saw that Randolph's troops were cutting their way free. Pulling back his men, Douglas told them, "The Earl of Moray has gained the day and since we were not there to help him in the battle let us leave to him the credit of the victory."

Randolph's victory, following on the heels of Robert's personal exploit, caused Scottish morale to surge, and it occurred to Robert that he might successfully attack with his infantry. That evening, according to Barbour, he gathered his officers, explained his plan, and added,

> Sirs, we have every reason to be confident of success for we have right on our side. Our enemies are moved only by desire for dominion, but we are fighting for our lives, our children, our wives and the freedom of our country. And so I ask and pray that with all your strength, without cowardice or alarm, you meet the foes whom you will first encounter so boldly that the ones behind them will tremble. See that your ranks are not broken so that, when the enemy come charging on horseback, you meet them steadfastly with your spears; and do not let any seek for booty or prisoners until the field is surely ours. Think on your manhood and your deeds of valor and the joy that awaits you if you are victorious. In your hands you carry honor, praise, riches, freedom, and felicity if you bear yourselves bravely, but altogether to the contrary if your hearts fail you. You could have lived quietly as slaves, but because you longed to be free you are with me here, and to gain that end you must be valiant, strong, and undismayed.
>
> I know not what more to say. You know what honor is. Bear yourself in such fashion as to keep your honor.

The following day, June 23, 1314, the Scots advanced upon the English line at dawn. At 100 yards, the Scots knelt and made a brief prayer. When Edward II saw them he exclaimed, "They kneel for mercy!"

One of his knights, Sir Ingram de Umfraville, responded, "For mercy yes, but not from you: from God for their sins. These men will win all or die."

The Scottish attacked, their bristling schiltrons pushing inexorably through the English ranks. The armies were so closely engaged that the English could not use their archers for fear of hitting their own men. Impaled horses threw their riders and then trampled them underfoot. As the English were forced back, the Scots shouted, "On them! They fail!" In their panic, so many of the retreating English plunged into the Bannockburn and drowned that they created a bridge of corpses. Afraid he would be captured, Edward II fled with an escort of 500. The Black Douglas pursued him with 60 knights, killing stragglers and harrying the main body so effectively that it was said that until it reached the safety of the castle at Dunbar, no English knight could so much as stop to pass water.

As the English troops saw the departure of the royal standard, their spirits flagged. It was at this point that Robert ordered a horde of camp followers and servants into the fray. Believing this to be yet another Scottish army, the English broke and ran.

It was the most humiliating defeat England had ever suffered. Its baggage train, which included money chests for the troops' wages and was valued at the then astronomical figure of £200,000, fell into the hands of Robert's men. So much loot was distributed that hardly a family in Scotland failed to benefit. Robert captured so many English barons, earls, and knights that he was able to trade for the freedom of his wife, whom he had not seen in six years, as well as family members and Scottish noblemen Edward II held captive. Many of the Scottish lords who had remained loyal to Edward II now allied themselves with Robert.

To keep England off balance, Robert launched devastating forays into its northern territories, many led by the Black Douglas. Even when he found himself confronting superior numbers of English knights, Douglas invariably attacked. On two occasions, he hacked a path to their leader and killed him in single combat, which had a decidedly dispiriting effect on the rest. Douglas's campaign of intimidation was so successful that "a hundred English would not hesitate to fly from two or three Scottish soldiers so grievously had their wonted courage deserted them," wrote Thomas Walsingham. The English were eventually forced to sue for peace and accept Robert's claim to the Scottish throne. He had successfully concluded the struggle that Wallace had begun.

The hapless Edward II came to a very bad end. In 1327, he was arrested by his lords and kept in dank dungeons for months in the hope he would sicken and die. When he proved too robust for this approach, he was tied down, a hollow bone was inserted into his rectum, and a red hot poker forced up it. No sign of violence marred the royal remains.

In 1329 Robert grew ill. Calling his friends around him, he expressed one great regret: his inability to fulfill the vow he had taken that if ever the war for Scottish independence were won he would go fight "the enemies of Christ." He asked that after he died, his heart be cut out and carried by one of his men on a crusade. The knights chose the Black Douglas for the honor. After Robert died, on June 7, his heart was encased in a small silver and enamel casket, which Douglas wore on a chain around his neck. The crusaders having been driven from the Holy Land, Douglas set out for Spain, and landed at Seville in 1330. Knights rallied to him as one of the most renowned fighting men in Christendom. On August 25, as the Saracens mounted an attack at Teba, Douglas led the charge and penetrated far into the enemy ranks until he was cut off and surrounded. Legend has it that he took off the casket and threw it into the ranks of the enemy before him, shouting, "Always before me, Great Heart!" (And this is how the gold-crowned red heart came to be in the Douglas coat of arms.) His body was recovered the following day, pierced with five mortal wounds and surrounded by a circle of enemy dead.

Douglas' bones and Robert's heart were recovered from the battlefield, returned to Scotland, and interred.

35 Ronald Rosser

I got even for Dick.
—Ronald E. Rosser

R onald Rosser was the oldest of 17 children growing up in the coal-mining town of Crooksville, Ohio. He saw it as his responsibility to protect his younger siblings from bullies and handed out black eyes and bloody noses to anyone who picked on them. At 17, in 1946, he dropped out of school to join the army, leaving his younger brother Richard to look after the others. After three uneventful years posted stateside with the 82nd Airborne Division, Ronald returned home and took a job in the mines. Richard joined the army in 1950, and with the outbreak of war was sent to Korea. In February 1951 he was killed in action.

After the funeral a few weeks later, Ronald told his family that he was reenlisting. "I'm going to get even with the commies for what they did to Dick. I'm going to kill as many of them as I can, and I'm not going to take any prisoners," he said.

To his chagrin, Rosser was posted with the 187th Airborne in Japan, rather than in Korea. He wrangled himself an assignment as a forward observer for a heavy mortar company with the 38th Infantry Regiment, Second Infantry Division. He saw his first combat at Bloody Ridge in late August and early September, where he not only directed mortar fire but frequently volunteered for raids and patrols.

Rosser was temporarily attached to L Company when on January 12, 1952, it was ordered to conduct a daylight raid on Hill 472, take a few prisoners, destroy whatever bunkers were found, and kill as many of the enemy as possible. Only light resistance was expected.

The temperature stood at -20°F, and there was a foot of snow on the ground as Company L crossed the broad valley below Hill 472 before dawn. Even in the dim light, the GIs were clearly silhouetted against the snow. Suddenly the Chicoms opened up with machine guns and mortars. Far from being lightly defended as intelligence had reported, the hill was held by hundreds of dug-in troops. Rosser radioed for mortar fire but didn't bother providing precise targeting coordinates. "Drop it in anywhere," he said. "There's so many of them up there you can't help but hit a Chinaman."

By the time L Company made it to the base of the hill it had suffered a dozen casualties. Captain Davies sent a platoon to the front of the hill to create a diversion while he attempted a flanking maneuver with the rest of his men, including Rosser. They met stiff resistance as they fought their way uphill through the trenches, and by the time they had gotten within 100 yards of the summit, only 35 of them were still standing. Captain Davies was badly wounded, as was his lieutenant. The only radio that still worked belonged to Rosser, and Davies borrowed it to call in a situation report to battalion headquarters. "I'm down to about three dozen effectives, we're low on ammo, and there's still one trench full of Chinese in front of us," he said. "What are my orders?"

After listening he turned to Rosser and said flatly, "They want us to take the hill."

Rosser, now the senior NCO, said, "I'll take 'em up for you, Captain."

Rosser arrayed the able-bodied men behind him and positioned the wounded on the flanks to provide covering fire. Bellowing, "Let's go!" he ran 50 yards through enemy fire, all the while shouting encouragement. When he took cover under the berm in front of the enemy trench, he discovered that not one GI had followed him. They had hit the dirt as soon as the enemy began shooting. He later recalled, "My first thought was to run like a rabbit. I was scared to death. Then I said to myself, 'This is what you wanted, why you're over here,' so I decided to make the best of it. I figured I was going to die and I'd just try to take as many of them with me as I could. I'd try to make them pay for Dick's death."

He leaped astride the trench. Beneath him, startled by his sudden appearance, were eight Chinese troops armed with submachine guns. He stuck the muzzle of his M2 carbine in the ear of the nearest one and fired. A soldier behind Rosser poked him in the back with his gun, apparently trying to take him prisoner. Rosser spun around and shot him in the neck. The soldier then grabbed his leg, so Rosser blasted him in the chest.

Flicking his selector to full auto, Rosser shot bursts into the rest of the soldiers as they scrambled to get away, killing five and wounding two. Two others made it to a bunker and disappeared inside. Rosser pulled the pin on a white phosphorous grenade and tossed it down the entrance, then gunned the men down as they crawled out of the smoke.

He shouted to the other GIs, "Come on! Let's go! I got them on the run!" Without waiting for a response he started down the zigzag trench. He could not see beyond a corner a short distance ahead, but over the top of the trench he could see a num-

ber of heads bobbing toward him. He stopped just short of the corner and shot the first enemy to come around it, then fired into the rest as they turned around. Rosser climbed out of the trench and ran alongside it, firing into the Chinese even as a hail of bullets was directed at him from other positions. He created a dozen more casualties before the rest of the enemy found refuge in a pair of bunkers.

Down to his last magazine, Rosser headed back down the trench toward his company. Near the point where he'd commenced his solitary rampage, he found a wounded GI who had attempted to join him. Rosser slung the man onto his back and brought him back to what was left of L Company.

Rosser gathered grenades and magazines from the dead and wounded and stuffed them into his field jacket. A friend begged him not to renew his assault, but Rosser responded, "Hell, they didn't get me last time. I can get back up there and get some more of them."

As he ran toward the trench, he realized that the enemy had reoccupied it and was waiting for him. Still running, he pulled the pin on a grenade and tossed a Hail Mary from about 50 feet. "It was about the most perfect throw I ever made," he later recalled. "It landed smack in the center of the trench." Before the smoke cleared Rosser jumped into the trench, firing bursts from his carbine and throwing more grenades. He made his way down its length, shooting everyone in sight. Grenades and mortar rounds exploded all around him, one blast lifting him high into the air. He slammed back to earth, got to his feet and fought on, wounded by shell fragments but seemingly as indestructible as Sgt. Rock of the comic books.

When he had expended the last of his ammunition, Rosser ran down the hill and again stuffed his pockets with ordnance. He tried to persuade others to go back up with him, but there were no volunteers, so he returned to the trench alone, in search of further targets. When the Chinese turned a machine gun against him, he decided "enough is enough," and returned to his company, still holding its small spot on the hill. He learned that the battalion had sent reinforcements, but they were blocked by enemy troops who had returned to the previously cleared trenches below them. The six American tanks in the valley didn't know where to direct their fire, so Rosser volunteered to go down and tell them, picking up a wounded GI along the way.

Rosser gave the tanks precise firing instructions, and under their covering fire L Company made its way to safety. That evening, a heavily bandaged Captain Davies visited Rosser to thank him for what he had done, telling him he'd be proud to have him in L Company.

"No thanks," replied Rosser. "I'd get killed for sure if I spent much time with you."

Not that he was ready to stop fighting. He refused an order to leave the front lines and remained in Korea another six months. When he returned home he told his mother, "I got even for Dick."

On June 27, 1952 Rosser received the Medal of Honor at a White House ceremony. His neighbors in Crooksville were amazed by his exploit. Gladys O. Heskett, his sixth-grade teacher, told *Time* magazine, "I can't for the life of me see little Ronnie Rosser slaughtering all those Chinese, although I'm sure they deserved it."

36 Hans-Ulrich Rudel

Only he is lost who gives up on himself.

—Hans-Ulrich Rudel

The Knight's Cross with Oak Leaves, Swords, and Diamonds was Germany's highest decoration until Hitler decided that one man's valor called for something more. He ordered that the medal be upgraded with *Golden* Oak Leaves. Twelve were made up in the expectation that others might be found worthy, but only Hans-Ulrich Rudel actually received it, on January 1, 1945. And although he shot down a handful of planes in his career, he was not among Germany's glamorous fraternity of top fighter aces but flew a slow and out-moded Stuka dive-bomber.

After completing his officer cadet and flight training in June 1938, Rudel entered the Stuka program. He did not demonstrate any particular aptitude, and his instructors were convinced he would never make it. They also found him odd; as one said, "He doesn't smoke, drinks only milk, has no tales to tell about women, and spends all of his free time at sports: Rudel is a strange bird!" In fact, his devotion to athletics bordered on the fanatical, and whenever he wasn't flying he was either organizing a game or training in track and field.

He served as a reconnaissance pilot during the invasion of Poland in 1939 and was then assigned to uneventful duty in occupied France. He eventually mastered the Stuka, but the poor reputation he had established early on dogged him when he sought a combat posting. In June 1941, he was sent east and participated in the opening stage of Operation Barbarossa, the invasion of the Soviet Union. At last he had an opportunity to demonstrate his prowess, bombing tanks, antiaircraft positions, and ammunition dumps. In a backhanded compliment, his squadron leader pronounced him "crazy" for his willingness to dive lower than anyone else to hit the target.

One of Rudel's first missions was to bomb a railroad station. A storm blew in, and even though the squadron was over the target, the leader called off the attack. He turned suddenly, forcing Rudel to bank too sharply. His plane stalled and, weighed down by its bomb, fell like a rock, plunging out of control for thousands of feet. He managed to pull out just over the ground, actually hitting some birch trees. With leafy branches sticking out of holes in his wings, his Stuka flew even more slowly than usual back to base. By the time he made it, his squadron leader had already delivered a short obituary speech: "Pilot Officer Rudel and his crew attempted the impossible. They tried to attack the set target by diving through the storm, and death has claimed them."

When Rudel told him that his dive was unintentional, his squadron leader responded, "Rubbish! You are exactly that kind of idiot. You were absolutely determined to attack the railway station."

Rudel protested, but his leader snapped, "The future will prove I was right."

· KIRCHNER ·

Proof that Rudel would press home an attack under any circumstances came soon enough, when the squadron was ordered to take on the Soviet Baltic Fleet, cruising the Gulf of Finland near the besieged city of Leningrad. The primary goal was to eliminate two battleships, the *Marat* and the *Oktyabrskaya Revolyutsiya*, which were using their long-range guns to deadly effect against the German infantry. Special 1,000-kilogram bombs were delivered for the mission, capable of penetrating the armored deck to explode deep within the hull.

On September 21, 1941, Rudel was second in a formation of Stukas flying at 10,000 feet toward Kronshtat harbor. The explosions of the antiaircraft flak were so dense that they looked like cloud banks. Rudel reminded himself that the gunners were putting up a screen, not firing at him in particular. It was no use flying evasively as some of the others were doing— as he often said, "War is not exactly a life insurance."

Ahead of him he saw the 23,000-ton *Marat*. He dived at an angle of 70 to 80 degrees, overtaking his group leader. The battleship's antiaircraft batteries opened up with a furious barrage, but Rudel pressed his attack, easing off the diving brakes and increasing his angle to close to 90 degrees as he closed in, his Stuka still rock-steady at 350 mph. At 900 feet, he could see sailors scurrying about on the deck directly beneath him as he released his bomb. He belatedly recalled a warning that unless he dropped the bomb from at least 3,000 feet he might be caught in the blast. Exerting all his strength against the stick, nearly blacking out, he managed to pull out of the dive—fortunately, the Stuka was nearly impossible to overstress. He skimmed a dozen feet above the water, below the effective range of the antiaircraft fire, as his rear gunner told him over the intercom, "*Herr Oberleutnant*, the ship is blowing up!" The bomb had evidently hit the *Marat*'s ammunition store. Congratulations flooded in over the radio from his fellow pilots. Asked later how he felt at that moment, Rudel replied, "As if I looked into the eyes of thousands of grateful infantrymen."

To Rudel the war on the Eastern Front was a crusade, and Germany Europe's vital bulwark against bolshevism. That bulwark was pushed steadily back as the Soviet Union poured its seemingly limitless quantities of men and materiel into battle. One by one his squadron mates died, incinerated in fireballs or smashed against the earth, and he wondered when his time would come. He had become a national hero, and when he had flown a thousand sorties he was encouraged to retire from active combat. He refused to consider it.

In February 1943, Rudel was introduced to an experimental modification of the Stuka, the Ju 87 G-1, dubbed the *Kanonenvogel* (Cannon Bird), or *Panzerknacker* (Tank Buster). Mounted under each wing was a 37mm automatic Flak 18 cannon with a six-round magazine. The two cannon fired in unison, using a special one-kilogram armor-piercing shell that could take out a T-34 tank with one hit in its rear-mounted engine. Rudel took a Cannon Bird back to his squadron, used it to destroy 70 Soviet landing craft in the Black Sea, and in March blew up his first tank. In July, on his first mission on the first day of Operation Citadel, he eliminated four tanks, and by the end of the day he had taken out 12. He was put in charge of a tank-buster squadron.

As the Ju 87 G-1 proved its effectiveness, the Soviets began to escort their leading tanks with mobile antiaircraft guns, forcing Rudel to plan his attacks carefully. Sometimes he would climb to 2,400 feet, above the flak level, and then scream down in a steep dive, weaving violently to dodge the wall of steel thrown at him. At a height of about 350 feet he would straighten out for an instant, fire, and then pull out. Other times he would approach at treetop level, again weaving, and in the one-second interval that the tanks were in range, dip the nose of the Stuka slightly and fire at a target roughly a meter square. Short of shooting skeet from a roller coaster, a more difficult shooting challenge would be hard to contrive, but Rudel excelled at it—his wartime tally was many times that of his nearest rival, and he destroyed as many as 18 tanks in a single day. Because his success rate was so high he flew as much as possible—10, 15, even 17 missions a day—landing only to refuel and reload his guns, or to switch to a new plane if his had been badly chewed up by enemy fire. He knew that every tank he stopped would not take its toll on the infantry, nor would it go on to ravage his fatherland.

As Rudel was awarded each higher order of the Knight's Cross, he received a personal audience with Hitler, who engaged him in lengthy discussions on the war. As much as Rudel appreciated the honor, it pained him to take even a brief reprieve from the front. Furthermore, Hitler invariably told him to stop flying, maintaining that he was now too precious to the nation to continue to risk his life. Rudel responded that if that was to be the price of a decoration he would refuse it. By the end of the war he was flying in direct defiance of the führer's orders.

Late in March 1944 Rudel was leading a bombing run against bridges on the Dniester River when a novice crew crash-landed behind Soviet lines. Rudel landed on a muddy field nearby to pick them up. He had performed such service six times before, but this time his Stuka became inextricably mired. With Russian troops approaching there was nothing to do but run for the Dniester, about four miles away. He shouted "Follow me!" to his rear gunner, Erwin Hentschel, and the two-man crew.

It was clumsy running in heavy boots and fur coats, but desperation spurred the Germans. They had increased their lead on the "Ivans" when they came to the high, almost perpendicular cliffs above the Dniester's banks. Rudel jumped, slowing his descent by grabbing at the thorny bushes which grew out of the face of the cliff. His companions followed suit, and by the time they reached the bottom all four men were bleeding from numerous lacerations, their clothes torn to ribbons. As they rested, the Soviet troops arrived at the top of the cliff. Unable to see the Germans beneath them, they gave up their search.

The Dniester, in flood stage, was 300 meters wide and just

a few degrees above freezing, with chunks of ice floating in it. Still, it was the only path to safety, and the Germans stripped off their coats and boots and plunged in. In seconds Rudel was unable to feel a thing, but years of athletic competition had given him stamina and discipline, and he forced himself to go through the motions of swimming. Along with the two novices he made it across, but Hentschel, a loyal friend with 1,490 missions behind him, succumbed to the cold. Rudel jumped back into the river and swam to the spot where he saw him go under, but it was too late.

He and the others intoned a solemn Lord's Prayer.

In their wet clothes and bare feet the Germans began to walk toward their lines, skirting inhabited places. It was three o'clock in the afternoon and Rudel, who had not eaten since dawn, was famished. After an hour he saw three armed figures ahead, silhouetted against the late afternoon sun. He hoped they were Romanians, allies of the Germans, but as they approached he saw that they wore red star insignia of the Red Army.

Rudel's pistol was taken from him—a .25 automatic, it probably wouldn't have helped him anyway. The situation seemed hopeless, but rather than accept defeat he suddenly bolted, crouching and swerving. He heard a shout of, *"Stoi!"* (Halt!) Two of the soldiers fired their rifles but missed. The third opened up with his submachine gun and hit Rudel in the shoulder. With bullets whistling by, he kept running. He marveled to think that moments before he was hardly able to put one foot ahead of the other, yet now he was sprinting faster than he ever had in all his years of competition. Blood spurted from his shoulder, but he slowly increased the gap between himself and his pursuers, who periodically stopped running to fire. "Only he is lost who gives up on himself," he repeated over and over again. As he neared the top of a hill he saw another 20 enemy Russians coming at him from the side. He ran down the far side of the hill and across a plowed field. He was a few hundred yards ahead of his pursuers when he tripped and fell into a furrow, where he lay panting, too exhausted to get up.

The Soviets reached the edge of the field and spread out. With his fingertips, Rudel scraped up bits of the frozen earth and threw it back over himself. His wet clothes were freezing on him, but he felt feverish with the expectation of imminent capture. One man approached within 20 paces and looked from side to side, but did not see him. At that moment Rudel's Stuka squadron roared overhead. He looked up at it longingly, but dared not move even a finger. He imagined the thoughts of his squadron mates as they searched for him: *This time even he has had it.*

At sunset more enemy soldiers arrived, with dogs. Rudel assumed he would soon be found, but, incredibly, they filed by him before forming a systematic line of search. He wondered why the dogs didn't catch his scent, but couldn't explain it. As darkness came the Soviets left.

Rudel stood up and headed on his way, guiding himself by the east wind, since it was too dark to see his compass. He tripped over unseen obstructions and walked into trees. Avoiding bridges, he waded across chest-deep rivers. His feet became badly cut and bruised, and he gradually lost all feeling. He was weak with hunger. Above all, he told himself, don't sit down—keep hobbling on. As he later wrote, "The will to live, to keep my freedom, urges me on; life without freedom is a hollow fruit."

At last he found an isolated farmhouse and knocked on the door. An old woman answered, and Rudel forced himself in. On a rough plank bed an old man lay asleep. The woman gave Rudel water and a chunk of moldy cornbread, and he lay down and rested between the couple. A few hours later he left, walking through the night in the rain. He estimated that he had covered 16 to 18 miles since he crossed the Dniester. At dawn he forced himself to run; he routinely ran six miles each morning, and he told himself that this day should be no different. Despite the excruciating pain in his feet, he managed that distance before exhaustion overwhelmed him. He found some deserted farmhouses and searched them for food, but even the old corn cobs had been picked clean.

A Romanian man and girl, fleeing the Soviets, approached in a wagon. They gave him directions, as well as rusks. As they rode off he asked himself why he had not taken their vehicle, but the idea had not entered his mind—they were refugees like him.

Outside the city of Floresti, Rudel encountered two German soldiers. He identified himself, but because he had no identification they remained suspicious until he pulled from his pocket his Knight's Cross with the Oak Leaves and Swords. He was reunited with his squadron.

His shoulder was bandaged, and he could barely move his arm, and his feet were so stripped of flesh that he couldn't operate the rudder bar, much less walk. He was ordered not to fly, but after a day in the aid station he had himself carried to the airfield and put in his plane. Radio Moscow had triumphantly announced that he had been captured, but it would soon learn otherwise. He killed 10 tanks that day, and 17 the next, when he immolated a tank column carrying drums of fuel. Within days he had raised his total score to more than 200. On March 29, Rudel became only the 10th German soldier to be awarded the Knight's Cross with Oak Leaves, Swords, and Diamonds. By June, he became the only pilot in history to fly 2,000 combat missions. An enraged Stalin put a reward of 100,000 rubles on his head.

Even though the Cannon Birds took a terrible toll on Soviet armor, it was not enough. By the autumn of 1944, Germany was falling back before the Soviet advance into Hungary.

On August 19, Rudel attacked a tank column 25 miles out of Budapest. He had expended his ammunition, leaving five tanks in flames, when he noticed that one of them was an unfamiliar model. He wanted to be able to describe it to headquarters, and ordered the rest of his formation back to base while he flew in for a closer look. A heavy machine gun opened up on him. He suddenly felt two hammer blows strike his plane and a searing pain in his left thigh. As his blood flowed, he felt his strength and consciousness fading. His rear gunner had no access to the cockpit and could do nothing for him. They were flying over sparsely settled country, and Rudel figured that if he made a forced landing he would bleed to death before he could get medical help. With no alternative, he flew to Budapest on sheer willpower.

One 12.7mm slug had to be removed from his leg; the other had passed clean through. He was ordered to take six weeks' recuperation, but after eight days he'd had enough and returned to his unit, his leg in a plaster cast.

By February 8, 1945, the Soviets had bridged the Oder and established a footing at Lebus, 50 miles from Berlin. As Rudel's Stuka wing tried to hold them back, it came under heavy flak from well-hidden Antiaircraft guns. Worried about the survival of the other, less experienced pilots, he told them to hold back while he attacked alone. He set four tanks ablaze before returning to base. After his second sortie he had to change planes because his had been badly torn up. By his fourth sortie he had taken out 12 T-34s and heavily armored Stalin tanks, but one Stalin defied him. Repeatedly he climbed to 2,400 feet and made his vertical dive, but the tank refused to burst into flames despite several solid hits on it. Finally, as he climbed for one last attempt, with one cannon jammed and only a single round left in the other, he asked himself whether it wouldn't be wiser to fly back to the base and reload. But the relentless taskmaster inside him responded: "You will say next that I will botch it because it is the thirteenth. Superstitious nonsense! You have one round left so stop wasting time and get on with it!"

Rudel dived, made his shot, and was jubilant to see the tank burst into flames, but as he pulled out of his dive, with ground batteries blazing at him, his plane was hit by two 40mm shells and red-hot steel tore through his right leg.

He wrote, "Everything goes black before my eyes, I gasp for

breath. But I must keep flying . . . flying . . . I must not pass out. Grit your teeth, you have to master your weakness."

They say God only gives you the pain you can stand, but Rudel was pushing Him. Battling for consciousness, unable to see, he flew by instinct. As he repeatedly drifted into a somnambulistic haze, his rear gunner shouted at him to pull back on the stick, snatching him momentarily back to alertness. At last he crash-landed on a patch of rough ground and passed out, his rear gunner managing to slow the bleeding enough to keep him alive.

He awoke in the hospital, his right leg amputated. The surgeon was mystified that he was flying at all, with his left leg in a cast. But Rudel would soon outdo himself: by Easter, he was flying with his left leg still in a cast and an artificial limb on his right! Since he was now flying against orders, his victories were credited to the squadron account.

In the course of the war Rudel flew an unparalleled 2,530 missions, including 400 in the Focke-Wulf 190. He fired more than 5,000 37mm rounds, 150,000 20mm rounds, and dropped over a million kilograms of bombs. He got confirmed kills on 519 tanks, 150 artillery pieces, 70 landing craft, and 800 combat vehicles, as well as a battleship, a destroyer, and a cruiser.

Even though his tank-killing Stuka was not set up for aerial combat, Rudel achieved ace status with it, accounting for five Soviet planes with its single-shot cannon. He shot down six more in the Fw 190. He was shot down 30 times and wounded five.

After Germany's unconditional surrender, Rudel led a Stuka squadron to the U.S.-occupied sector. He ordered his pilots to pancake in, so as not to surrender any serviceable aircraft. (A quixotic gesture, since by 1945 the Stuka was a museum piece.) An American approached Rudel and tried to snatch the Knight's Cross with Golden Oak Leaves from around his neck but was shoved brusquely away. Rudel did not consider himself vanquished. As he saw it, he had never been defeated in the air, on his merits, but only by the sweeping tide of men and materiel on the ground.

"Only he is lost who gives up on himself" continued to be Rudel's motto, and once he had had a suitable prosthesis made he participated in sports with the same indomitable spirit with which he had made war. He won diving, tennis, and skiing competitions in which he was given no special consideration for his handicap. In 1949, he placed in the top class in the world skiing championships at Bariloche. In 1953, he became the first man to climb the 6,739-meter Llullaillacu volcano in the Andes.

Unlike other well-known Luftwaffe aces, Rudel never renounced the cause he had fought for. A hero to the German far right, he became something of an embarrassment to the postwar government.

He died in 1982 at age 66.

37 Shaka

A young beauty named Nandi, bathing in a woodland pool, was observed by Senzangakona, a Zulu noble, who became aroused and had his way with her. Because they were both from the same clan, their union violated a taboo, so a few months later, when she notified his family that she was with child, they claimed she was merely infested with I-Shaka, an intestinal worm believed to cause false pregnancy. The boy she gave birth to was named after that worm, and he and his mother were reluctantly and unceremoniously accepted into his father's kraal, or homestead, in about 1787.

At age six, Shaka was put to work tending sheep, but Senzangakona was furious with him after a wild dog killed one of them. Nandi interceded on his behalf, and both were expelled from the kraal. Although they were taken in by Nandi's family, life was difficult. Shaka was cruelly teased by the older boys, not only for his poverty and bastardy but for his unusually small penis. As the childhood trauma of a man who would become one of Africa's greatest warriors this might sound unduly Freudian, but herd boys went naked up till puberty, and Shaka's inadequacy was apparent to all. Nandi had instilled in him a fierce pride, though, and he was not afraid to fight. When he was 11 two older boys cried, "Look at his penis; it is just like a little earthworm!" He attacked them with his stick and, though they were bigger and armed with similar sticks, nearly killed them before other boys pulled him away.

At age 13 Shaka killed a deadly black mamba. He was taken before a tribal chief who rewarded him with a goat and said, "Boy! Today you have done a brave man's deed."

As Shaka reached puberty he began to grow, dramatically. He soon stood half a head above other men, and as far as his development in other areas, suffice it to say that he eschewed the apron favored by most young men in favor of the less concealing foreskin cover. He excelled in all physical activities and was especially skillful with the *assegai*, or light spear. He practiced until he could hit a tuft of grass at 50 yards with two throws out of three.

When famine struck in 1802, Nandi and Shaka were again forced to wander in search of a home, until they at last found refuge in Mtetwaland.

When Shaka was 19, his dogs treed a leopard that had attacked his flock. Normally, in such a case one would round up a group of warriors and their dogs to face the beast, and even then several of the men could expect to be mauled. Shaka took on the leopard alone, armed with two spears and a heavy club. His first spear hit the cat, but entered its chest too far back, behind its heart. The leopard dropped out of the tree, and with fierce grunting sounds charged him. As the cat leaped, Shaka speared it through the chest and brought the club down

· KIRCHNER ·

on its head, killing it instantly. For his bravery he was rewarded with a cow.

In his 20s Shaka served in the army of the Mtetwa empire.
Intertribal warfare at the time was largely symbolic and bloodless. The sides faced off and tossed their *assegais* from a distance while protected behind ox-hide shields. Each side picked
up the spears that landed nearby and threw them back until one
had had enough and left the field. That side was considered the
loser. This was not war to Shaka's liking. Rather than toss away
his weapon, he preferred to close with his enemy—whose shield
he would hook aside with his own—and stab him with his
spear. Shaka realized that the traditional *assegai* was too light
and fragile for his fighting technique, so he came up with a new
design and visited a master blacksmith to have it made, holding
him to exact specifications as to its length, shape, weight, and
balance. Shaka's spear occupies a place in Zulu lore comparable
to that of Excalibur in Arthurian legend. To forge it, virgin ore
was used and a new forge built; work was done during the proper phase of the moon and the most auspicious hours of the
night; incantations were muttered; demons were summoned
and addressed; and the blade was tempered in human fat. Every
specific type of Zulu spear has a name, but Shaka would not
name his yet—not until he had killed with it.

As Shaka marched to his next battle, against the Butelezi,
his comrades wondered why he carried a single heavy spear
rather than three light ones as did they. The armies faced off
at 100 yards, and the most renowned Butelezi warrior
stepped forward. With taunts and insults, he challenged any
man of Shaka's regiment to face him in single combat. Shaka
called out to him, "You dried-out old cow's bladder full of
wind, I will make you eat your words, and my spear too. Now
fight." Then he advanced. This was unprecedented—usually
both men would hurl *assegais* at each other from a distance of
40 to 50 yards. If one man dropped his *assegais* and fled, his
life was spared.

As Shaka closed to within 35 yards, his opponent threw his first *assegai*. Shaka deflected it with his shield and began to run toward him. At 15 yards, his opponent threw his second *assegai*, which Shaka also caught on his shield. Then Shaka was upon him. He hooked his shield and wrenched it sharply to the left, blocking the man's right arm and preventing him from bringing his last *assegai* into play, then thrust his broad-bladed spear under the man's exposed nipple, through his heart, and out his right side. As the Butelezi warrior fell, Shaka pulled his spear free and roared the Zulu victory cry, "*Ngadla!*" (I have eaten!)

The two opposing forces watched in silence, their wonder growing as Shaka proceeded to advance alone against the Butelezi line. His best friends, Nqoboka and Mgobozi, hurried forward to cover his back, and the rest of his army followed.

Shaka was promoted to the rank of captain of one hundred after that day's victory and given 10 head of cattle. Nqoboka and Mgobozi were each given three head of cattle, and their regiment as a whole was rewarded with 100. As for his spear, Shaka named it *Ixwa*, for the sucking sound it made when he pulled it from a deep body thrust.

Shaka had achieved the glory he had craved ever since childhood, and when his father died the paramount chief, Dingiswayo, installed him as chief of the small tribe of Zulus. From his 10-square-mile territory, Shaka scraped together an army of 500, which he armed with short, stabbing spears like his own. He ruthlessly drilled his men in his fighting methods, killing on the spot anyone who failed to obey orders instantly. He developed tactics in which his force would divide into four elements: a "chest," which engaged the enemy frontally; two "horns," which swept around the enemy flanks; and "loins," a tactical reserve. Shaka's men did not fight ritualistically, they fought to kill; their motto, Conquer or Die. Once they defeated an enemy, they gave survivors the option to join Zulu ranks or be executed. Shaka's army grew rapidly.

After the death of Dingiswayo, Shaka attained total power.

He rewarded all those who had befriended him during his years of struggle but was merciless with his enemies. He rounded up those who had teased him as a boy or shown disrespect to his mother, some three dozen in all, and recounted each and every slight. Those who could recall some mitigating good deed were granted a quick death by clubbing, while those who could not were sentenced to be impaled upon the sharpened upright fence posts of Shaka's kraal. As they were led away, he called out cheerfully, "Sit you well!"

Shaka installed Nandi as chief noblewoman and declared her "Mother of the Nation," and she was his closest adviser and confidant. Upon her death in 1827 he seemed to slip into psychosis, declaring Draconian terms for a year of mourning: no crops were to be cultivated; cows' milk was not to be drunk, but poured onto the ground—and if any woman became pregnant, she and her husband were slain. Anyone deemed insufficiently mournful was summarily executed, and Shaka picked out various groups for wholesale slaughter, declaring, "You can only rule Zulus by killing them."

In 1828, at 41 years of age, he was assassinated by his half brothers.

With his innovative tactics and fighting techniques, Shaka conquered 2 million square miles of Africa, an area larger than Europe. In the 12 years of his reign, he created a Zulu nation of 250,000. Sixty-three years after his death, it took a British army of 20,000 infantrymen and cavalry, armed with breech-loading rifles, Congreve rockets, and artillery to subdue his people.

38 Egil Skallagrimsson

> *Once I carved up eight,*
> *Aye, twice sliced eleven;*
> *I, alone, the bane of all,*
> *Gave the wolves a meal.*
> *Hot blows we traded,*
> *Making shields shudder;*
> *From my bold hard hand,*
> *My swordflame flashed red.*
> —Egil Skallagrimsson

The loosely knit Nordic societies of a thousand years ago were among the most honor bound on earth. The potential for violence lurked in every encounter as relative status was constantly contested, and only the man who would not tolerate a slight could lay claim to honor. Perceived insults had to be paid for in blood, and killings resulted in feuds that raged for generations—the Vikings were "battle-glad" and "strife-eager," in the words of one of their poets. That a people who spent so much time fighting among themselves still had the energy to invade, colonize, and pillage their neighbors might be seen as a testament to the human spirit. Providing insight into this world are the sagas, stories of Viking heroes. Though the sagas are not considered reliable history, Egil's is at least within the realm of possibility even if, like James Bowie or Robert the Bruce, he is credited with more heroics than seem likely in one lifetime.

Born in Norway in 910, the son of one Skallagrim, Egil became the most illustrious member of "a very mixed family, in that some were the most handsome people ever to be born . . . but most of the men...were outstandingly ugly." His brother Thorolf was among the handsome few, but, according to his saga, Egil fell on the ugly side. He was prematurely bald, and though a head taller than most men, he nevertheless resembled a troll, with bushy eyebrows of the sort that join in the middle, a large nose, and massive chin. He was ill tempered and greedy, but had an artistic bent that expressed itself in poetry after a few horns of mead or a battle well fought, and he was as famous a poet as he was a warrior.

As his saga would have it, even as a child of three Egil was trouble. Before his family left for a gathering of the clan, Skallagrim told him, "You're not going. You don't know how to behave yourself when there's company gathered and a lot of drinking going on. You're difficult enough to handle when you're sober." At age six, Egil went to a district festival and took part in a game organized for the boys. He was to play against Grim, five years older and considerably stronger. Egil grew frustrated when Grim got the better of him and tried to strike him with a bat. Warding off his blows, Grim threw him to the ground and beat him. Egil left the field, returned shortly with an ax, and drove it through Grim's skull. The festival broke up in a fracas that cost seven lives. Back at home, Skallagrim made it clear that he was not pleased with his son, but his proud mother said that Egil had the makings of a real Viking and when he was old enough ought to be given a ship.

Again as the saga would have it, Egil attended a feast for King Eirik Bloodaxe and Queen Gunnhild given by Bard of Atley Island. The young, drunken Egil grew annoyed with his host over some breach of Viking etiquette and, as he left the gather-

·KIRCHNER·

ing, stabbed him dead. When Bard's body was discovered, the king sent out men to capture Egil. A group of nine rowed to a nearby island, where three guarded the boat while six searched for him. Egil jumped the men by the boat, killing one on the spot. Another started to run up a slope, but Egil swung his sword and cut his leg off.[22] The third jumped into the boat and started pushing off with a pole, but Egil grabbed the mooring rope, pulled the boat back, and jumped in, too. After a brief exchange of blows he killed the man and threw him overboard. Egil sailed off and found refuge with a powerful chieftain, Thorir.

The following spring, Egil and his brother Thorolf mounted an expedition to the Baltic Sea. They fought many battles and the plundering was good. Egil forged inland with a dozen men at Courland. Finding a deserted farming village they did a bit of looting, but as they left a large force of Courlanders blocked their return to the sea, showering them with stones and spears. Wounded and exhausted, Egil and his men were bound and taken prisoner. The village chief was in favor of killing them on the spot, but his son convinced him to save them for the following day, so that everyone could enjoy their suffering as they were tortured.

The prisoners were locked in a room in a strongly constructed building. Because of his obvious strength, Egil's captors took the additional precaution of tying him hand and foot to a stout post set in the middle of its dirt floor, then went into a nearby hall to eat, drink, and plan the next day's merriment.

Egil struggled against the post, and through repeated twisting and jerking succeeded in pulling it from the ground. He slid his hands and feet off it, untied his bonds with his teeth, and freed his companions.

The door was bolted and the walls were strong, but with the

22. The frequent references in Viking sagas to cutting off a leg with a single stroke of the sword are not exaggerations. Forensic analysis of over a thousand remains from the Battle of Visby, Gotland, in 1306 indicated that more than 70 percent suffered serious leg wounds, with thigh and shin bones broken or sheared. In several cases both legs had been severed.

uprooted post the Vikings managed to batter down an interior partition. They found themselves in another room of the long building and heard voices coming from a trapdoor in the floor. They opened it and discovered a deep pit holding three other prisoners, a wealthy Danish farmer named Aki and his two sons, who had been captured the year before and held as slaves. They had enjoyed the run of the place until they tried to escape, after which they were kept in the pit. They eagerly joined Egil's group. After battering down several other partitions the Vikings found themselves in a room with a door that led outside.

His men wanted to escape as quickly as possible, but Egil was in no great hurry. He asked Aki where the chieftain kept his weapons and valuables. Learning that they were in the sleeping loft, Egil rushed in, grabbed an ax, and killed the servants there. He and his men then armed themselves, broke into the treasure vault, and gathered up what they wanted. They headed for the woods, but Egil had misgivings. "This is a poor sort of expedition," he announced. "It's not warrior-like. We've stolen the farmer's property and he doesn't know it. We mustn't let a shameful thing like that happen. We'll go back to the farmstead and tell people what's been going on."

His comrades protested, but Egil went back to the farm, where the chieftain and his men were still feasting. From a fireplace in a nearby building Egil pulled a flaming log, carried it to the great hall, and shoved it under the eaves. In moments, its thatched roof was ablaze. As the ceiling burst into flames, the carousers rushed for the door, but Egil cut them down as they attempted to get out. When the building had burned to the ground, not one man who had been inside was left alive.

That was warrior-like.

In 937, Egil and Thorolf took their men to England[23] as mercenaries, fighting for King Aethelstan against the forces of a Viking ruler, Olaf, in Scotland, led by Earl Alfgeir and the broth-

---

23. In the 10th century nearly half of England was ruled by the Vikings.

ers Jarl Hring and Jarl Adils. In the midst of the battle, Thorolf went into a berserker fury, swinging his shield onto his back and taking hold of his spear with both hands. He charged forward, hewing down the enemy until he cleared a path to the banner of Hring, killing the man who carried it and Hring himself.

In the following day's battle, the force from Scotland took its vengeance. Thorolf was ambushed and killed by Adils' warriors. Enraged, Egil plunged into the fray wielding the sword he called Adder, hacked his way to Adils, and slew him.

As the guest of honor at that night's victory feast, Egil was seated across the table from King Aethelstan. Egil was sullen: his helmet was still on his head, his shield at his feet, and his sheathed sword across his lap. Over and over he pulled his sword partway from its scabbard and then thrust it back. He refused to touch his drink, and "did nothing but pull his eyebrows up and down, now this one, now the other."

With a keen understanding of the human soul, the king drew his sword and, removing a heavy gold bracelet from his arm, hung it on its point and stretched it toward Egil. Without a word, Egil reached across the table with his own sword and took the bracelet on its point. He weighed the bracelet in his hand. He studied it closely. He clasped it around his arm. He sheathed his sword. He stopped glowering.

After Egil had spent some time in England, it occurred to him to return to Norway, marry his widowed sister-in-law, Asgerd, and take over his brother's large estate. When he was ready to leave, King Aethelstan gave him two chests of silver to present to his father as compensation for Thorolf's death.

Egil married his sister-in-law, but Eirik Bloodaxe disallowed his claim to his brother's lands. Although his friends had paid *wergeld*, or blood money, to absolve him of the murder of Bard, the king still had not forgiven him. Egil demanded a hearing. Eirik rejected his case and gave Thorolf's estate to Berg-Onund, one of his supporters. Egil stormed out of the meeting, swearing vengeance on those who had sided against him. As he set off in a fast skiff, the king sent men in pursuit. In a furious fight, 10 of Egil's men were slain, but he threw a spear that killed one of Eirik's most valued retainers. Crossing a submerged sandbar the king's ship could not clear, Egil escaped. Eirik declared him an outlaw throughout Norway. Any man could now legally kill him with impunity; at least, they were free to try.

A few years later, Egil happened to land near a royal estate. From a herdsman he learned that Berg-Onund was visiting there with Rognvald, the son of King Eirik and Gunnhild, and Frodi, their foster son. Egil told the herdsman that he had spotted a bear in the brush nearby and asked him to get help from the estate. As the herdsman ran off, Egil concealed himself. Onund arrived with Frodi and another man, and they began searching the brush. Egil popped out of hiding and killed each of them in turn. When the herdsman returned, Egil advised him, "Keep an eye on your master Onund and his companions. We don't want birds and beasts ripping up their corpses!"

As Egil and his men rowed away, they encountered Rognvald and 12 companions in a galley. The men had learned of Egil's presence in the area and were heading to warn Berg-Onund. After Egil's crew carved them into fish fodder, the bard waxed poetic:

> We battled a boatload
> With no fear of vengeance,
> I reddened my blade
> In Bloodaxe's boy.
> Perished on one pinnace
> The prince and twelve liege-men;
> Busy, these battle-hands,
> A good day's work done.

With the blood of Eirik's son on Egil's hands, it would seem that their feud could end only with death. Strangely enough, if we may believe the saga, it ended with a poem.

In 948, Egil was shipwrecked on the shore of the royal domain. Rather than attempt to escape, he went to Eirik's castle and requested a hearing, which was granted for the following day. He stayed up the entire night composing an epic poem extolling King Eirik, and the following morning presented himself to the court. To suggest that the audience was hostile would be an understatement—Egil was as welcome as the cholera. But as he began to recite they listened, transfixed, as his poem introduced them to the English end-rhyme technique, which had never before been heard in Nordic verse. The effect was electrifying. As hard as it may be to believe that the sycophantic effort cooled Eirik's wrath, the king no doubt imagined it resounding through the ages, ensuring that his name and glory would never die. Egil was allowed to depart unharmed.

Old Skallagrim's health began to fail, and Egil went to Iceland to help him run his lands. One morning, Skallagrim raised an awkward point. "It seems to me, Egil," he observed, "that you're in no great hurry to give me the money that King Aethelstan sent me. What do you think should be done with it?"

"Are you really hard up, father?" asked Egil. "I didn't know that! When I think you're short of silver I'll give it to you, but it so happens that I know you've still got the odd chest-full."

Skallagrim went out and buried his treasure where Egil would never find it shortly before he died.

Some time later, Egil visited the kin of his good friend Arinbjorn, son of his late protector Thorir, in More, Norway. Egil had no complaints about the food and entertainment, but he detected a pall over the household. It seems the son, Fridgeir, was scheduled to fight a duel the following day with a berserker, Ljot the Pale. Berserkers worked themselves into a mad frenzy before battle, tearing their shirts off, howling, and chewing their steel-rimmed shields. They were held in dread for it was said that "iron could not bite them." Ljot had come from Sweden and had made a good deal of money dueling, acquiring the estate of every man he defeated. After his request to marry Fridgeir's sister had been refused, he issued a challenge to Fridgeir. Fridgeir was not strong and had never fought a duel in his life, so Egil accompanied him. When they arrived, Egil looked over Ljot and mocked him in verse:

> It suits not young Fridgeir
> To fight with this warrior,
> Grim gnawer of shield-rim
> Who hears Valkyries' song.
> Much better I meet him,
> And rescue the maiden;
> The madman stares fearsome
> With doomstruck eyes.

"You, big man, come over here to the field and fight me, if you're all that keen," replied Ljot. "We'll try each other out. It would be more of a match than fighting Fridgeir. I wouldn't think more highly of myself just for laying him out."

Egil accepted with another rhyme:

> Ljot asks such a small favor,
> 'Twould be rude to refuse him.
> I'll play with the pale one
> Swinging sword upon mail.
> So busk we for battle,
> But raise no hope of pity,
> Merry bout with the wordsmith
> Is all that I promise.

Egil walked onto the dueling field carrying a shield and his father's sword Dragvendil, which held a keen edge and had drawn a good deal of blood over the years. From his belt hung his sword Adder. The muse once again struck him:

Hew we with the steel-flash
Hack we at the shield,
My iron tongue's thirsting
For a taste of his blood.
And when the game's done
Ljot won't have much life left;
Steel quells the quarrel-seeker,
Come eagles to dine.

The bout commenced. Egil drove Ljot back with every blow until he forced him outside the stone markers that indicated the boundary of the dueling area. Ljot asked for a break, which Egil granted. After the men caught their breath, they went at it again. Egil pressed Ljot closely, then knocked his shield aside and cut off his leg just below the knee. He bled to death on the spot.

After Fridgeir congratulated him, Egil spouted this verse:

Fallen lies the wolf-feeder,
Foul worker of mischief,
The bard lopped his leg off
Leaving Fridgeir in peace.
From the bright golden river,
No reward am I seeking,
For pure sport of sword-din
I played with pale foe.

Caught up in the moment, Egil had declined payment, but months later, with time to reflect, he became increasingly covetous of Ljot's estate, now his by rights. However, it had been seized by King Hakon, successor to Eirik, who had no love of the belligerent bard. In 950, Egil sent Arinbjorn to plead his case, but Arinbjorn only succeeded in straining his own relationship with the king. Egil was unwilling to drop the matter and grew increasingly sullen. Arinbjorn finally paid him out of his own pocket, with 40 marks (about 20 pounds) of silver. Egil's good cheer returned.

Perhaps awakened to the rewards of dueling, Egil challenged Atli the Short, brother and heir of Berg-Onund, for possession of the estate that had belonged to Egil's wife, Asgerd.

Egil took the field with a helmet on his head, a shield on his left arm, a spear in his right hand, and his sword Dragvendil. Atli, a strong man and a seasoned duelist, was likewise equipped. Running at each other, they threw their spears, but both weapons went wide and hit the ground. The fighters then closed, hammering at each other's shields with their swords. His shield finally shattered by Egil's blows, Atli tossed it away and, gripping his sword with both hands, furiously fought back. Egil got in several good blows, but his edge had been so blunted against the steel rim of Atli's shield that it would not bite. By this time Egil's own shield had been smashed into uselessness, so he threw shield and sword away, launched himself at Atli, knocked him to the ground and tore out his throat with his teeth, "best of swords at need."

Egil went on to fight numerous other battles. During a raid in Frisland, after jumping across a stream, Egil found himself separated from his men and surrounded by the enemy. He single-handedly killed 11 of them. On another occasion, he was warned that he and his men would be ambushed by Värmlanders when they traveled through the Eida Wood. Egil was not dissuaded, but the warning did inspire a verse:

> If four men do flank me,
> No six could you find,
> Who'd barter their sword blows
> 'Gainst my shield-shearing might.
> And with eight men beside me,
> No twelve men could shake
> The heart of the black-browed
> Bard of the battle-storm.

And indeed, in the ambush and the running battle that followed it, 25 of the Värmlanders were killed. Egil killed 8 in one skirmish and 11 in another. He received a number of wounds, but none were serious.

Egil lived his later years in Iceland. When he was 51, he lost his second and most-favored son, Bodvar, in a shipwreck. He took the death hard and for three days lay in bed and would not eat or drink. His daughter Thorgerd implored him to write a eulogy, and he finally assented. As he worked on the poem, his spirits began to lift. When he finished "Lament for My Sons," he proudly read it to his family. It is considered his finest work.

The admonition that he who lives by the sword shall die by the sword would be regarded as more of a promise than a threat to the Vikings. It was said that they feared nothing save a quiet death, and, ironically, that was to be the fate of Egil. In his final years he lived with his niece Thordis and her husband, Grim Svertingsson. He stumbled around the household, his sight and hearing gradually fading, trying to stay out of the way of the servants as he warmed himself by the cook stove, ruing the indignities of old age:

> Like hobbled steed I stumble
> Bang bald head when I fall,
> Cock, limp like lamb's tail, useless
> As my dead man's ears.
> Blind near the fire I wander,
> Beg of the fire-maid pardon,
> That I might take a seat;
> What sorrow these sightless eyes bear!
> Yet England's mighty monarch
> Once gave me greatest honor;
> And princes once with pleasure
> The poet's wordcraft heard.

He gathered his strength one day and set out with two slaves and the two chests of silver he had received from King

Aethelstan. The next day he returned alone; after the slaves buried his treasure, he had killed them. It was never found.

In the autumn of 990, at age 80, Egil died.

In the 12th century, a set of bones was found under the altar of a church built by Grim Svertingsson, who had been converted to Christianity. They were thought to be Egil's because they were larger and heavier than the ordinary, and the skull was thick and ridged all over like a scallop shell. The priest put it on top of a fence post and struck it hard with the back of an ax. The skull neither broke nor was dented on impact, reinforcing the belief that it was indeed that of Egil Skallagrimsson.

39 Sokaku Takeda

> If there is any reserve or hesitation, even a skilled practitioner can be easily defeated. Hear the soundless sound, see the formless form. At a glance, control your opponent and attain victory without contention.
>
> —Sokaku Takeda

Born into a samurai family on October 10, 1859, Sokaku Takeda was a child during the Aizu War, when the Japanese shogunate was crushed and imperial rule reestablished. The spectacle of combat delighted him—he used to pack himself a lunch of rice balls, sneak out of his house, and walk as many as eight miles to watch battles taking place. When caught, he was chastised and sent home, but he kept returning.

Though he grew up during Japan's rapid transition from a feudal to a modern society, when the skills of the samurai were no longer in demand, his father, Sokichi, and grandfather Soemon were determined to school him in the martial arts. They taught him the sword, the spear, and the long staff (*bo*), as well as *daito-ryu aikijujutsu*, a fighting system kept secret within the Aizu clan for hundreds of years. Sokichi, a 240-

· KIRCHNER ·

pound sumo wrestler ranked at the highest level, trained him in that art as well. Discipline was severe. Sokichi would burn incense on Sokaku's hands if he failed to master a technique quickly enough, but Sokaku was too passionate about learning martial arts to require such punishment often; it was in other areas that he was delinquent. He regularly disobeyed his father's injunction against participating in local amateur sumo contests and had such an aversion to academics that he never learned to read or write. "Others will read and write for me," he predicted confidently.

354

At 14 Sokaku was apprenticed to kendo master Toma Shibuya, but rather than finish his program, Sokaku drifted from school to school, frequently getting into scrapes. He studied with the famed Kenkichi Sakakibara, at whose school he met and trained with the top swordsmen of the day, many of them retainers of the last shogun. He also mastered the half-bow (*hankyu*), short staff (*jo*), and throwing darts (*shuriken*).

In the spring of 1875, Sokaku was crossing a bridge in Inawashiro when rival gangs swarmed toward him from either end. Caught in the middle of their fight, he drew his sword and fended them off, cutting the legs of four or five before jumping into the river to escape.

With the death of Sokaku's elder brother in the autumn of the following year, all of Sokichi's expectations fell on Sokaku, and he was summoned home from Tokyo to study for the Shinto priesthood. Near Aizubange he had to cross a desolate mountain pass where a trio of bandits had been robbing and murdering travelers. Sokaku ignored warnings not to attempt the pass alone and was ambushed. With a vigorous counterattack he killed one of the bandits and left the others with crippling injuries.

Back home, Sokaku was sent to study with Saigo Tanomo, a distinguished scholar, martial artist, and priest. Tanomo soon realized that Sokaku was not cut out for the spiritual life, and instead passed along to him *oshikiuchi*, a secret unarmed fighting technique of blows, locks, pins, and throws, which involved *ki*.[24] *Ki* is a vital energy that one can channel when he or she finds his balance and achieves harmony with nature. When highly developed, *ki* is supposed to enable the martial artist to anticipate an opponent's moves and respond to them with almost irresistible speed and force. It was not until 1899 that Tanomo considered Sokaku to have finished his *oshikiuchi* training and wrote out the following enigmatic verse as a sort of diploma:

24. Also spelled *ch'i*.

All people, know this!
When you strike
a flowing river
no trace remains
in the water.

Sokaku's initial training with Tanomo was interrupted when he decided to join the Satsuma Rebellion led by Takamori Saigo, but by the time he arrived in Kyushu it had been crushed. He drifted around Japan on a warrior pilgrimage, looking for opportunities to sharpen or test his fighting skills and earning his expenses by taking on all comers at local fairs. He was barely five feet tall and weighed about 100 pounds, small even for Japan at the time, but he was acknowledged as a true *budoka*, or fighting master. He was dubbed the Little Tengu of Aizu, the *tengu* being mythological long-nosed demons renowned for their expertise in the martial arts. He is said to have been involved in hundreds of no-holds-barred contests and to have killed a number of opponents.

While demonstrating a sword defense against three men armed with spears, he lopped off a spearhead, which flew up and knocked out his front teeth, giving his mouth a permanently grim set. This, along with his piercing gaze and a voice that he always employed at top volume, made him a rather intimidating character.

While traveling through Kumamoto Prefecture with a troupe of acrobats, Sokaku saw a man demonstrating *Okinawa-te*, an early form of karate. Sokaku challenged the man to a fight and won, but was sufficiently intrigued to spend two years in Okinawa mastering the art.

In 1880, back in Kyushu, Sokaku was involved in his most famous imbroglio, with 40 to 60 construction workers who were repairing the road between Sendai and Tokyo. As Sokaku was passing the workers, among whom were a number of criminals, they tried to get his goat, and then attacked with tools, iron rods, and bricks. He drew his sword and killed eight or nine but sustained so many injuries, including a pick wound in the back, that he lost consciousness just as the authorities arrived and rescued him. After spending a month in jail, he was tried for manslaughter but acquitted on the basis of self-defense. However, his heirloom sword, dating from the 17th century and made by Kotetsu, one of Japan's most renowned swordsmiths, was confiscated. "The age of the samurai warrior is over," the judge scolded him.

From this battle Sokaku concluded that the traditional *seigan* stance, in which the sword was held horizontally, was less effective against multiple attackers than the *jodan* stance, in which the sword was held over the head, allowing for faster counterblows. As with all such hard-won knowledge, he incorporated it directly into his teaching.

Sokaku traveled extensively, teaching *daito-ryu aikijujutsu* to police, military forces, and noblemen. In 1888 he married and started a family, but his wife died giving birth to their second child. When his house burned down shortly thereafter, he placed his children with relatives and resumed his wandering life.

In 1904 Charles Parry, an American who taught English at Sendai Second High School, encountered Sokaku as he was traveling by train. Parry didn't like the look of the scruffy, scarred man sharing his first-class compartment and asked the conductor to check his ticket. When Sokaku demanded to know why his ticket was being reexamined, the conductor told him of Parry's complaint. Enraged, Sokaku got out of his seat and faced the American. Parry, who was over six feet tall, stood up and raised his fists, expecting his diminutive challenger to be cowed. Instead, Sokaku grabbed his fists, applied a paralyzing pressure-point hold, and tossed Parry into the corner of the compartment. Parry was so impressed he asked to train with Sokaku and later wrote to President Roosevelt about his remarkable skills. Roosevelt expressed such interest that Sokaku sent a disciple, Shunso Harada, to the United States.

For three years, Harada gave instruction to the president and other government leaders.

During this period, a brigand was terrorizing the populace of Fukushima Prefecture, attacking travelers at night. After weeks in which the police had been unable to apprehend him, he was discovered one morning dead in a field beside a road, his head nearly twisted from his body. Though it was never proven that Sokaku had killed the man, he was giving a series of nighttime courses in the area and made it a practice to walk the most isolated roads alone.

In 1911, when he was in his 50s, Sokaku was hired by Sanehide Takarabe to train police forces in Hokkaido. The lightly populated northern island was Japan's frontier, attracting a rough mixture of smugglers, gamblers, gangsters, and highwaymen who had recently sacked several police stations. When gang leaders learned of Sokaku's arrival, they put a tail on him and found out that he visited the public baths every morning. Six toughs were sent to teach him a lesson. The ensuing mayhem is delightful to imagine, if difficult to believe: Sokaku is said to have fought off his attackers with a wet towel, projecting his *ki* through the improvised weapon as he flicked it at them, cracking their ribs and knocking them senseless. (Aikido expert Steven Seagal performed a similar stunt in *Out for Justice*, pulverizing a pool hall full of toughs with a bar towel, but he took the precaution of slinging a cue ball in it.) Afterward, gang members seeking revenge surrounded Sokaku's hotel. He threatened to litter the streets with their corpses if they made a move against him. Their leaders arranged a hasty truce.

In the course of his lifetime, Sokaku trained some 30,000 people. Though he could not read the written word, he is credited with an uncanny ability to read his fellow man. Before starting with a new group of students he would look each one in the eyes and then dismiss a few for no apparent reason. When asked to explain, he might say, "The first is a drunkard, the second a womanizer and the third a troublemaker. I don't teach such people." His intuitions invariably proved correct.

In 1912 Sokaku married a female student less than half his age, who bore him seven children. But domesticity was not for him. He would leave home for months at a time, bidding farewell to his family with a terse "Don't expect me back."

In 1915, Sokaku met the man who was to become his most famous pupil, Morihei Ueshiba. Morihei, who had never lost a fight, was a recognized *budoka* in his own right. When he heard that the *daito-ryu* master was giving lessons at an inn, Morihei made a point to attend, and when Sokaku, 25 years his senior, easily defeated him in a bout he sought an apprenticeship. Their association lasted nearly 30 years, but their relations became strained when Morihei came under the influence of the messianic religious leader Onisaburo Deguchi.[25]

In 1930 journalist Yoichi Ozaka interviewed Sokaku, and accepted a challenge to try to strike the 72-year-old master. He wrote, "Every time, I am downed even before I can figure out how. Before I know it the old man has my neck and both of my arms tied up in a pin with his legs. My arms feel as if they will break, and I can hardly breathe." In *daito-ryu aikijujutsu*, the legs are used to hold an opponent so that the hands are free to pull back his head and cut his throat.

When Sokaku demonstrated *kata* (movements) with a short sword, Yoichi wrote, "The whitish blade makes a mysterious whistling sound each time it whips in front of my eyes, under

---

25. To those familiar with the history of Japanese martial arts, it may seem strange to profile Sokaku rather than Morihei, who is celebrated as the founder of modern aikido. However, to accept accounts of Morihei's exploits demands unconditional surrender of the critical faculty. His disciples claim he was able to uproot trees, leap 20 feet into the air, dodge bullets, and knock down enemies with a gesture. Fantastic abilities of this sort are attributed to many martial arts masters of the East, making them difficult to include in a collection such as this, which steers clear of the Greek demigod and the shape-changing Viking. The mind-over-matter approach was put to the test during China's Boxer Rebellion in 1900, when kung fu fighters took on European troops confident that their *ki* would render them impervious to bullets. Such did not prove to be the case.

my nose, and around my shoulders." Sokaku told him, "If it doesn't make this whizzing sound when you swing it, you won't be able to cut a man satisfactorily."

Sokaku remains a controversial character. Unlike the classic martial arts hero, he is not described as having found inner peace through his discipline. He took pride in having killed a great number of men but feared reprisal from their friends and relatives. After the Meiji Restoration of 1867, when samurai were prohibited from wearing their swords, Sokaku always armed himself with a sword cane or an iron staff and concealed a dagger under his kimono. While eating, he always kept a pair of sharpened brazier chopsticks beside his plate to use as weapons. He would not enter any building, even his own home, until someone he knew came to the door to escort him, and he moved his bedding several times nightly to foil assassins. He was so fearful of being poisoned that he would not drink even tea he had prepared himself until after a disciple had tasted it. He never let a man walk behind him. He was once at Morihei's home, engrossed in a game of *go* with his host, when a neighbor entered, his face part covered by a scarf. Sokaku leapt to his feet and beat the man senseless with the game board, later explaining, "I thought it was one of my enemies, out to get me." His critics see in such behavior proof that he was a madman—Onisaburo said of him, "The man reeks of blood and violence"—but perhaps Morihei had it right when he described Sokaku as "the last of the old-time warriors," one whose mindset, however unsuited to polite society, had carried him through countless deadly encounters.

Sokaku died at 83 on April 25, 1943.

40 Lance Thomas

*I'm not a murderer. I gave
my attackers until the last
possible instant of their lives
not to go through with it.*

—Lance Thomas

L ance Thomas never looked for trouble; it sought him out. He became a gunfighter not because he wanted to, but because he had to—yet he defended himself with a deadly resolution unsurpassed by any hero of the Old West.

He was born in 1940 in a tough part of San Diego, his father a career naval officer and professional welterweight boxer. After Thomas saw other kids being harassed and beaten in the schoolyard, he asked his father how he should respond if bullies came after him. His father advised him to ignore insults and walk away from trouble because violence was not something to take lightly. There was only one reason to fight and that was in defense of your life. In that case, you don't play around, he told his son—if you have to, you kill. Thomas took the advice to heart.

In 1973, Thomas left his job as a successful IBM salesman to pursue his interest in antique clocks and classic watches. He is regarded as one of the first to recognize the potential market for prewar Elgins, Walthams, and Gruens. In 1974, he opened The Watch Co. at 12118 Santa Monica Boulevard. Business thrived, and Thomas was worth well over a million dollars by the mid-1980s. Handsome, dynamic, six feet tall, and powerfully built, he enjoyed all the trappings of success. Renouncing his conservative upbringing as a Seventh Day Adventist, he indulged himself in fancy cars and a steady flow of beautiful women. Seeking to further scale the high life, he invested in a dozen racehorses and sold shares in their prospective winnings. Unfortunately the horses didn't do their part. By 1988 they had plunged him $350,000 in debt, and, at the same time, The Watch Co. was burglarized of more than $20,000 in watches for which Thomas was not insured. Bankrupt at 48, and with limited employment prospects, Thomas decided he would simply put in as many hours at The Watch Co. as it might take to pull himself out of his financial hole. The trouble began when he hung a neon Rolex sign in his window. It attracted robbers like moths to flame, and the nearby freeway on-ramp made his store appear an easy target.

At 10:30 A.M. on August 10, 1989, Thomas attended to a customer as two men waited quietly in line. Thomas was looking through a drawer containing repaired watches when he heard a thud. His customer had been knocked to the floor by a pistol blow from the man standing behind him, S. Livingstone. Striking a combat stance, Livingstone turned his 9mm on Thomas and shouted, "Gimme the watches! Gimme the watches!"

Concerned about a rash of jewelry store robberies, Thomas had recently armed himself with a .38-caliber Smith & Wesson model 36, a snub-nosed five-shot revolver. It happened to be lying on the counter near his right hand, out of Livingstone's sight. Thomas momentarily pretended to comply with Livingstone's demand, then snatched it up and pumped out three rounds. The first struck Livingstone just under the nose, and the next two hit the front door as Livingstone dropped.

"That was it. It was as simple as that. I just decided not to be a victim—in an instant," Thomas said.

He swung his revolver to cover the second man, who had a weapon tucked in his belt. "Get out of here," Thomas ordered.

The man grabbed Livingstone and dragged him out the door. The customer who had come to pick up his watch climbed out from under the table where he'd been cowering, clutching his head in pain.

"Are you all right?" Thomas asked. Without a word the customer ran out the door, never to return, leaving his watch behind.

Dropped off at Cedars-Sinai hospital, Livingstone was arrested after Thomas identified him from mug shots and was later sentenced to five years. Thomas' slug had broken Livingstone's jaw and then split in two, the halves carving two grooves in his face. A Santa Monica detective suggested to Thomas that he upgrade to the Glaser Safety Slug, then regarded as something of a silver bullet by law enforcement. Designed to impart the maximum energy to its target while eliminating the problem of overpenetration and ricochets, the conventionally jacketed bullet contains shot. Its promoters claim it offers two to three times the stopping power of a conventional hollowpoint.

Beyond the practical considerations, he felt he must eliminate any trace of moral confusion from his mind so that he could respond to an attack decisively. After a legal hearing Thomas was told he was free to go about his business, but that was easier said than done. He was shaken by the incident, playing it over and over in his mind. What if his gun had not been within reach? Worse yet, what if the trouble was not over—if Livingstone had friends who would seek revenge? He pondered the fact that in any robbery the timing and circumstances would be chosen by the robber, gun in hand, while he himself would inevitably be surprised, empty-handed and possibly outnumbered. At the same time he realized that he had a certain advantage. The robber, after all, was pointing a gun at him not to kill him, but to establish a relationship—that of predator and prey—and would probably prefer not to pull the trigger. Thomas, on the other hand, had no interest in a relationship— he just needed to eliminate a threat. Action beats reaction every time, and by going for his gun he would seize the initiative. He was convinced that if he could draw and fire in less than a second he would be able to shoot a man who had the drop on him.

He began an exercise program so that he would be "fast, able, and alert" if his store were struck again. He bought three .357 magnum revolvers: a Colt Python with a six-inch barrel, a stainless-steel Ruger Security Six, and a Smith & Wesson model 19. He screwed their holsters against the back of his counters at regular intervals so that he would always have one within reach. When his store was empty he practiced his draw until he was satisfied with his speed. He decided that as soon as the shooting started he would throw off his assailant's aim by dodging quickly to the right, figuring that it is harder for a right-handed man to track to the left than to the right. Rather than worry about reloading, he would grab another gun if the need arose. Beyond the practical considerations, he felt he must eliminate any trace of moral confusion from his mind so that he could respond to an attack decisively.

He knew from his religious training that, properly translated, the Sixth Commandment reads "Thou shalt not murder," as opposed to "Thou shalt not kill," and, anyway, Thomas was convinced that the survival instinct programmed into every living organism superseded any law or religious edict. Simply put, his position, was, "I have a right to survive. Anyone who would take my life must be resisted." He considered resistance to force a moral duty.

Mentally, physically, and tactically prepared, Thomas was no longer afraid. "Fear is an emotion evoked from the unknown," as he saw it. "If you are prepared, you don't fear the arena."

Meanwhile, a five-man gang comprising Kriss Sumlin, Gaylord Smith, the brothers Tony and Char-Ru Currie, and an unidentified driver was robbing jewelry stores throughout the Los

Angeles area. The driver would remain in the car while the four others approached the chosen premises. Sumlin would stay outside as a lookout while Tony and Char-Ru Currie walked in brandishing guns. On their heels, Smith, carrying a sack, would then enter and collect the merchandise. The gang had honed its modus operandi to perfection, but its victim selection process was faulty: on the evening of November 27, 1989, it struck The Watch Co.

There were two customers in store at the time, an unidentified man and a former girlfriend of Thomas named Geri. Thomas, whose back was to the door, turned when he heard a scuffle to see Tony Currie holding Geri by the throat and pointing a .25 automatic at her head. "Move and you're dead," Tony said quietly.

Char-Ru Currie, wearing a heavy leather jacket and waving a high-capacity 9mm MAC-10, shouted, "Give it up or we'll kill all of you!"

Your money or your life: the classic proposition overlooks an obvious third possibility. Thomas, grabbing his Ruger, shouted "Hit the deck!" to his customers. Smith, just outside the door, emptied his five-shot revolver through the glass, narrowly missing him. Char-Ru dove behind one end of the U-shaped counter, where he was momentarily out of the fray. Tony fired eight rounds at Thomas with his .25 auto, hitting him three times in the right shoulder and once in the neck, while at the same time Thomas fired back. His first bullet hit a ledger book, creating a surreal snowstorm of confetti that drifted through the air, but his next five shots went into Tony, killing him. The three-second exchange felt like an eternity to Thomas—he can't remember hearing the shots, but the click of his hammer on a spent shell brought him instantly back to reality. He tossed the empty gun at Tony and grabbed his .38, firing it through the door at Smith. People ran screaming from a nearby bus stop and customers at a burrito stand across the street went over the counter to take cover. Smith and Sumlin ran back to their getaway car, nearly getting run over as they crossed Santa Monica Boulevard. (They were later arrested.)

As Char-Ru fired bursts at him over the countertop with the MAC-10, Thomas dialed 911. Shots can be clearly heard on the tape as Thomas calmly gives his store's name and address. When he talked blood blew out of the hole in his neck, but he was unaware of any pain and determined to resist as long as he lived. "I was pissed off," he said. "These guys really messed up my day." He remembers the gun battle in stroboscopic slow motion, feeling as if his life had already ended. As strange as it sounds, he saw bullets streaking toward him, illuminated by flashes of light that seemed to burst out of, then be sucked back into, the gun barrels, followed by puffs of smoke.

Thomas picked up another .357 and emptied it into Char-Ru Currie, killing him.

Arriving upon the nightmare scene, the police were amazed that amid all the blood, broken glass and spent brass, the only dead bodies were those of the perpetrators. One bullet had passed through Geri's pocketbook, leaving a grazing wound along her buttock. Thomas, still on his feet but severely wounded, was taken away by ambulance.

Don Kladstrup, interviewing Thomas for ABC's *Turning Point*, asked, "How could you keep shooting—fighting back—with a bullet wound in the neck and three bullets in the shoulder?"

After a moment's reflection Thomas answered, "They hadn't killed me yet and I hadn't run out of ammunition."

After a week in the hospital Thomas returned to his business. His friends couldn't believe he would reopen the store, but he knew no other way to make a living, and he refused to be intimidated. He cleaned the blood from his carpeting, which, fortuitously, happened to be red. He put in a video camera, backed his door with bulletproof Lexan, and set up a door-buzzer security system. A detective friend gave him a Kevlar vest, but Thomas found it too uncomfortable to wear. Other friends lent him guns to tide him over while his were held by the police during their investigation.

The spectacular shootout brought with it unwelcome attention. Thomas refused numerous requests for interviews from the press, but agreed to meet with an FBI agent who was impressed by his management of close interpersonal crises. The agent gave Thomas the benefit of his expertise on firearms, recommending that he switch to semiautomatics for their greater magazine capacity and stick to one model so that he could accustom himself to its feel and function. He specifically recommended SIG-Sauers for their quality, accuracy, and reliability. With his taste for fine machinery, Thomas found the high-end German import appealing. He bought three model 220 .45s, which held seven plus one (seven in the magazine plus one in the chamber), and one model 225 9mm, which held eight plus one.

Thomas was disappointed with the performance of the Glaser rounds, which he believed had largely spent themselves against Char-Ru's leather jacket. The agent recommended he switch to the Federal Hydra-Shok round, a hollowpoint that expands as it penetrates tissue, resulting in a larger-diameter wound channel.

He also took Thomas to a shooting range and coached him on the modern pistol technique. He taught him the two-handed Weaver stance, and to grip the pistol properly and consistently. He stressed focusing on the front sight and pressing the trigger for a "surprise break." The quality of the gunfighter that is the most difficult to inculcate—mind-set—was one in which Thomas needed no instruction.

At 1:45 P.M. on December 4, 1991, 6-foot 5-inch, 250-pound Valdeas O'Neal entered The Watch Co. accompanied by an attractive woman. After a short, friendly conversation, the woman handed Thomas a broken watch and asked whether he could repair it. As Thomas bent over it, O'Neal vaulted the counter and pressed a 9mm Glock to his neck. Seeing the SIG 225 lying eight inches from Thomas's right hand, he said, "Don't reach for it—I'll kill you."

What went through Thomas's mind? *Motherfucker, you should have already pulled the trigger.*

He jerked his head to the side and grabbed his SIG. O'Neal immediately shot him through the neck, then hesitated for an instant. Perhaps he assumed he had killed Thomas, perhaps he had not mentally prepared himself for a victim who fought back, but that instant was all Thomas needed. Not even taking the time to bring his pistol forward, he twisted his wrist at a right angle and pumped three 9mm rounds into O'Neal's chest. Then the SIG jammed.[26]

Even though he reeled backward, O'Neal fired twice more, wildly, before Thomas grabbed a .45 and stitched him from his knee to his head with five shots. The second shot seemed to lift O'Neal off his feet, and he hit the floor gushing blood. His female accomplice fled.

Then? "I went to the hospital," recalls Thomas. "[The bullet] didn't sever my spinal cord or my jugular . . . so a Band-Aid sufficed and I was back to work the next day."

In his interview, Kladstrup asked Thomas to explain his action: "He said, 'Don't do anything or I'll kill you'—*so why do anything?* I mean, you reached for your gun. If you hadn't reached for your gun, maybe you wouldn't have gotten shot. Maybe he would have gotten a few of your watches, but it would have been over."

"It would've been up to him, wouldn't it?" responded Thomas quietly.

As he told the *Los Angeles Times*, "When you pull out that gun, you and I will battle to the death over meaningless valuables, whether it is a dollar or a million dollars." This was not to say that he valued his life less than the goods the robbers sought—he simply refused to barter for it or be cowed by violence. It was not as important to him that he win as that he fight, that he not allow aggression to go unresisted, that he not allow himself to be cast in the role of prey. "Maybe I'm more afraid of being a victim than I am of dying," he mused.

26. It jammed due to the awkward angle at which Thomas held it. To cycle properly, an automatic must be gripped firmly.

O'Neal had been released from prison three months earlier after serving eight years for armed robbery. When the police searched his body they found his parole card in his shirt pocket, neatly punched by a round.

With his third successful armed encounter, the tall mustachioed bachelor was compared to Wild Bill Hickok. Neighboring storekeepers were supportive. "He's tough," said Tavi Castor, owner of a photocopying business. Sharon Mnich, owner of the balloon shop across the street, said that she was not surprised by the latest incident: "He's said before that if anyone comes in there [to rob him] they're not coming out." Her manager kept Thomas' telephone number posted on a bulletin board. "If we ever need any help, we'll definitely call him," she said. Edmond Hakami, owner of a yogurt shop, told a reporter, "It's like having a private security guard across the street. It sends a message: Don't mess around." Thomas received a number of letters of support. One correspondent, along with congratulations, enclosed two $5 bills "to pay for more ammo." Several were from people whose loved ones had been killed by armed robbers even after they had complied with the robbers' demands.

One evening Thomas heard a woman screaming from a parking lot on the other side of Santa Monica Boulevard. Running out of his shop and across traffic, he scared off a rapist who had already pushed his intended victim to the ground and torn open her clothing. As Thomas returned to his shop, Castor, who had been drawn outside by the ruckus, asked him why he hadn't just called 911.

"I *am* 911," replied Thomas.

Thomas installed a "cage" type double-door security system and hired a retired cop as a clerk, but shortly after 4 P.M. on February 20, 1992, robbers struck again. As one news story put it, "They keep trying, and they keep dying." Or, in the words of another, "They take a lickin' and Lance keeps tickin'."

Lance buzzed in two teenagers, Tremichael Garret, 19, and

William Shannon, 17. They said they wanted to buy a watch for their father, feigned interest in one, then left. A few minutes later they returned. Their nervousness aroused Thomas's suspicions and he surreptitiously pulled a .45 from its holster. Suddenly Garret shouted, "You're dead!" and both teens pulled semiautomatic pistols. Ironically, shouting "You're dead!" cost them their lives because it allowed Thomas time to raise and fire his .45. ("When you have to shoot, *shoot!*—don't talk," as Eli Wallach observed in *The Good, the Bad, and the Ugly.*)

Garret fired a shot that just missed the ex-cop's head before Thomas pumped the better part of a magazine into him, killing him. Shannon, trying to use the door as a shield, got off one shot before Thomas, grabbing another .45, finished him with four rounds. Shannon collapsed in the doorway, blocking it open. By this time, the ex-cop had managed to get his weapon into action, putting five shots through the walls and display cases and hitting Shannon's already dead body once.

When Monet Delapaz, a clerk at the balloon store, heard the first shots, he assumed it was a car backfiring. But as the fusillade went on, he knew better. "Another one bites the dust," he thought to himself.

Squad cars converged on the scene, sirens wailing. Officers drew their weapons and pointed them at The Watch Co.'s door, from which a pool of blood was spreading. A hundred or so owners and patrons of nearby shops gathered across the street, wondering whether their homegrown Hickok had met his end. Following orders barked through a police bullhorn, Thomas walked out of store with his hands in the air. As the crowd broke into enthusiastic cheers, Thomas balled his upraised hands into triumphant fists.

Garret and Shannon turned out to be members of the Crips gang. One of them was suspected of having shot a man in front of his eight-year-old son the day before.

In the course of four gun battles Thomas had killed five robbers and wounded one. Shooting predators seemed to be becoming a habit; he admitted it no longer bothered him. "A frightening thing about this is that it becomes easier," he told a reporter. To those who expected him to feel remorse, he was defiant. "Remorse? Remorse connotes error," he observed.

"Lance Thomas was totally justified in everything he did," said Detective Lee Kingsford, who investigated the shootings. "All of the suspects had extensive criminal records. They knew what they were doing; they just didn't know who they were doing it against."

Thomas used only necessary force and never shot anyone who had ceased to present a threat. On one occasion, a young man looking at an $8,000 Rolex "President" suddenly ran out of the store with it. Thomas chased him. When the thief climbed onto the back of a partner's motorcycle and sped away, Thomas commandeered a Porsche and gave chase. After a moment's reflection, he called it off. A vehicular chase could only endanger others, and the man posed no threat. Criminals could flee from Thomas in safety; they just could not point a gun at him.

Nevertheless there was criticism. Although he had never displayed a desire to do anything but run his business unmolested, some decried him as a vigilante. Ruth McNair, a freelance paralegal whose two sons were killed in the November 1989 robbery attempt, filed suit against Thomas and against the city for not prosecuting him. "I just feel that someone needs to do something to stop him because he's a danger," she said, apparently without irony. (Her case was thrown out.) Laura Levenson, a professor at Loyola Law School, questioned whether Thomas could be said to be responding out of a reasonable fear for his life, as self-defense law demands, when he didn't seem to be particularly afraid of anyone. In her view, he was acting with the "make my day" attitude of Dirty Harry. Her argument seemed to be that anyone who consistently and successfully resisted violence was psychologically suspect. It also suggested that criminals should ultimately determine who was permitted to operate a business in the city.

As it happened, that was the way it worked out.

The police informed Thomas that L.A. gangs had put a price on his head, and that the next time he was hit he wouldn't get a chance to shoot back. He and any customers who might be with him would be the victims of a drive-by shooting. He shut his store for a few weeks as he considered his options, and during that time groups of Crips came around looking for him, asking his neighbors for his whereabouts. What's more, political pressures being what they were, the police warned him that he would be indicted after another shooting, whatever the circumstances; he apparently wasn't trying hard enough to avoid confrontation. In April 1992 he decided not to buck the odds any longer.

"Wild Bill Hickok got shot in the back, Jesse James was shot in the back, and, frankly, I was next," he said. He closed his shop and began dealing watches from his home and, later, over the Internet at www.watchcompany.com.

After a few months two men came to the glass front door of his home. The one who knocked was clean-cut and smiling, but standing a short distance behind him was a cohort with ex-con written all over him. As Thomas put it, "When you've been in this situation as many times as I have, your ability to read it becomes almost telepathic." The handle of the Lexan-backed door was to his right. He opened it a few inches with his left hand, holding his SIG in his right, down against his leg.

"I have a Mickey Mouse watch I'd like you to take a look at," said the closer man in friendly fashion, as his partner stood back and said nothing.

Thomas swung the door wider to give himself a clear shot and spoke loudly and deliberately to the man standing back. "I don't want your *stinking Mickey Mouse watch*! Do you *hear me*? Do you *understand*?"

Evidently they did—they quickly backed away.

Three months after that Thomas was looking out his front window when he saw a car containing four gangbanger types pull up and idle. Holding his pistol out of sight, he walked into the street and stood 25 feet in front of them. He said nothing, but waited, his eyes alight, his teeth bared in a grin. The men in the car squirmed and ducked their heads, and after a few moments reversed, turned, and drove away.

"I wasn't challenging or insulting them," said Thomas, "but I didn't want them to challenge or insult me. I wanted them to recognize me as a fellow warrior. *I am not a rabbit.*"

Is Thomas a hero? As the term was defined throughout most of history, of course: a hero was a fighter of spectacular courage and prowess, one who could single-handedly turn the tide of a battle. Today, though, we seem to apply the term more often to victims—the police officer killed in the line of duty, the disabled veteran, the POW. Their sacrifice, their suffering, seems to give them moral superiority over the man who fights and wins, whose violence overwhelms that of his enemy. The Lance Thomas type makes many of us uncomfortable, for he seems to have more in common with those he fights than he does with us. Beyond that he shames us, for we know that unlike him, when the predator comes, we will likely be prey.

Author's note: Thomas is the only subject in this book with whom I had the opportunity to talk and meet. Before he would discuss his story with me he wanted to know why I was interested. He had no desire to titillate the morbidly curious or give fodder to people who would misinterpret his motives.

I met him at his modest villa-style home, cluttered with antique clocks and watches. He found it amusing that I would lump him together with the likes of Bowie, Hickok, and Murphy—"I just sell watches," he said—but obviously there is a common thread. All are men for whom honor is more important than life. As Thomas put it, "It's not what a man owns, or what his title is that's important, but *who* he is. That he does what he thinks is right. That he lives by a principle. Isn't that why anybody remembers anybody?"

Thomas feels conflicting emotions about his experience,

what one newspaper described as "a mixture of pride and bitterness." When pressed for details of his encounters he seemed momentarily to relive them, and I saw some of that physical transformation that contemporaries observed in Nathan Bedford Forrest—the flushed skin, the fiery eye, the feral grin. He is clearly a very dangerous man to push, and I was surprised that anyone in the business of selecting victims would mistake him for one.

Throughout our interview, he sat catercorner from me at a desk. When I got up to leave, he snatched a pistol from beneath it in a move as quick as the snapping of a rattrap. "I had you covered all the time," he said mischievously, pointing it safely to my right. He released the magazine, jacked the round from the chamber, and handed the .45 SIG over to me. Judging by its heel-mounted magazine release and Browning-embossed grips, it was a late 1970s or early 1980s import, the bluing on its slide worn and pitted from frequent handling. As I examined it, it occurred to me that, knowing Lance Thomas, he had another one, loaded, close at hand.

41 Nancy Wake

*She is the most feminine
woman I know—until the
fighting starts. Then, she is
like five men.*
　　　　　—Maquis Colonel
　　　　　　　　　Tardivant

T hough many women served in the underground armies of Western Europe, few held as high a leadership position, participated in as much combat, or experienced as many close calls as did Nancy Wake.

Wake was born in New Zealand in 1912 and raised in Australia. At age 20, she sailed out of Sydney Harbor in search of adventure. After visiting New York and London, Wake settled in Paris in 1934, supporting herself as a freelance journalist until she married the wealthy Marseilles industrialist Henri Fiocca in November 1939. (She became Mme. Fiocca but was subsequently known by so many code names that, for clarity, we will stick with her maiden name.) Formerly accustomed to meager circumstances, Wake now lived in luxury. She spent her mornings in a leisurely bath, snacking on caviar and sipping champagne. Afterward she shopped, visited the beauty salon, and dropped into Basso's or the Hotel du Louvre for aperitifs. In the evening, she and her husband would dine at a fashionable restaurant, sometimes journeying 150 miles to try out a new one.

When Germany invaded, Henri was called off to war. Before he left, Wake insisted that he have one of his firm's trucks converted to an ambulance so that she too might serve by ferrying the wounded back from the front. Henri was perplexed. "But why do you want to help?" he asked. "War isn't for women." Finally, under her stubborn insistence, he gave in.

As France crumbled under the blitzkrieg, Wake's ambulance work became increasingly dangerous, with the roads blocked by bombed-out vehicles, clogged with fleeing refugees, and regularly strafed by German planes. She persevered until Paris surrendered, after which she returned to Marseilles where Henri rejoined her a few weeks later. The city was now part of unoccupied France, ruled by the collaborationist Vichy régime. Nancy and Henri began secretly using their wealth to help out friends and neighbors with food, bypassing the strict rationing system.

While having her customary afternoon drink at the Hotel du Louvre, Wake was surprised to see a young man at the bar reading an English-language book, and she struck up a conversation with him. He was a British officer, one of 200 who were interned in nearby Fort Saint-Jean but permitted an occasional outing on their sworn promise to return. Ever eager to defy the authorities, Wake arranged to meet him the next day, offering him cigarettes and a visit to a black-market store where he could buy food. She lay in bed that night worrying that the man might actually be one of the German agents with whom Marseilles was crawling, but the following day when she saw him approach with two friends her doubts vanished, for one of them had a huge, ridiculous mustache of the sort that only an Englishman would wear proudly. Wake invited them all to her

KIRCHNER

apartment for dinner and after that entertained groups of four or five Englishmen daily. They were honor-bound not to try to escape while on these outings but felt no compunction about using the time to plan escapes. Wake committed herself to helping them and before long, working with the French Resistance, she established an escape route that eventually repatriated more than a thousand Allied servicemen. Henri was concerned about his wife's activities, knowing the fate that awaited those caught defying the Gestapo, but as a patriotic Frenchman he would not stand in her way. He even provided her with a generous allowance for her work.

Wake expanded the scope of her activities while maintaining her cover as a spoiled, self-indulgent society wife. She rented an apartment as a safe house for escaped prisoners and Resistance operatives, explaining to the real estate agent that she was having an affair and needed a discreet lovers' nest, always a plausible reason in France. The risk she was running was brought home to her when she visited the premises with a load of groceries, only to have her downstairs neighbor inquire sympathetically about her "bad colic." Instinctively, Wake did not contradict her, but replied, "How very kind of you to concern yourself. How did you know?"

"Because your cistern goes 20 times a night," the old woman replied. Wake assured her she was feeling much better, then went to the apartment and delivered a tongue-lashing to the men, concluding with, "In future, more security and less lavatory flushing."

After the arrest of Ian Garrow, an escaped British officer and one of her Resistance contacts, Wake boldly began writing and visiting him at the Fort Saint-Nicolas Jail, posing as his cousin. She continued to visit him even when he was transferred to a prison camp at Meauzac, bringing food parcels and even smuggling in brandy in bottles labeled "hair tonic" or "cough medicine." As she hoped, she was eventually approached by a guard who offered to help Garrow escape in exchange for a large bribe. Henri wired her the money.

The next day, when she showed up at the prison, she was taken to the office of the commandant. "Madame, I am informed that you have just received a large amount of money from Marseilles. Why?" he demanded.

Wake feigned surprise. "Me? A large amount of money? I have received no large amounts of money, I assure you."

The commandant shouted, "The post office has told me, Mme. Rocca, that yesterday afternoon you received by telegram 40,000 francs. That is a very large sum. Why was it sent to you? Why?"

Wake stared at him coolly. "Monsieur le Commandant,"

she said, "perhaps, to you, 40,000 francs is a lot of money. I don't know. But to me, I assure you, it is nothing . . . pin money, in fact."

"Pin money?" gulped the commandant.

"Nothing at all," declared Nancy. "I needed it for drinks at the bistro."

After the deflated commandant excused her, Wake was ushered in to see Garrow and whispered to him that his escape had been arranged for the coming weekend. A week later, she remained in Marseilles and attended several social affairs to establish her alibi. When a gendarme showed up at her door to inform her that her "cousin" had broken out of prison, she expressed delight and immediately telephoned Henri to tell him the news, though she suspected that her line was tapped. Why? Because that was what she would have done had she not been involved. No matter how flagrantly she flouted the law, Wake instinctively comported herself as if she were innocent. It was her brazenness, as much as her courage, that made her such a successful operative.

Once, while traveling by train, she had to figure out how to get a heavy suitcase full of black-market pork through a railway station checkpoint. She began flirting with a Gestapo officer in her compartment, and when they arrived in Marseilles he offered to carry her bag. She cheerfully agreed, though when she saw how he strained under the load she took him to task. "The way you are carrying my bag the police will think it's full of black-market stuff. You'll get me into trouble! *Faites comme ça.* Swing it like this!" she ordered, pantomiming how she would carry a light handbag. With gritted teeth, the German held his back erect and took the suitcase through the checkpoint, waving his Gestapo ID. Wake was certain he had begun to suspect it was full of contraband but didn't know how else to get himself out of the situation.

Resistance work became far more dangerous in November 1942, when the Germans occupied all of France. They were aware of a highly effective female operative they dubbed the White Mouse but had no idea of her identity. Nevertheless, Wake soon noticed that she was being followed, and she heard strange clicking sounds when she picked up her telephone. The Resistance was rife with informers and others had been betrayed. She discussed her predicament with Henri, and they decided that she should escape to England.

With the occupation, security was tighter than ever. Wake's train was stopped near Toulouse, and the passengers were told to get onto trucks. She leapt off her car and ran through the city streets but was swept up in a police dragnet and taken to jail. Although her interrogators didn't know she was the sought-after White Mouse, they worked her over for days. She told them nothing. On her fourth day, as she sat in a corridor, battered and bruised, she was startled to see a member of her underground group standing between two policemen. She first assumed that he too had been arrested, but to her astonishment she learned that he had come to get her released. He had convinced the commissaire that she was his lover and was only trying to protect him from her jealous husband.

In the next few weeks Wake made five unsuccessful attempts to approach the Spanish border by train. On her sixth, a conductor ran through the corridor warning the passengers that there was a German inspection ahead. Wake climbed through a window and jumped off the train before it came to a stop. She ran through a vineyard toward an emergency rendezvous point as machine-gun bullets slashed at the vines around her.

She met her contact and at last crossed the Pyrenees after a nonstop, 47-hour climb along steep trails, through intermittent snowstorms, all the while evading German patrols. Once in Spain she contacted the British consul, who had her transported to England.

In July 1943, after a month's rest, Wake signed up with the First Aid Nursing Yeomanry, a cover group that trained women as saboteurs to be dropped into occupied Europe. Wake found the training rather silly, having worked in the Resistance for two years without once swinging on a rope or jumping off a 20-foot platform. The director wasn't pleased with her attitude, and when she answered him with what her biographer describes as an "army word," she was dismissed.

Her old friend Garrow, now back in London, got her into the Special Operations Executive (SOE). Wake was sent to a camp in Scotland, the only woman in a group being trained in explosives and automatic weapons, land navigation, night operations, radio transmission, parachuting, and techniques of silent killing. If this were a current-day Hollywood movie, Wake would undoubtedly outshine the men, but it was real life, and she had her difficulties. She couldn't toss a grenade properly and capsized a boat during a rowing exercise. She did receive a compliment from her instructor for not shooting high with the Sten gun, a typical error of male trainees, but she refrained from telling him it was only because she could barely hold the barrel up. When she refused to scale a vertical obstacle, her instructor asked, "What will you do if you have to climb a wall like this in France?"

"I've never seen a wall like this in France," she responded. "And if I ever do—even if the whole German army's after me — I won't even *try* to climb it . . . I'll just stay on my side of it and talk myself out of trouble."

Whatever her physical limitations, Wake received high marks for her nerve, morale, and natural leadership—and, of course, she had already proven herself in action, so she was the first of her training group to be sent out. On February 29, 1944, she flew to France in the belly of a Liberator, with two revolvers in the pockets of her coveralls and a handbag containing a million francs. The bomber was bounced by bad weather and flak, so she spent most of the trip throwing up and was only too happy to jump out when the time came.

Wake was assigned as a British liaison to the 7,000 maquis in the province of Auvergne, a rugged, forested, highland area ideal for guerrilla activity. The maquis were fragmented into various groups under different leaders, but Wake soon bent them to her will. As the *chef du parachutage* who arranged the drops from England, she controlled the distribution of cash, supplies, and armaments. Some of the leaders tried to manipulate or intimidate her, but she was used to handling men. If she had to cajole them she did, and if she had to curse them out like a drill sergeant, she could handle that as well. On a few occasions they tried to get her drunk, but after she proved she could drink them under the table her credibility was established.

As the German presence was weak in Auvergne, the maquis were able to travel by car. Making her rounds, Wake always wore a brace of revolvers and carried a Sten gun on her lap. On several occasions she encountered enemy patrols and had to shoot her way out.

Everywhere she saw victims of German reprisals—bodies hanging from trees and the charred remains of men, women, and children outside of burned-out farmhouses. As much as she hoped that death would be quick if her time came, she knew that in all likelihood it would be preceded by months of degradation and torture, and for that reason she always carried a poison pill hidden in a button on her sleeve.

At dawn on June 20, 1944, the Germans attacked the stronghold of Wake's group, the plateau above Chaudes-Aigues, with 22,000 Waffen-SS troops supported by air power and artillery. All day long, the French held them off from their fortified positions, planning to withdraw under cover of darkness. Wake drove from group to group distributing weapons and ammunition as shells burst around her. Her car came under fire from a Henschel 126, and it was only by a skillful application of the brake and accelerator that Wake escaped its bullets through three strafing passes. As it came around again, she gathered up some personal items from the backseat—a jar of face cream, a saucepan, a packet of tea, and a red satin cushion—and ran off just as the car exploded under the plane's guns.

That night, Wake slipped though the German cordon, crossing the fast-running Truyère River on a bridge of rocks and timbers the maquis bands had constructed just beneath the river's surface, invisible to German reconnaissance. Most of the maquis escaped the plateau; only 100 were killed, at a cost of 1,400 Germans.

Unfortunately, during the initial phase of the attack, Wake's radio operator had destroyed his transmitter and codes out of fear that they would be captured. It was vital that Wake reestablish contact with London, but to make a connection with a Resistance transmitter she would have to travel 300 miles by bicycle through occupied territory. German security was tighter than ever and she didn't have the newly issued ID papers, or even a change of clothes, since she had left her spare clothing behind when she fled the plateau. The journey was the most dangerous she had ever undertaken, but she completed it in 72 hours. Of all her wartime exploits, Wake would later say that she was most proud of "the bike ride." It had at least one amusing moment, when she approached a bistro whose proprietor was a friend. He rushed outside to warn her, "You must not come in. . . . There's a Communist here! He says he will shoot you!"

It wasn't wise to get between Wake and a well-earned drink. She strode into the bistro, sat down next to the Communist, slammed her revolver on the table, and said, "I hear that you are going to shoot me. Well, you'll need to be very quick on the draw. *Patron*, a cognac!"

With the Allies driving the Wehrmacht back, the Resistance grew bolder, and Wake took part in a number of ambushes of German convoys. During a daring daytime attack on the Montluçon Gestapo headquarters, she ran into the building tossing grenades; 38 of the enemy were killed. In a nighttime raid on a factory, she was supposed to knock out a German sentry with a blow from behind. However, at the last moment he turned toward her, and she was forced to silence him. Jamming her forearm under his chin, she snapped his neck as she had been taught in SOE training and felt a chill as he slumped lifelessly in her arms.

Wake struck her last blow of the war in the dining room of the British officers' club in Paris, just after the liberation. She was seated with an Englishwoman who was struggling to place an order *en français* with their French waiter. Assuming that they would not comprehend, the waiter muttered to himself that he would take the Germans over the English any day. As he headed into the kitchen, a livid Wake followed, and after a few colorful comments in fluent French, she punched him out. Moments later, a furor broke out when his unconscious body was discovered. Waiters surrounded Wake and her friend, shouting at them, but Wake pretended not to understand. She and her friend were able to dine in peace only after a secretary of the British embassy informed the manager that a few weeks previously Wake had been lustily killing Germans, and it might be best not to rile her unduly.

After the war, Nancy Wake's valor was recognized by three of the Allied powers. From England, she received the George Medal; from America, the Medal of Freedom with a Bronze Palm; and from France, two Croix de Guerre with Palm and a Croix de Guerre with Star, as well as the sparingly bestowed Resistance Medal. She had paid a high price, though. Henri had been arrested by the Gestapo in May 1944 and executed five months later, after he had refused to provide information about her activities, even under torture. The family fortune was gone, seized by the Germans. Still, Wake never regretted her decision to fight. As she told her biographer, "I hate wars and violence but, if they come, then I don't see why we women should just wave our men a proud good-bye and then knit them balaclavas."

42 Lewis Wetzel

*The border needed Wetzel.
The settlers would have
needed many more years in
which to make permanent
homes had it not been for
him. He was never a pio-
neer, but always a hunter of
Indians.*

—Zane Grey

How we view yesterday's heroes depends largely on the fashions of today. As the expansion of the American West has come to be regarded by the politically correct as more genocidal conquest than Manifest Destiny, those who fought the Indians have fallen into disrepute, though they faced warriors as determined and skillful as ever existed, who were frequently as well armed as the white man and usually had the advantage of numbers. It is hard for many to accept that the American Indian, now portrayed as a tragic victim, was once seen as a terrifying presence and a serious military threat. (And ironic, as well, for while an Indian warrior might have taken pride in being feared, he would find our pity unbearable.)

Few men had more Indian blood on their hands than Lewis

Wetzel, who spent most of his life pursuing a remorseless vendetta against the red man. Even in his own day he was a controversial figure—a hero to many, to others a homicidal maniac.

Born in August 1763 in Lancaster County, Pennsylvania, Wetzel moved with his family to the frontier area that later became Wheeling, West Virginia, when he was a baby. John Wetzel, Lewis' father, schooled his five sons from earliest childhood in the skills that would ensure their survival in the wilderness: hunting, stalking, woodcraft, and fighting. In August 1777, Lewis and his 11-year-old brother Jacob were alone at the farm when it was attacked by Wyandot Indians. A bullet fractured Lewis' sternum but glanced off. The Indians looted the house, taking Old John's rifle and some other goods, then tied the boys' hands and roughly marched them off. Lewis made little of his pain, knowing that if he showed courage he might be adopted into the tribe, but any sign of weakness would get him killed. At the second night's camp, after their captors had fallen asleep, Lewis managed to work his rawhide bonds loose and untie his brother. The Indians had taken their shoes from them, so he crept among the sleeping braves to take two pairs of moccasins that were drying near the fire and then recovered his father's rifle. The boys set out. A few hours later they heard sounds of pursuit. Rather than try to stay ahead of their pursuers, they hid and let them pass, then fell behind them at a safe distance. When the Indians gave up the search and headed back, the boys hid again as they passed by in the other direction. They had to hide once more as two Indians made a second sweep on horseback, but the boys finally made it to the Ohio River, crossed on a bundle of logs, and returned to the settlement at Wheeling. Then and there, Lewis vowed that he would kill every Indian that crossed his path as long as God let him live.

Later that year Lewis Wetzel participated in the defense of Fort Wheeler.

In 1780, Wetzel, who at 16 already had a reputation as an excellent woodsman, a crack shot, and a steady man in a pinch, was invited to accompany a group of settlers in pursuit of three Miami Indians who had stolen some horses. The settlers tracked them into what is now Belmont County, Ohio, where they found the horses grazing near a spring and the Indians napping nearby. Startled, the Indians fled into the woods. The settlers decided to break into two parties, the larger to return home immediately with the recovered horses and the smaller to stay long enough to allow the horses they had been riding to rest. When the Indians suddenly reappeared, the whites who had remained took to their heels, leaving the horses behind. They soon caught up with the rest of their group and explained the situation. Most of the settlers wanted to avoid a fight, but not Wetzel, who was loath to return home without his father's mare. Only two men would join him. They crept along until they spotted the Indians, who saw them at the same time. Wetzel and the Indians then "treed" (hid behind trees) while seeking a clear shot at about 50 yards' distance. Wetzel looked around for his companions and saw them running off into the distance. He was on his own.

Employing a well-worn ruse, he hung his hat on his rifle's muzzle and stuck it out from behind the tree trunk. Three muskets fired nearly at once, knocking the hat away, and Wetzel fell theatrically to the ground, clutching his chest. The Indians laid down their muskets and came forward, brandishing tomahawks. Wetzel stood up, shot the lead one, and began to run. The two others, in no fear of his empty rifle, chased him. But Wetzel had mastered an extraordinary skill—he was able to reload while running at full tilt. He turned and killed the second of his pursuers, then reloaded again and shot the last—"it was his last sickness," as he was fond of saying. Collecting their scalps and his mare, Wetzel rejoined his fellows. The deed made him a hero throughout the region and earned him frequent employment as a scout.

Wetzel had occasion to perform this stunt again two years later when he and one Thomas Mills, while trying to recover a stolen horse, came upon a raiding party of 40 Delawares. Wetzel fired and killed one, and Mills was wounded in the return fire. Wetzel and Mills fled. Mills was quickly overtaken and killed, but Wetzel, chased by four men, was able to reload on the run and winnow them down, although the second Indian he turned to shoot was close enough to grab his gun barrel. They "had a severe wring" for it, but Wetzel was able to bring the muzzle to his opponent's chest and fire. Two more men chased him. When he stopped to fire in a clearing, one treed himself behind a trunk too narrow to offer cover. Wetzel shot him in the thigh, and he quickly bled out. The fourth chose not to continue the pursuit.

In August 1786, Wetzel was traveling the Ohio River by canoe with his father, two brothers, and two other men, when they came under fire from Indians on shore. His father was killed, and one brother was mortally wounded. After this Wetzel's vendetta against the red man took on a crazed quality. He would disappear into the wilderness for weeks at a time on guerrilla-type forays, stalking and killing small hunting parties he came across, sometimes hiding motionless for an entire day to get a shot. Between the years of 1779 and 1788 he claimed to have collected 27 scalps.

Wetzel was a striking figure, about 5 foot, 10 inches and muscular, with a dark complexion deeply pitted from smallpox, and pierced ears from which he hung silk tassels and other ornaments. He kept his thick black hair in braids; when combed out, it reached nearly to his knees. He joked that a scalp as sought after as his should be a worthy prize. His Indian foes described him as "the man whose gun was always loaded," and for his speed and endurance gave him the sobriquet Old Death Wind.

Wetzel once demonstrated his remarkable stalking skills on a self-styled mountain man whose bragging annoyed him. Wetzel wagered that if the man stood anywhere he chose to in the woods, Wetzel would be able to sneak up on him and touch him on the shoulder before he was aware of Wetzel's presence. Taking the bet, the man took a position near an open field, fig-

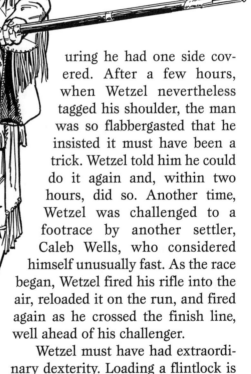

· KIRCHNER ·

uring he had one side covered. After a few hours, when Wetzel nevertheless tagged his shoulder, the man was so flabbergasted that he insisted it must have been a trick. Wetzel told him he could do it again and, within two hours, did so. Another time, Wetzel was challenged to a footrace by another settler, Caleb Wells, who considered himself unusually fast. As the race began, Wetzel fired his rifle into the air, reloaded it on the run, and fired again as he crossed the finish line, well ahead of his challenger.

Wetzel must have had extraordinary dexterity. Loading a flintlock is a multistep process: one must pour a charge down the barrel, fit a ball to a patch and push it into the muzzle, draw the ramrod from its slot and ram the ball home, return the ramrod to its slot, cock the hammer, flip up the pan cover and prime the pan, and then close the pan cover. Of these operations, using the ramrod and priming the pan would be the most difficult to perform on the run. Some firearms experts therefore suspect that Wetzel used some shortcuts. He may have stored some undersized balls in his cheek that he could spit into the muzzle. Unpatched, they would have rolled down the barrel without the assistance of the ramrod if he smacked his flintlock's butt against the ground. If he had enlarged his rifle's touch hole, the same jolt would prime the pan with some of the main powder charge. The loose-fitting projectile would be effective only at short range but adequate for Wetzel's purposes.

When James Madison's brother John came to the frontier to stake claim to lands along the Big Sandy, Wetzel was the obvious choice as guide and bodyguard. Shepherding a city slicker through the woods was not Wetzel's favorite occupation, but the money was persuasive. From the winter of 1785 through the spring of the following year Wetzel worked for Madison, but on May 13 they were attacked, probably by Shawnees, and Madison was killed. Reloading on the run, Wetzel was able to kill three Shawnees as he made his escape.

Wetzel was a ruthless proponent of the view that the only peace fit for an Indian is that which a bullet gives him. In 1791, a Seneca chief named Tegunteh was traveling to Fort Harmar for negotiations when Wetzel cold-bloodedly shot him in the back. He was arrested and put in irons. Allowed outside for exercise in manacles, but without his leg irons, Wetzel escaped. He was recaptured, but sentiment for him ran so high in the community that he was released on a writ of habeas corpus and never called to trial.

In the late 1790s, in New Orleans, Wetzel innocently passed counterfeit currency he had received in payment for furs and was imprisoned for two years. For Wetzel, accustomed to the feral freedom of the wilderness, confinement was an almost unbearable torment.

Wetzel never settled down, married, or farmed. He died in 1808, probably from yellow fever. His cousin's wife insisted that his rifle, Old Kill Devil, be buried with him, saying that a gun that had killed so many men would haunt any house it was kept in.

Wetzel County in northwestern West Virginia is named for him.

43 Sam Whittemore

War is generally a young man's game. Physical decline, as well as the waning lure of adventure and idealistic causes, incline most men over 40 toward a seat on the sidelines. Nevertheless, there are exceptions, perhaps the most notable being Sam Whittemore, a prominent farmer in 18th-century Menotomy (now Arlington), Massachusetts. At 50 he served as a captain in a Royal Dragoon regiment and participated in the capture of the French fortress at Louisburg, Nova Scotia, in 1745. He returned to his farm with an engraved, silver-mounted French saber as a souvenir, reporting that its previous owner had "died suddenly." Thirteen years later, at 64, Whittemore rode off on his swaybacked nag to take part in the reconquest of the fortress at Louisburg, and a year later he was with General Wolfe at Quebec. He returned astride a fine stallion and carrying a pair of expensive dueling pistols. Again, they came from an enemy officer who had "died suddenly." In 1763 Chief Pontiac of the Ottawa organized a massive Indian uprising against British rule. Whittemore, then 68, reenlisted and fought in the Great Lakes region for 13 months.

On April 19, 1775, Whittemore was working his fields when he got news that the elite light infantry and grenadiers of the British foot regiments were making an orderly withdrawal to Boston from Concord, where they had attempted to seize local militia munitions and had fought the self-styled Patriots at Lexington. Whittemore, a civic leader who had served as a town assessor and selectman as well as in other capacities, was on the side of independence. He immediately stopped what he was doing and went home, where he armed himself with his saber, dueling pistols, and musket; slung his powder horn and shot pouch over his shoulder; and told his astonished family to stay safely indoors while he went to fight the British.

The 80-year-old Whittemore joined a group of minutemen heading toward Cooper's Tavern, where the route to Medford turned off to the north. He staked out a position behind a stone wall 150 yards off the road, where he would be in the path of flanking elements of the British force.

As the redcoats came into view, the minutemen around Whittemore began taking potshots, then sprinting away to reload in safety. Whittemore held his fire until the British were almost upon him. He then fired his musket, killed a regular, and put his pistols to work, dropping one man and mortally wounding another. With no time to reload as the British surrounded him, he drew his saber and slashed at them. One soldier fired his Brown Bess musket into Whittemore's face, tearing half his cheek away and knocking him to the ground, and others bayoneted him and clubbed him with their gun butts, leaving him for dead.

When the British had marched on, local residents ventured

out to reclaim Whittemore's body. To their amazement they found him not only conscious, but feebly attempting to reload his musket for another shot. They carried him to Cooper's Tavern where Dr. Nathaniel Tufts was tending the wounded. After stripping off Whittemore's blood-soaked and bayonet-rent garments, Tufts counted no less than 13 stab wounds, many into internal organs. He was mystified that the old man should still be alive and offered no hope for his survival. Nevertheless, the locals insisted Tufts do what he could, so he dressed Whittemore's wounds and sent him home to die.

Evidently Whittemore didn't get the word. He was soon out of bed, and with farmwork as physical therapy made a full recovery. Though disfigured and slightly lame, he lived another 18 years, dying on February 3, 1793, at age 98. To his dying day he expressed pride at the part he had played in the War for Independence.

There is a stone monument to Whittemore on Massachusetts Avenue in his hometown. In 2000 another Arlington octogenarian, Tommy Rawson, the 1935 New England boxing champion who still coaches boxing at Harvard, pushed his state representatives to propose Samuel Whittemore as the official "Hero of the Commonwealth." Representatives of other towns objected, claiming that they had their own unsung heroes who were equally deserving.

If seniority counted for anything, it would be no contest.

44 Alvin C. York

> *Get determined to get the other fellow before he gets you, keep on thinking about it and with that determination you'll come through.*
>
> —Alvin C. York

E ven as the 20th century ushered in the age of mechanized war—of tanks, machine guns, artillery, and poison gas—battles still hinged on the courage and skill of extraordinary individuals. In World War I America's greatest warrior was a reluctant one, Alvin Cullum York.

York grew up in the Cumberland Mountains of Tennessee, 20 miles from the Kentucky border. His father was a blacksmith, but he did most of his work in the evening, reserving the daylight hours for hunting and shooting. The marksmanship advice he gave his son was to "always be accurate." Alvin hunted food for the family table and recalled that his father threatened "to muss me up right smart if I failed to bring a squirrel down with the first shot or hit a turkey in the body instead of taking its head off."

His father died in 1911, and as the oldest son still living at home, Alvin inherited the responsibility to support his brothers and sisters. He earned a few dollars as a farmer, blacksmith, and day laborer but also helped provide for his family with his uncanny shooting ability. In turkey shoots, where men took turns shooting at the bobbing head of a turkey tethered behind a log, York usually won the bird as well as whatever he had bet on the side. In another popular target competition, entrants put up money to purchase a beef. It was divided into five parts, with the best shot getting first choice, the second best getting second choice, and so on. Competition was fierce, and differences in shot placement were carefully measured to determine the winner. On one occasion York placed all five of the best shots and took home the entire beef. He was also a crack shot with a pistol, with either hand. He practiced shooting from horseback, riding through the woods and firing at the spots on beech trees.

As a young man York had a reputation as a hell-raiser; he gambled, drank, and brawled. His nickname was Big 'Un, and he claimed he was never beaten or even knocked down in a fight. He was slow to anger but, once roused, would "go through with the job and there'd be a hurting." His mother, a deeply religious woman, begged him not to drink, worrying that he would be killed in a brawl, as was his best friend. Shaken by his friend's death and concerned about how his rowdiness was affecting his family, York sought help from religion. He joined the fundamentalist Church of Christ in Christian Union, studied the Bible, and experienced personal salvation on January 1, 1915. Within two years he was the second elder of his church.

When war was declared in April 1917 York's loyalties were divided. As he put it, "I loved and trusted old Uncle Sam and I have always believed he did the right thing. But I was worried clean through. I didn't want to go and kill. I believed in my Bible. And it distinctly said Thou shalt not kill."

York was working as a $1.60-a-day laborer, building a highway, when in June 1917 he received his draft notice. He applied

National Archives

for conscientious objector status, but his bid was rejected and his appeal denied. With deep misgivings he submitted to induction.

In boot camp York was issued a bolt-action rifle, possibly an '03 Springfield. He considered it no more accurate at 100–150 yards than the muzzle-loader he had grown up with, but allowed as how its box magazine might be an asset in combat. He was amazed at the lack of shooting skill among the city-born recruits. Some of them not only missed the targets at 100 yards, he noted, they missed the embankments on which the targets were set. He himself found army shooting "tolerably easy."

York proved himself one of the ablest recruits but continued to believe that he was doing wrong by being in the army. His captain sent him to talk with the battalion commander, Maj. George E. Buxton, who took York's concerns seriously and engaged him in lengthy discussion. Drawing on his own extensive knowledge of the Bible, Buxton made a persuasive case for the doctrine of just war.

York was given a 10-day pass to go home and collect his thoughts, and after a night in the wilderness he experienced an epiphany. He was convinced that God wanted him to fight for his country and would protect him from harm. He returned to his unit with his mind at peace, having dovetailed his Biblical convictions with the Allied mission in Europe. As he put it, "We were to be peacemakers. . . . That was we-uns. We were to help make peace, the only way the Germans would understand."

York was shipped to France with Company G, 328th Infantry Regiment, 82d Division. There the men turned in their U.S. rifles for what York termed "British guns"—.303-caliber Enfield Mark 1s. Based on the British P-14 design, this rifle was manufactured by Remington at its Eddystone plant. York considered it less accurate than the rifle he had trained on.

By the end of June 1918 he was in combat. His company came under small-arms fire, artillery barrages, and gas attacks, and even though many of his comrades were wounded and killed, he maintained his faith that God would protect him.

On October 8, 1918, during the Meuse-Argonne offensive, as his battalion crossed an open valley several hundred yards wide, it came under heavy machine gun fire from the surrounding hills. York wrote, "Our boys just went down like the long grass before the mowing machine at home." Sgt. Harry Parsons ordered three squads, one led by York, to outflank the machine gun positions. Three squads normally numbered 24 men in all, but casualties had reduced them to a total of 17. Parsons felt he was sending them "to what looked to be certain death. But I figured it had to be done. I figured they had a slight chance of getting the machine guns."

The patrol got around the flank of the Germans and surprised 20 or 30 of them at breakfast, including an officer who spoke fluent English, a Lieutenant Vollmer. They immediately surrendered.

About 30 German machine guns positioned on a ridge about 40 yards away turned and fired on the American patrol. The captured Germans dropped to the ground, saving themselves, but six Americans were killed and three wounded. Corporal York was the only surviving noncom. As York described events in his journal, "Those machine guns were spitting fire and cutting down the undergrowth all around us something awful. And the Germans were yelling orders. You never heard such a racket in all your life. I didn't have time to dodge behind a tree or dive into the brush. I didn't even have time to kneel or lie down."

York demonstrated the shooting skill he had honed at turkey shoots. "All I could do was touch the Germans off just as fast as I could," he wrote. "I was sharpshooting. I don't think I missed a shot. It was no time to miss. In order to sight me or to swing their machine guns on me, the Germans had to show their heads above the trench, and every time I saw a head I just touched it off. All the time I kept yelling at them to come down. I didn't want to kill any more than I had to. But it was they or I. And I was giving them the best I had."

The prisoners around York squirmed under the incoming bullets, but he made them remain where they were to restrict their compatriots' fire.

From a trench about 25 yards away, a German lieutenant and five infantrymen charged York with fixed bayonets, perhaps figuring that at least one of them would get him, since his Enfield held only five rounds. If so, they had overlooked the fact that his Colt .45 held seven. York described what happened: "I changed to the old automatic and just touched them off too. I touched off the sixth man first, then the fifth, then the fourth, then the third, and so on. I wanted them to keep coming. I didn't want the rear ones to see me touching off the front ones. I was afraid they would drop down and pump a volley into me." Within seconds, all six lay on the ground.

York returned to his rifle and continued to cover the machine guns, and each time he fired a man fell dead. As a captured German officer later observed, "Such marksmanship is bound to have a most demoralizing effect on the men who are the targets." While York's attention was elsewhere, Vollmer drew his Lüger. No doubt he was trying to emulate York's performance, but he only succeeded in demonstrating the inefficiency of a pistol in unskilled hands, emptying his magazine in York's direction without hitting him once.

York had faced massed machine gun fire, a bayonet charge, and Vollmer's pathetic assault and emerged unscathed. Twenty-eight Germans lay dead. York pointed his .45 at Vollmer's head and told him "If you don't make them stop firing I'll take off your head next." To Vollmer it must have seemed like a good time to call it quits. He handed his pistol to York, then blew his whistle and ordered the remaining Germans to throw down their arms. York describes what followed: "They came down and began to gather around and throw down their guns and belts. All but one of them came off the hill with their hands up, and just before the one got to me he threw a little grenade, which burst in the air in front of me. I had to touch him off. The rest surrendered without any trouble."

With a surviving force of only seven, York had to escort 80 to 90 German prisoners back through their own lines. He organized them into a double file and made them carry the American wounded. He put three of his men on either side of the column, with one at the rear, and stationed himself at the head with Vollmer and two other officers around him as cover. Vollmer, who had thought he was the victim of a large-scale American assault, noticed the disparity of numbers, and asked, incredulously, "How many men have you got?"

Fixing him with a cold gaze and the muzzle of his .45, York answered, "I have got a-plenty."

"And so I marched them straight at that old German front line trench," York wrote.

> And some machine guns swung around and began to spit at us. I told [Vollmer] to blow his whistle or I would take off his head and theirs too. So he blew his whistle and they all surrendered—all except one. I made [Vollmer] order him to surrender twice. But he wouldn't. And I had to touch him off. I hated to do it. But I couldn't afford to take any chances and so I had to let him have it.

As he approached the American lines, York was concerned that his column might be mistaken for a German attack, but his luck held. Relief squads that had been sent forward to help him were astounded when they counted his prisoners—there were 129 enlisted men and three officers, far too many to be accommodated at battalion headquarters. York was ordered to proceed to regimental headquarters, but no one there had any idea what to do either, so York was sent on to division headquarters. On the way, the column came under heavy shelling and York had to double-time his prisoners to get through safely. "There was nothing to be gained by having any more of them killed or wounded," he wrote. "They had surrendered to me, and it was up to me to look after them. And I did."

When he arrived, the brigade commander stepped out of his post and said, "Well, York, I hear you have captured the whole damned German army."

York saluted and answered, "No sir, I have only 132."

Tellingly, York's main concern was to get his prisoners taken off his hands so that he could return to the lines. It was still early in the day. He remained in combat until November but had come close to being killed on October 12 when a shell exploded so close to him that it blew him into the air. When he left the lines, he was promoted to sergeant and, to his surprise, began to be treated as a hero. After the November 11 Armistice, he met President Wilson in Langres, France. He came home to a ticker-tape parade in New York and an appearance before a joint session of Congress. The Tennessee highway he had been working on when he was drafted was named in his honor. He was awarded the Medal of Honor, the Distinguished Service Cross, the Croix de Guerre, and so many others that he claimed he would have needed two jackets to wear them all. He was offered a fortune to make product endorsements and personal appearances, but refused because he felt it would be wrong to profit from serving his country. He turned down a Rotary Club-sponsored triumphal nationwide tour, saying it was "merely a vainglorious call of the world and the devil." At a testimonial dinner his senior commanding officer, General Duncan, asked him to say a few words about that day in the Argonne. York declined, explaining, "It is one of those things I want to forget." But no one else could forget that in three hours on that October morning he had performed one of the most spectacular feats in the history of individual combat. With a rifle and a pistol he had killed 28 of the enemy, silenced 35 machine guns, and taken an unheard-of number of prisoners. An army surrenders when it loses hope of victory: York was able to provoke that collapse of morale through his own astonishing prowess.

There were other awesome feats of arms in World War I. A professional soldier, Lt. Samuel Woodfill, cleaned out five machine gun nests on October 12, 1918. He killed more than a dozen German gunners with his rifle and pistol, and when he ran out of ammunition, leaped into the last machine gun nest and wiped out its crew with an entrenching tool. Woodfill was the soldier General Pershing most wished to see honored, but the public responded to York's character as much as his deed. He represented an ideal from a bygone era: the humble, God-fearing patriot who is slow to violence but invincible in a just cause. As the *New York Times* put it, "One likes to think that the United States was built and protected by such men, simple and pure men who provided the foundations on which the more brilliant and imaginative could build."

York devoted the rest of his life to bringing education to the backwoods of Tennessee and established a vocational school that still exists. In the late 1930s, as war again loomed on the horizon, he was entreated to allow a movie to be made of his World War I exploit. Disillusioned by the results of "the war to end all wars," he was at first unwilling, but consented in 1940 with the stipulation that his story be portrayed accurately and that a share of the profits go to Tennessee schools.

After Pearl Harbor, York's misgivings vanished. He enthusiastically signed up for the draft in the same general store where he had reluctantly registered 25 years before. "If they want me for active duty I'm ready to go. I'm in a mighty different mood from that other time," he said. He was offended that the military was rejecting many of his Kentucky and Tennessee brethren because of their illiteracy and offered to lead a battalion of illiterates into combat. He insisted that all mountain folk were crack shots, the best soldiers in the world, and that "every one of them will be able to endorse his first army paycheck." York's offer was turned down (possibly delaying victory by months!) and he himself, arthritic and overweight, failed his army physical.

York died at age 76 in 1964. In accordance with his wishes, he was not buried at Arlington National Cemetery, but where he felt at peace, in his family graveyard in Jamestown, Tennessee.

York's story raises an interesting issue: as much as we may claim to respect those who hold strong religious beliefs, we show a higher regard for those who obey the law of honor, which often contradicts them. A recurring character in popular entertainment is the hero who has forsworn violence but who is provoked until he finally employs it against his enemies. Far from being disappointed when he discards his pacifism, the audience is invariably delighted. Evidently most of us prefer to fantasize about vengeance rather than martyrdom. The underlying dilemma is that we cannot judge a man by the motives he claims, only by his actions. A pacifist may claim that it requires courage not to fight, but unless he is willing to face death for his belief, how can he prove it? After all, cowardice is a much more likely reason not to fight. When a man has proven his valor as conclusively as did Sergeant York, we are more apt to accept at face value his professed beliefs—even if, paradoxically, they concern the evils of violence.

Just as Alexander, the hero who fought for pure glory, seemed a good place to begin this collection, so York, the hero who found no glory in war, seems a good place to end.

Bibliography

Alexander the Great

Arrian. *The Campaigns of Alexander*. Translated by Aubry de Sélincourt. New York: Dorset Press, 1986.

Green, Peter. *Alexander the Great*. New York: Praeger Publishers, 1970.

Plutarch. *Lives of the Noble Grecians and Romans*. Translated by John Dryden. New York: The Modern Library, 1932.

Wright, F. A. *Alexander the Great*. New York: Robert M. McBride & Company, 1935.

Tom Allen

The Junction City Union, Junction City, Kansas, April 25, 1885.

Kansas State Historical Society. (ed. George W. Martin.) *Collections of the Kansas State Historical Society,* Volume IX, 1905–1906.

Penfield, Thomas. *Western Sheriffs and Marshals*. New York: Grosset & Dunlap, 1955.

James Bowie

Garst, Shannon. *James Bowie and His Famous Knife.* New York: Pocket Books, 1955.

Hopewell, Clifford. *James Bowie: Texas Fighting Man.* Austin, Tex.: Eakin Press, 1994.

Gregory "Pappy" Boyington

Boyington, "Pappy." *Baa Baa Black Sheep.* New York: G. P. Putnam's Sons, 1958.

Gamble, Bruce. *The Black Sheep.* Novato, Calif.: Presidio Press, 1998.

Walton, Frank E. *Once They Were Eagles: The Men of the Black Sheep Squadron.* Lexington: The University Press of Kentucky, 1986.

Delf A. "Jelly" Bryce

"Auto Theft Suspect Near Death from Police Bullets." *The Daily Oklahoman,* March 11, 1929.

Chaffin, Kym B. "Jelly Bryce, the FBI's Legendary Sharpshooter." *Oklahombres* IV, 3 (Spring 1993): 1–10.

"Editor's Corner: Meet an SAC." *The Investigator* (July 1957): 22–24.

"Jelly Bryce—A Legend with a Gun." Hobart, Okla.: Kiowa County Historical Society, *Pioneering in Kiowa County* 3 (September 1978): 175–181.

"'Jelly' Bryce Was Legend with Gun." *Oklahoma City Times,* May 14, 1974.

"One Dead, Another Shot by Detectives in Fight." *Oklahoma City Times,* March 11, 1929.

Owens, Ron. *Oklahoma Justice: The Oklahoma City Police.* Paducah, Ky.: Turner Publishing Company, 1995.

"Police Launch City Cleanup Drive After Fatal Shooting." *The Daily Oklahoman,* July 19, 1934.

"Speaking of Pictures . . . G-Man Can Draw a Gun Faster Than You Can Read This." *Life* 19 (November 12, 1945): 12–13, 15.

"Subject: Delf A. Bryce," Federal Bureau of Investigation, Freedom of Information Act file number 67-38692.

"Theft Suspect Shot by Police." *The Daily Oklahoman,* November 8, 1928.

Lloyd L. Burke

Jacobs, Bruce. *Heroes of the Army.* New York: W. W. Norton, 1956.

Murphy, Edward F. *Korean War Heroes.* Novato, Calif.: Presidio Press, 1992.

Ned Christie

Coffey, Ivy. "He Refused to Hang." *The Daily Oklahoman,* November 10, 1957.

Hamilton, Roy, and Gene Norris. *Ned Christie: A Family Remembers.* Stilwell, Okla.: Roy Hamilton, 1995.

McKennon, C. H. *Iron Men: A Saga of the United States Marshals Who Rode the Indian Territory*. Garden City, N.Y.: Doubleday & Company, 1967.

Steele, Philip W. *The Last Cherokee Warriors*. Gretna, La.: Pelican Publishing Company, 1993.

Winston S. Churchill

Churchill, Winston. *My Early Life*. London: Thornton Butterworth, Ltd., 1940.

Churchill, Winston. *The Malakand Field Force*. London: Octopus Publishing Group, 1989.

Ty Cobb

Stump, Al. *Cobb: A Biography*. New York: Workman Publishing Co., Inc., 1994.

Hannah Duston

Axelrod, Alan. *Chronicle of the Indian Wars: From Colonial Times to Wounded Knee*. New York: Prentice-Hall, 1993.

Caverly, Robert B. *Heroism of Hannah Duston, Together with the Indian Wars of New England*. Boston: B. B. Russell & Co., 1875.

Lincoln, Charles. *Narratives of the Indian Wars—1675–1699*. New York: Barnes & Noble, 1959.

Rehm, Jeffrey. "The Story of Hannah Duston." http:/vader.castles.com/ftprints/web50205.html@1996

Nathan Bedford Forrest

Anders, Curt. *Fighting Confederates*. New York: G.P. Putnam's Sons, 1968.

Duke, Basil. *Reminiscences of General Basil W. Duke, C.S.A.* Garden City, N.Y.: Doubleday, Page & Co., 1911.

Goodloe, Albert. *Confederate Echoes*. Nashville: Publishing House of the M.E. Church, 1907.

Henry, Robert Selph. *"First with the Most" Forrest*. New York: Smithmark Books, 1991.

Hurst, John. *Nathan Bedford Forrest: A Biography*. New York: Alfred E. Knopf, 1993.

Jordan, Gen. Thomas, and J.P. Pryor. *The Campaigns of Lt. Gen. N.B. Forrest and of Forrest's Cavalry*. (Reprint of a 19th century text.) Dayton, Ohio: Morningside Bookshop, 1977.

Taylor, Lt. Gen. Richard. *Destruction and Reconstruction*. New York: Appleton and Co., 1879

Wyeth, John Allen. *That Devil Forrest: Life of General Nathan Bedford Forrest*. New York: Harper & Brothers, Publishers, 1959.

Peter Francisco

Cook, Fred J. *What Manner of Men: Forgotten Heroes of the American Revolution.* New York: William Morrow & Co., 1959.

Gustaitis, Joseph. "One Man Army." *American History* (October 1998): http://www.earlyamericanhom.com/American History/ articles/1998/10982_text.htm

Hamilton, Charles Henry. *Peter Francisco: Soldier Extraordinary.* Richmond, Va.: Whittet & Shepperson, 1976.

Geronimo

Barrett, S. M. *Geronimo: His Own Story.* New York: Penguin Books, 1996.

Burbank, E.A., and Ernest Royce. *Burbank Among the Indians.* Caldwell, Idaho: 1944.

Roberts, David. *Once They Moved Like the Wind: Cochise, Geronimo, and the Apache Wars.* New York: Simon & Schuster, 1994.

Gurkhas: Jitbahadur Rai, Dwansing Basnet, Lachhiman Gurung

Arvidson, Maj. John S. "Britain's Gurkhas: Mercenaires Extraordinaires." *Soldier of Fortune* (February 1983): 58–63, 68–70.

Bolt, David. *Gurkhas.* New York: Delacorte Press, 1967.

Caplan, Lionel. *Warrior Gentlemen: "Gurkhas" in the Western Imagination.* Providence, R.I.: Berghahn Books, 1995.

Farwell, Byron. *The Gurkhas.* New York: W. W. Norton, 1984.

James, Harold, M. C., and Denis Sheil-Small. *The Gurkhas.* Harrisburg, Penn.: Stackpole Books, 1966.

Frank Hamer

Frost, H. Gordon, and Jenkins, John H. *I'm Frank Hamer.* Austin and New York: The Pemberton Press, 1968.

Webb, Walter Prescott. *The Texas Rangers: A Century of Frontier Defense.* Boston and New York: Houghton Mifflin Company, 1935.

Nancy Hart

Bannister, Ruby Nell Heaton. *A Portrayal of Nancy Hart.* Hartwell, Ga.: The Sun Press, 1985.

Clyne, Patricia Edwards. *Patriots in Petticoats.* New York: Dodd, Mead & Company, 1976.

Ellet, Elizabeth Fries. *Revolutionary Women in the War for American Independence: A One Volume Revised Edition of Elizabeth Ellet's 1848 Landmark Series.* Westport, Conn., London: Praeger, 1998.

"History of Nancy Hart." http://georgiamagazine.com/tosee/n_hart.htm

Erich Hartmann & Hans-Joachim Marseille
Bekker, Cajus. *The Luftwaffe War Diaries*. Garden City, N.Y.: Doubleday & Company, 1968.
Constable, Trevor J., and Toliver, Col. Raymond F. *Horrido! Fighter Aces of the Luftwaffe*. New York: MacMillan, 1968.
Constable, Trevor J., and Col. Raymond F. Toliver. *The Blond Knight of Germany*. New York: Doubleday & Company, 1970.
Kurowski, Franz. *German Fighter Ace Hans-Joachim Marseille*. Atglen, Penn.: Schiffer Military History, 1994.
Musciano, Walter A. *Messerschmitt Aces*. Blue Ridge Summit, Penn.: 1989.
Sims, Edward H. *The Greatest Aces*. New York: Harper & Row, 1967.
Spick, Mike. *Luftwaffe Fighter Aces: The Jagdflieger and their Combat Tactics and Techniques*. Mechanicsburg, Penn.: Stackpole Books, 1996.

Wild Bill Hickok
Cooper, Jeff. "How Good Was Hickok?" *Guns & Ammo* (March 1960): 22–27.
Rosa, Joseph G. *They Called Him Wild Bill*. Norman, Okla.: University of Oklahoma Press, 1974.

Andrew Jackson
Encyclopaedia Britannica. Eleventh edition. New York: Encyclopædia Britannica, Inc., 1910–1911.
James, Marquis. *The Life of Andrew Jackson*. New York: The Bobbs-Merrill Company, 1938.
Johnson, Gerald. *Andrew Jackson: An Epic in Homespun*. New York: Minton, Balch & Co., 1927.
Nolte, Vincent. *Memoirs of Vincent Nolte*. New York: G. Howard Watt, 1934.
Wyatt-Brown, Bertram. "Andrew Jackson's Honor." *Journal of the Early Republic* 17 (Spring 1997): 1–36.

Jean-Louis
Alaux, Michel. *Modern Fencing*. New York: Charles Scribner's Sons, 1975.
Hutton, Alfred. *The Sword and the Centuries*. London: Grant Richards, 1901.
Gautier, Théophile. *Captain Fracasse*.
    http://sailor.gutenberg.org/by_title/xxx255.html.
"German Duelling." *Colburn's New Monthly Magazine* 40: 140 (1834): 470–477.
Lynch, Col. Arthur. "French and Italian Schools of Fence." *Outing* 39 (March 1902): 673–683.
Truman, Ben. *The Field of Honor*. New York: Fords, Howard, & Hulbert, 1884.

"Turkey Creek" Jack Johnson
Lake, Stuart. *Wyatt Earp: Frontier Marshal*. Boston: Houghton Mifflin Company, 1931.

413

O'Neal, Bill. *The Encyclopedia of Western Gunfighters*. Norman: University of Oklahoma Press, 1979.

Charles E. "Commando" Kelly
Kelly, Charles E. (with Pete Martin). *One Man's War*. New York: Alfred A. Knopf, 1944.

Kelly, Charles E. (ed. Pete Martin). "One Man's War." *Saturday Evening Post* July 1, 1944; July 8, 1944; July 15, 1944; July 22, 1944; July 29, 1944.

_____. "Heroes All." *Newsweek* 23:40 (May 8, 1944).

_____. "Kelly Earns a Medal." *Time* 43:33 (March 20, 1944).

_____. "No Place Like Home." *Time* 43:13 (May 8, 1944).

Murphy, Edward F. *Heroes of World War II*. Novato, Calif.: Presidio Press, 1990.

Schott, Joseph L. *Above and Beyond: The Story of the Congressional Medal of Honor*. New York: G. P. Putnam's, 1963.

José "Pepe" Llulla
Downey, Fairfax. *Our Lusty Forefathers*. New York: Charles Scribner's Sons, 1947.

Hearn, Lafcadio. *An American Miscellany,* vol. 2. New York: Dodd, Mead, and Company, 1924.

Kendall, John S. "The Humors of the Duello.*" Louisiana Historical Quarterly* 23 (January, 1940): 445–470.

Frank Luke
Donovan, Frank. *The Medal: The Story of the Medal of Honor*. New York: Dodd, Mead & Company, 1962.

Exhibit notes, Champlin Fighter Museum, Tempe, Ariz.

Robertson, Bruce. *Air Aces of the 1914–1918 War*. Letchworth, Hertsfordshire: The Garden City Press, 1959.

Schott, Joseph L. *Above and Beyond: The Story of the Congressional Medal of Honor*. New York: G. P. Putnam's, 1963.

"The 27th Pursuit Squadron and the Saga of Frank Luke Jr." www.geocities.com/Athens/Acropolis/7133/

Bat Masterson & Luke Short
DeArment, Robert K. *Bat Masterson: The Man and the Legend*. Norman: University of Oklahoma Press, 1989.

Horan, James. *The Lawmen*. New York: Grammercy Books, 1996.

Masterson, W. B. (Bat). *Famous Gun Fighters of the Western Frontier*. Silverthorne, Colo.: Vistabooks, 1996.

Short, Wayne. *Luke Short: A Biography*. Tombstone, Ariz.: Devil's Thumb Press, 1996

Trachtman, Paul. *The Gunfighters*. New York: Time-Life Books, 1977.

La Maupin
Burrows, Jim. "Mademoiselle Maupin Home Page."
   www.ultranet.com/brons/LaMaupin
Gilbert, Oscar Paul. *Women in Men's Guise*. London: John Lane, 1932.
Rogers, Cameron. *Gallant Ladies*. New York: Harcourt, Brace and Company,
   Inc., 1928.

Donald McBane
Hutton, Alfred. *The Sword and the Centuries*. London: Grant Richards, 1901.
McBane, Donald. *The Expert Sword-Man's Companion: Or the True Art of
   Self-Defence*. Glasgow: James Duncan, 1728.
Wise, Arthur. *The Art and History of Personal Combat*. Greenwich, Conn.:
   Arma Press, New York Graphic Society, Ltd., 1971.

Mgobozi
Bond, Geoffrey. *Chaka the Terrible*. London: Arco Publications, 1961.
Ritter, E. A. *Shaka Zulu*. London: Penguin Books, 1978.

Usamah ibn-Munqidh
Usamah Ibn-Munqidh. *An Arab-Syrian Gentleman and Warrior in the Period
   of the Crusades*. Princeton, N.J.: Princeton University Press, 1987.

Audie Murphy
Graham, Don. *No Name on the Bullet: A Biography of Audie Murphy*. New
   York: Viking, 1989.
Morgan, Thomas B. "The War Hero." *Esquire* (December 1983): 597–604.
Murphy, Audie. *To Hell and Back*. New York: Holt, Rinehart and Winston, 1967.
Simpson, Col. Harold B. *Audie Murphy: American Soldier*. Dallas, Tex.: Alcor
   Publishing Company, 1982.
Whiting, Charles. *Hero: The Life and Death of Audie Murphy*. Chelsea, Mich.:
   Scarborough House, Publishers, 1990.
www.audiemurphy.com

Miyamoto Musashi
King, Winston L. *Zen & the Way of the Sword*. Oxford: Oxford University
   Press, 1993.
Musashi, Miyamoto. *A Book of Five Rings*. Woodstock, N.Y.: The Overlook
   Press, 1982.
Sugawara, Makoto. *Lives of Master Swordsmen*. Tokyo: The East
   Publications, Inc., 1985.
Yoshikawa, Eiji. *Musashi*. New York: Harper & Row, 1981.

Charles Nungesser

Jullian, Marcel. *Le Chevalier du Ciel: Charles Nungesser*. Paris: Amiot-Dumont, 1953.

Longstreet, Stephen. *The Canvas Falcons*. New York: Barnes & Noble Books, 1995.

Mason, Jr., Herbert Molloy. *High Flew the Falcons*. Philadelphia and New York: J. B. Lippincott Company, 1965.

Norman, Aaron. *The Great Air War*. New York: Macmillan, 1968.

Robertson, Bruce. *Air Aces of the 1914–1918 War*. Letchworth, Hertsfordshire: The Garden City Press, 1959.

Francisco Pizarro

Innes, Hammond. *The Conquistadors*. New York: Alfred A. Knopf, 1969.

Prescott, William H. *History of the Conquest of Peru*. New York: E. P. Dutton & Co., 1921.

Shay, Frank. *Incredible Pizarro: Conqueror of Peru*. New York: The Mohawk Press, 1932.

Wilcox, Desmond. *Ten Who Dared*. Boston: Little, Brown & Company, 1977.

Robert the Bruce

Barbour, John. *The Bruce: Being the Metrical History of Robert the Bruce, King of the Scots*. Compiled A.D. 1375; translated by George Eyre-Todd. Glasgow: Gowans & Gray, Limited, 1907.

Davis, I. M. *The Black Douglas*. Boston: Routledge & Kegan Paul, 1974.

Montross, Lynn. *War through the Ages*. New York: Harper & Brothers Publishers, 1944.

Scott, Ronald McNair. *Robert the Bruce: King of the Scots*. New York: Peter Bedrick Books, 1989.

Robert Rosser

Jacobs, Bruce. *Heroes of the Army*. New York: W. W. Norton, 1956.

Murphy, Edward F. *Korean War Heroes*. Novato, Calif.: Presidio Press, 1992.

Time 60 (July 7, 1952): 19.

Hans Ulrich Rudel

Cooper, Jeff. *Fireworks*. Rogue River, Ore.: The Janus Press, 1980.

Just, Günther. *Stuka-Pilot Hans-Ulrich Rudel*. Atglen, Penn.: Schiffer Military History, 1990.

Parada, George. "Hans-Ulrich Rudel." www.actungpanzer.com

Rudel, Hans Ulrich. *Stuka Pilot*. Costa Mesa, Calif.: The Noontide Press, War and Warriors Series, 1987.

Shaka
Bond, Geoffrey. *Chaka the Terrible*. London: Arco Publications, 1961.
Ritter, E. A. *Shaka Zulu*. London: Penguin Books, 1978.

Egil Skallagrimsson
Jones, Gwyn. *Egil's Saga*. New York: Syracuse University Press, 1960.
Pálsson, Paul, and Paul Edwards, translators. *Egil's Saga*. Harmondsworth, Middlesex, England: Penguin Books, 1976.
Wernick, Robert. *The Vikings*. Alexandria, Va.: Time-Life Books (The Seafarers Series), 1979.

Sokaku Takeda
Pranin, Stanley A. *Daito-ryu Aikijujutsu*. Tokyo: Aiki News, 1996.
Stevens, John. *Abundant Peace: The Biography of Morihei Ueshiba, Founder of Aikido*. Boston: Shambala, 1987.
"Takeda Sokaku: Reviver of Daito-ryu Aiki Jujutsu."
http://www.daito-ryu.org/takedaso.html

Lance Thomas
Los Angeles Times, December 5, 1991, February 21, 1992; February 22, 1992; March 1, 1992; April 26, 1992.
ABC-TV. *Turning Point*. "Guns & Self Defense: When Can You Shoot?" Copyright 1994.
Thomas, Lance. "American Gunfighter." Movie script, 7/10/2000.

Nancy Wake
Braddon, Russell. *The White Mouse*. New York: W. W. Norton & Company, 1957.
Laffin, John. *Women in Battle*. London: Abelard-Schulman, 1967.
Wake, Nancy. *The White Mouse*. Melbourne: Australian Large Print, 1987.

Lewis Wetzel
Allman, C. B. *Lewis Wetzel, Indian Fighter*. New York: The Devin-Adair Company, 1961.
Carroll, George. "Lewis Wetzel: Warfare Tactics on the Frontier." *West Virginia History* 50 (1991): 79–90.
Pierce, James B. "Lewis Wetzel, Dark Hero of the Ohio." *Early America Review* 1: 4 (Spring 1997).
http//www.animus.net/ ~ earlya/review/spring97/wetzel.html

Sam Whittemore

Galvin, John R. *The Minute Men.* New York: Hawthorn Books, Inc. 1967.

Leonard, Patrick J. "A Veteran Long before the War for Independence, Sam Whittemore was America's Oldest, Bravest Soldier." *Military History* (June 1996).
http://columbiad.com/militaryHistory/articles/06963_text.htm

Leonard, Patrick. "The Indestructible Captain Sam." *Yankee* (April 2000): 42–43.

Alvin C. York

American Family Enterprises. *America: An Illustrated Diary of Its Most Important Years.* Valencia, Calif.: American Family Enterprises, Inc., 1972.

Brandt, Nat. "Sergeant York." *American Heritage* (August–September 1981): 56–64.

Cowan, Sam K. *Sergeant York and His People.* New York: Funk & Wagnalls Company, 1922.

Lee, David D. *Sergeant York: An American Hero.* Lexington: The University Press of Kentucky, 1985.

Perry, Sgt. John. *York: His Life, Legend & Legacy.* Nashville, Tenn.: Broadman & Holman Publishers, 1997.

York, Sgt. Alvin C. "Alvin C. York's Diary."
http://volweb.utk.edu/Schools/York/diary.html